Delivering on Doha

FARM TRADE AND THE POOR

Delivering on Doha

FARM TRADE AND THE POOR

Kimberly Ann Elliott

CENTER FOR GLOBAL DEVELOPMENT
INSTITUTE FOR INTERNATIONAL ECONOMICS
Washington, DC
July 2006

Kimberly Ann Elliott, senior fellow, has been associated with the Institute for International Economics since 1982 and holds a joint appointment with the Center for Global Development. She is the author or coauthor of *Can Labor Standards Improve under Globalization?* (2003), *Corruption and the Global Economy* (1997), *Reciprocity and Retaliation in US Trade Policy* (1994), *Measuring the Costs of Protection in the United States* (1994), and *Economic Sanctions Reconsidered* (2d. ed., 1990).

INSTITUTE FOR INTERNATIONAL ECONOMICS
1750 Massachusetts Avenue, NW
Washington, DC 20036-1903
(202) 328-9000 FAX: (202) 659-3225
www.iie.com

C. Fred Bergsten, *Director*
Valerie Norville, *Director of Publications and Web Development*
Edward Tureen, *Director of Marketing*

CENTER FOR GLOBAL DEVELOPMENT
1776 Massachusetts Avenue, NW
Washington, DC 20036
(202) 416-0700 FAX: (202) 416-0750
www.cgdev.org

Nancy Birdsall, *President*

Typesetting by Circle Graphics
Printing by Kirby Lithographic Company, Inc.

Printed in the United States of America
08 07 06   5 4 3 2 1

Library of Congress Cataloging-in-Publication Data

Elliott, Kimberly Ann, 1960–
    Delivering on Doha : farm trade and the poor / Kimberly Ann Elliott.
        p. cm.
    Includes bibliographical references and index.
        ISBN 0-88132-392-6
            (978-0-88132-392-4 : alk. paper)
        1. Produce trade—Government policy. 2. Commercial policy. 3. Poverty—Developing countries. I. Title.

HD9000.6.E45 2006
382'.41—dc22   2006017081

Contents

Preface   ix

Acknowledgments   xiii

1   Introduction   **1**
Why Is Agricultural Liberalization at the Center
of the Doha Round?   3
Why Is a Doha Agreement on Agricultural Liberalization
Not Enough?   9
Plan of the Book   10

2   The Problem: Rich Countries Supporting Rich Farmers   **13**
Mechanisms for Supporting Farmers   13
The WTO Framework for Negotiating on Agriculture   17
Patterns of Support Across Countries   20
Patterns of Support Across Commodities   28
Implications for the Doha Round   31
Appendix 2A   Producer Support Estimate for US Cotton   32

**3   Prospects for Reform: Lessons from US and European
Experience**   **35**
The Evolution of US and European Agricultural Policy   36
Decoupled EU, US Subsidies: Implications for the Doha Round   47
Reform Obstacles and Opportunities in 2006   52

4   Opportunities and Challenges for Developing Countries   63
Agricultural Trade and Developing Economies   64
The Opportunities: What Do Developing Countries Export?   67
What Are the Challenges?   75
Domestic Obstacles to Grasping Trade Opportunities   83
Sanitary and Phytosanitary Standards: Both a Challenge
   and an Opportunity   87

5   The Devil in the Doha Details   91
Export Subsidies and the Role of Food Aid   92
Domestic Support   95
Market Access   108

6   Delivering on Doha's Promise   115
Special and Differential Treatment   117
Aid-for-Trade and Supply Constraints   122
Recommendations for a Doha Package Deal   126

Glossary   133

References   137

Index   143

Tables
Table 1.1   Average applied tariffs, 2001   5
Table 1.2   Estimated gains from global free trade   7
Table 1.3   World Bank estimates of gains from Doha liberalization
             scenarios   8
Table 2.1   OECD estimates of support to agricultural producers,
             average 2002–04   23
Table 2.2   Average agricultural tariffs in selected rich countries 26
Table 2.3   Tariff escalation on selected products   27
Table 2.4   Producer support estimates by country and commodity,
             average 2002–04   29
Table 2.5   Average applied tariffs, tariff peaks, and tariff-rate
             quotas, 2001   30
Table 2A.1   Government assistance to US cotton producers,
             1995–2003   33
Table 2A.2   Percentage PSE and NAC calculation, 1995–2003   34
Table 3.1   US and EU agricultural subsidies   50
Table 3.2   Concentration of US farm subsidy payments, 1995–2003   55
Table 4.1   Agricultural indicators for developing countries   64
Table 4.2   Distribution of developing-country exports   65
Table 4.3   Developing countries most dependent on agricultural
             exports   66
Table 4.4   Agricultural trade positions in developing countries   67

Table 4.5   Most important commodities among developing-
               country agricultural exports   72
Table 4.6   Sources of daily calories in developing countries   77
Table 4.7   Price effects of complete global trade liberalization,
               selected countries and commodities   78
Table 4.8   Indicators of trade preferences for agricultural products   81
Table 4.9   Possible winners and likely losers from US and EU
               sugar policy reform   84
Table 4.10   Indicators of infrastructure quality and trade costs   85
Table 4.11   Firm perceptions of major or severe obstacle to doing
               business   86
Table 5.1   Potential impact of Doha domestic subsidy proposals
               on EU agricultural support   99
Table 5.2   Potential impact of Doha domestic subsidy proposals
               on US agricultural support   100
Table 5.3   US countercyclical payments   106
Table 5.4   Key tariff-cutting proposals, March 2006   110
Table 6.1   Possible indicators for differentiating special and
               differential treatment under an agricultural agreement   121
Table 6.2   Categories of aid for trade   125

Figures
Figure 2.1   Uruguay Round agreement for reducing
               domestic support   18
Figure 2.2   Producer support estimate as percent of gross
               farm receipts, 1986–2004   22
Figure 2.3   Most trade-distorting support as share of total
               producer support, 1986–2004   24
Figure 2.4   Subsidies and prices, 1986–2004   25
Figure 3.1   EC-10 agricultural trade (excluding intra-EC trade),
               1970–2003   39
Figure 3.2   Evolution of the European Common Agricultural Policy,
               1960–2005   41
Figure 3.3   US agricultural trade, 1970–2003   44
Figure 3.4   Evolution of US agricultural policies, 1960–2005   48
Figure 3.5   Partially or mostly decoupled subsidies as a share
               of producer support, 1986–2001   49
Figure 3.6   Share of population dependent on agriculture, 1960–2003   54
Figure 4.1   Shares of middle-income country agricultural exports,
               1970–2002   70
Figure 4.2   Shares of low-income country agricultural exports,
               1970–2002   71
Figure 5.1   Japanese farm support as measured by OECD and WTO   97
Figure 5.2   US aggregate measurement of support with
               and without market price support   101
Figure 5.3   USDA payments for selected commodities   105

Boxes

Box 3.1   Policy reform options   37
Box 3.2   The political economy of US sugar policy   57
Box 4.1   Sugar preferences in the United States
           and the European Union   73
Box 5.1   Potential implications of the Doha Round for the 2007
           US farm bill   102

Preface

As this book was going to press in summer 2006, differences over agriculture were once again threatening the successful conclusion of an international trade negotiation. The Uruguay Round was wrapped up in the early 1990s after a three-year delay when American and European negotiators finally hammered out a deal that appeared to cut agricultural trade barriers and subsidies by 20 to 36 percent but that in fact left farm policies largely untouched. The risk is that the impasse will not be broken this time, and the Doha Round will fail or result in a minimalist agreement.

This book, by Senior Fellow Kimberly Ann Elliott, explains why progress on agriculture is politically the key to breaking the impasse—and why a breakthrough on agriculture by itself would yield only a modest "development" result. The first key to breaking the Doha Round impasse is to scale back the demands for flexibility in the rules on agriculture. Excessive flexibility in the Uruguay Round Agreement on Agriculture undercut the intended discipline and let the farm sectors in OECD countries off the hook. Hence far more attention is being paid this time to the devils in the details. Besides discontent with the Uruguay Round outcome, real progress on agriculture is also necessary because the elimination of quotas on textiles and apparel in 2005 left the rich countries with little else to put on the negotiating table. Brazil and the other developing-country members of the Group of 20 will not agree to significant opening of their own markets for nonagricultural products and services unless they get increased access to rich-country agricultural markets. In addition, American farmers will not agree to cuts in present subsidies they receive unless they receive additional market access abroad.

In addition to the politics, the conventional wisdom is that the Doha Development Agenda, as this round is officially known, cannot succeed unless it helps the hundreds of millions of desperately poor people living in the rural areas of poor countries. But Elliott's analysis shows why agricultural liberalization alone would be a modest step in reducing global poverty. With the important caveat that they exclude services, most models show that the majority of gains from further trade liberalization would indeed come from agriculture because that is where the remaining barriers are the highest. But most of the gains would go to the consumers and taxpayers in the rich countries, who pay most of the costs of supporting farmers in their countries. Developing countries as a group are likely to gain from agricultural reform in the rich countries, but the benefits would not be evenly distributed, and some poor countries could even lose from higher food prices and the erosion of their preferential access to European and American markets for sugar and other commodities. And in the poorest countries, many poor farmers will see little change if inadequate infrastructure, the lack of credit, or perverse government policies prevent their taking advantage of new market opportunities.

For these reasons, Elliott concludes that agricultural liberalization is only part of the package that is needed to deliver on the promise of the Doha Development Agenda. Breaking the impasse over agriculture is the necessary first step. But reductions in the high tariffs that rich countries maintain on textiles, apparel, footwear, and other labor-intensive light manufactures are also important for many countries. Because trade negotiations are reciprocal, and because taking these steps would be politically difficult for policymakers in Europe, Japan, the United States, and other rich countries, a deal will only be possible if their exporters receive increased access as well, including in manufacturing and services in the more advanced emerging markets such as Brazil, China, and India. A final part of the package has to be a credible program of broadly defined aid-for-trade that helps developing countries both address the adjustment costs associated with trade liberalization, including preference erosion and tariff revenue losses, and take advantage of new trade opportunities.

This book is a follow-up to William Cline's *Trade Policy and Global Poverty*, which was published jointly by the Center and the Institute in 2004. That book documented the potential gains from further liberalization and concluded that as many as 500 million people might be pulled out of poverty by moving to global free trade. This book complements that analysis by focusing on the details that need to be addressed to ensure that a new WTO agreement on agriculture is truly liberalizing and on the complementary policies that are needed to ensure that developing countries reap the largest possible gains.

The Center for Global Development is an independent, nonprofit policy research organization dedicated to reducing global poverty and inequality and to making globalization work for the poor. Through a combination of research and strategic outreach, the Center actively engages policymakers and the public to influence the policies of the United States, other rich countries, and such institutions as the World Bank, the International Monetary Fund, and the World Trade Organization to improve the economic and social development prospects in poor countries. The Center's Board of Directors bears overall responsibility for the Center and includes distinguished leaders of nongovernmental organizations, former officials, business executives, and some of the world's leading scholars of development. The Center receives advice on its research and policy programs from the Board and from an Advisory Committee that comprises respected development specialists and advocates.

The Center's president works with the Board, the Advisory Committee, and the Center's senior staff in setting the research and program priorities and approves all formal publications. The Center is supported by an initial significant financial contribution from Edward W. Scott Jr. and by funding from philanthropic foundations and other organizations. This book was made possible in part by funding from the MacArthur Foundation.

■ ■ ■

The Institute for International Economics is a private, nonprofit institution for the study and discussion of international economic policy. Its purpose is to analyze important issues in that area and to develop and communicate practical new approaches for dealing with them. The Institute is completely nonpartisan.

The Institute is funded by a highly diversified group of philanthropic foundations, private corporations, and interested individuals. Major institutional grants are now being received from the William M. Keck, Jr. Foundation and the Starr Foundation. About 33 percent of the Institute's resources in our latest fiscal year were provided by contributors outside the United States, including about 16 percent from Japan.

The Institute's Board of Directors bears overall responsibilities for the Institute and gives general guidance and approval to its research program, including the identification of topics that are likely to become important over the medium run (one to three years) and that should be addressed by the Institute. The director, working closely with the staff and outside Advisory Committee, is responsible for the development of particular projects and makes the final decision to publish an individual study.

The Institute hopes that its studies and other activities will contribute to building a stronger foundation for international economic policy around the world. We invite readers of these publications to let us know how they think we can best accomplish this objective.

NANCY BIRDSALL
President
Center for Global Development
June 2006

C. FRED BERGSTEN
Director
Institute for International Economics
June 2006

Acknowledgments

This is my first book as a joint fellow with the Center for Global Development and the Institute for International Economics, and I benefited greatly from being able to draw on two groups of excellent colleagues. I would like to thank the participants in the October 2005 study group for their feedback on the manuscript and especially Kym Anderson, Mac Destler, Bob Fisher, Jim Grueff, Lawrence MacDonald, Catherine L. Mann, Maureen Lewis, David Roodman, Susan Sechler, and Ann Tutwiler for reading the entire manuscript and providing thoughtful comments. Peter Timmer called into the study group at an inhumanly early hour from California and cheerfully responded from around the world to emails on various agriculture and development issues. I am also grateful to Dani Rodrik for reviewing the entire manuscript and for pointing out several ways to improve it. David Orden is due special thanks for reading multiple drafts and serving as a guide to the arcana of US agricultural policy. While any remaining errors are mine alone, they surely would have been numerous without the help I received from David and others.

The book would not have been possible without the support of Fred Bergsten and Nancy Birdsall, and I would especially like to thank Nancy for taking such a strong interest in the project and encouraging me throughout. I would also like to thank Sebastian Sotelo and Ceren Özer for research assistance and Valerie Norville and the Institute's publications team and Lawrence MacDonald and the CGD communications team for their help in producing this book in a timely fashion.

1

Introduction

The trade talks launched in Doha, Qatar, in November 2001 were the first of the nine rounds of multilateral trade negotiations held since World War II to "place the needs and interests [of developing countries, especially the poorest] at the heart" of the talks. This commitment, contained in the ministerial communiqué launching the Doha Development Agenda, was a response to an increase in the number of developing-country members in the World Trade Organization (WTO), more active involvement by these countries in negotiations, and the dissatisfaction of many of them with the results of the previous round. Since many developing countries have a comparative advantage in agriculture and since many of the world's poor live in rural areas, it seems logical that increased agricultural market access subsequently emerged as a central issue in the talks.

But even without the development focus, agriculture would have been central because it is the major piece of unfinished business from previous trade rounds. This means that it is the sector with the highest remaining barriers in rich countries and the greatest potential gains from further liberalization of merchandise trade. And it is not just key developing countries, such as Brazil, and poor commodity-dependent regions, such as sub-Saharan Africa, that are interested. US agricultural exporters have traditionally been an important part of the pro–free trade coalition, and they will give up some of their subsidies only if they get increased market access abroad. Thus, agricultural liberalization is the key to a successful Doha Round because that is what key countries want and most of what the rich countries have left to contribute in a reciprocal negotiation.

1

The implications for development and for poverty alleviation in poor countries are more complicated, however. Developing countries and groups within them are diverse, and farm policy reforms in rich countries will affect them in different ways. Farmers stand to benefit from higher world prices for agricultural products, but poor consumers could lose. Some countries will see their preferential access to developed markets eroded. Within countries, many rural poor live in remote areas that are isolated from national, much less international, markets. Connecting the rural poor to markets and increasing demand for their products, including through exports, would contribute to reduced global poverty, but increased market access alone is not be enough to achieve that goal. Many countries, especially the poorest, also need to adopt complementary policies to create an environment in which the poor can grasp new trade opportunities and where the losers are compensated. And the rich countries should help them.

Before tackling those challenges, however, rich countries must be persuaded to reduce subsidies and increase access to their markets. It is no accident that agricultural protection sticks out like a sore thumb. Agricultural products were largely excluded from international trade rules from the start of the postwar system, and negotiations have had little impact on farm policies in the industrialized countries since then. Even when this policy area was finally addressed, in the 1986–93 Uruguay Round, the conclusion of the negotiations was delayed for three years over farm policy, and the Agreement on Agriculture, when finally reached, was shaped by the content and scope of internal reforms in key countries rather than the reverse. In the current round of talks, the ministerial meeting planned for the midterm of the round in Cancún failed, in part over US and European unwillingness to be more forthcoming on agriculture. And a year after the scheduled January 2005 end date for the Doha Round passed, yet another ministerial meeting, in Hong Kong, concluded with minimal progress because of a continued impasse over agriculture.

This account of the history is not meant to discourage the pursuit of ambitious goals for agricultural policy reform; rather, it is intended to inform it. Compromise will no doubt be required, and careful attention to the details could lead to an agreement that is politically feasible in the rich countries and also delivers meaningful benefits to developing-country exporters. With a view to putting reform efforts in context, the present chapter first briefly reviews the history of attempts to discipline agricultural policies through trade negotiations and analyzes what is at stake in these talks. The challenges poor countries face in taking advantage of new trade opportunities and the need for complementary policies to address domestic supply constraints are then described. The chapter concludes with a preview of the remainder of the book.

Why Is Agricultural Liberalization at the Center of the Doha Round?

Agriculture is the key to getting a deal in the current round of trade talks because previous negotiations failed to deliver significant reforms in this sector. The Uruguay Round created a more transparent framework for measuring and capping agricultural support, but it did little to lower the level of applied subsidies or trade barriers. Since the eight previous trade rounds reduced average tariffs on manufactured goods (other than textiles and apparel) to the low single digits in rich countries, agriculture is what remains as a market-access target, especially for key developing countries.

The Uruguay Round Was Only a Start

The Uruguay Round of trade negotiations (1986–93) was the eighth under the General Agreement on Tariffs and Trade (GATT), and the first to seriously address agricultural trade distortions. From the creation of the GATT after World War II, agriculture received special treatment.[1] Export subsidies and import quotas were prohibited for manufactured goods but were permitted for agricultural and primary products under conditions designed to limit the impact on international markets (Jackson 1991, 44, 101). But the constraints were weak, and agricultural policies from the 1950s through the 1970s were set largely in response to domestic political demands.

With US farmers increasing exports in the 1960s, US policymakers came to regret their role in resisting international disciplines on agricultural trade. Beginning with the "Chicken War" in the early 1960s (over European barriers to poultry imports), US negotiators used both bilateral and multilateral trade negotiations to try to restore some restraint, particularly on European subsidies and import barriers. Bilateral pressure and threats of trade retaliation produced some limited successes in constraining the EU Common Agricultural Policy (CAP), but agricultural policies remained mostly beyond the GATT's reach. Finally, in September 1986, with strong backing from Australia, New Zealand, Brazil, and other members of the Cairns Group of agricultural exporting countries, US negotiators succeeded in getting agreement to address agricultural subsidies and trade barriers in the GATT negotiations launched in Punta del Este, Uruguay.

What finally emerged, but only after the United States and the European Community came close to a trade war over oilseeds (Iceland 1994), was a deal that produced much less reform than many had hoped for. While roundly condemned by the Cairns Group and other agricultural exporters,

---

1. There are many excellent treatments of postwar agricultural trade policies; Hathaway (1987) provides a succinct summary. Also see the references in chapter 3.

it was ultimately accepted as the best possible deal at the time.[2] The most important contributions of the resulting agreement include

- affirmation of the principle that trade negotiations must address trade-distorting domestic subsidies, as well as export subsidies and trade barriers;

- creation of a framework for measuring and reporting on agricultural support policies that has increased the transparency of support measures; and

- movement toward eliminating quantitative restrictions.

But with the exception of export subsidies, whose use has declined substantially, the resulting reductions in trade barriers and subsidies were minimal.[3]

The result was very little increased market access, including for middle-income developing countries in the Cairns Group. Developing countries had conceded on adoption of the intellectual property standards of the wealthier countries, as well as new rules on opening service sectors. These concessions supposedly were in return for increased market access for agricultural and clothing exports, where many of the developing countries have a comparative advantage. Disappointment with agricultural liberalization in practice, along with a back-loaded schedule for eliminating quotas under the Agreement on Textiles and Clothing, contributed to the perception among the developing countries that they had gotten a "bum deal" in the Uruguay Round.[4]

Lingering dissatisfaction with the results of the Uruguay Round and the feeling among some developing-country negotiators, especially from Africa, that their concerns were being ignored, contributed to the failure of efforts to launch a new round in Seattle in 1999. The focus on development in the communiqué that finally launched the round in 2001 was crafted to avoid a similar outcome. A legacy of this history, however, is the sluggish pace of the Doha Round amid developing countries' complaints over the lack of progress on their issues. These simmering grievances came to a boil in August 2003, when US and EU negotiators announced a joint proposal on agriculture. The Cairns Group and other developing-country exporters interpreted the proposal as an attempt to cut a deal that would protect sensitive sectors of the US and European economies at the expense of other

---

2. For a comprehensive and detailed history of the Uruguay Round, including agriculture, see Croome (1998).

3. For more on the details, see Josling (1998, chapter 3).

4. The most restrictive quotas generally were not liberalized until the end of the 10-year phaseout period; see Bhattacharya and Elliott (2005).

Table 1.1 Average applied tariffs, 2001 (percent)

Category	European Union	Japan	United States	High-income countries	Developing countries
All partners, import weighted					
Agriculture	13.9	29.4	2.4	16.0	17.7
Textiles and apparel	5.2	9.7	9.8	7.5	17.0
Other manufacturing	2.2	1.4	1.8	1.9	9.0
Total merchandise	3.2	5.2	1.8	2.9	9.9
Developing-country partners, production weighted					
Agriculture	34.4	158.1	5.0	n.a.	n.a.
Total merchandise	7.5	26.9	2.8	n.a.	n.a.

n.a. = not available

Sources: Anderson, Martin, and van der Mensbrugghe (2006); Roodman (2005).

countries. The negative reaction to the proposal triggered formation of the "Group of 20," a coalition of developing countries whose principal demand is significant liberalization of the more affluent countries' agricultural policies. The developing countries' reaction to the proposal also contributed to the failure of the midterm ministerial meeting in Cancún a month later.

Farm Trade Is Where the Barriers Are—and the Potential Gains

With the long-awaited end of the global quota system restricting trade in textiles and apparel in January 2005, agriculture has no competitors for the title of most distorted sector of the global economy. It is now the only sector where both quantitative restrictions (tariff-rate quotas) and export subsidies are still permitted, and the level of protection for agriculture is far higher than that for manufactured goods. Clearly, agriculture offers the choicest targets for liberalization.

The data in table 1.1 give only a hint of the distortions of global agricultural trade, which are analyzed in detail in chapter 2. On average, agricultural tariffs applied by high-income countries are more than five times higher than the average tariffs they apply to merchandise overall, and almost eight times higher than those they apply to manufactured goods other than textiles and apparel. An alternative calculation presented at the bottom of the table mostly uses the same underlying data but a different weighting scheme. These adjustments result in higher tariff levels but a similar ratio between agricultural and total merchandise tariffs in the European Union and Japan, which is the key point here.[5] The apparently low US figures are misleading because they do not include the effect of domestic subsidies, which the United States uses more heavily than trade measures.

All of the figures likely underestimate the overall distortionary effects of rich countries' farm policies for at least two other reasons. First, it is difficult to be precise about the protective effects of tariff-rate quotas, and they are almost certainly not fully reflected in table 1.1. Another potential problem is that the data include detailed information on bilateral applied tariffs that take into account preferential tariff arrangements, such as the European Union's Everything But Arms program and the United States' Africa Growth and Opportunity Act. On the one hand, this dataset is an improvement over previous ones, which mostly ignored these preference programs. On the other hand, the approach that is used also results in underestimation of the average applied tariff because the compilers of the dataset assumed that all exports eligible for preferential treatment receive it. Numerous studies suggest otherwise (see chapter 4).

Because its rates of protection are well above average, the agricultural sector offers the largest potential gains from further liberalization of merchandise trade, even though agriculture is a small part of the global economy.[6] Table 1.2 shows the results of three recent efforts to model the benefits from moving to global free trade (Bouet 2006, Cline 2004, Anderson, Martin, and van der Mensbrugghe 2006). Although the overall levels of benefits differ, the distribution of gains and the distribution of the sources of gains are broadly similar.[7] All three models show developing countries gaining relatively more as a share of national income than high-income countries; they also show developing countries capturing around 30 percent of total global gains, which is roughly 50 percent more than their share of global income. All of the models also show that agricultural liberalization accounts for roughly 60 percent of the total, with the caveat that services liberalization is not included.

Still, these numbers are quite small, relative either to trade or national income. Moreover, the new World Bank estimates of the gains from global

---

5. Import weights are commonly used for calculating average tariffs but can lead to underestimation because imports will be low or nil when tariffs are prohibitive. See Roodman (2005) for a detailed discussion.

6. Many analysts believe, and the few empirical analyses that exist suggest, that the benefits from services liberalization would be greater. But most models exclude services liberalization because the data on services are often of poor quality and the quantification of barriers to trade in services is in its infancy and subject to uncertainty because of the difficulties in distinguishing market-improving and market-distorting regulations. A few efforts to estimate the benefits from liberalizing services have been made, however, and they suggest that the gains could be far larger than those from liberalizing agriculture. See, for example, Hertel and Keeney (2006).

7. For a discussion of the differences in the models and the results, see Elliott (2005a), Bouet (2006), and van der Mensbrugghe (2006).

Table 1.2 Estimated gains from global free trade

Computable general equilibrium model results	Cline (2004)	Anderson et al. (2006)	Bouet (2006)
Base year	1997	2015	2015
Model type	Static	Dynamic	Dynamic
Total (billions of dollars)	228	287	100
Relative to national income (percent)			
High-income countries	0.87	0.60	0.30
Developing countries	1.09	0.80	0.4–0.8[a]
Share of global gains (percent)			
Captured by developing countries	30	30	26
Resulting from agricultural liberalization	55	63	55
Resulting from textiles and apparel liberalization	11	14	n.a.

n.a. = not available

a. 0.4 for middle-income countries and 0.8 for low-income countries.

free trade, when adjusted for greater comparability, are far smaller than Cline's results and also far smaller than earlier World Bank estimates (World Bank 2002). Two key differences in the baseline most likely account for the smaller gains indicated by the new World Bank figures. The first is the use of the new database incorporating detailed information on bilateral and regional preference arrangements, which lowers the observed rate of protection against developing countries—and also likely leads to underestimation of the remaining gains from freer trade as noted above. The second difference from most previous studies is that the baseline scenario incorporates the final implementation of the Uruguay Round, including the end of the textile and apparel quotas in 2005, China's membership in the WTO, and the accession of 10 Eastern European countries to the European Union. In sum, the new World Bank estimates do not indicate smaller benefits per unit of liberalization. Rather, there is less liberalization remaining to be done than previously assumed.

These studies and others not discussed here find that almost all developing countries gain from a move to free trade, but the distribution becomes more uneven under some of the less ambitious partial liberalization scenarios. Table 1.3 shows results from several Doha Round scenarios analyzed by Anderson, Martin, and van der Mensbrugghe (2006).[8] A scenario

---

8. Other scenarios may be found in Bouet, Mevel, and Orden (2005) and Polaski (2006), but they are not included because of differences in assumptions and models that make them difficult to compare.

Table 1.3 World Bank estimates of gains from Doha liberalization scenarios

Group	Agricultural liberalization, no sensitive products: Scenario 1 (billions of dollars)	Agricultural and nonagricultural liberalization, no sensitive products: Scenario 7 (billions of dollars)	Same as scenario 7 but developing countries take same cuts on manufacturing (billions of dollars)	Share of liberalization gains due to agriculture: Scenario 7 (percent)
World	74.5	96.1	119.3	77.5
High-income countries	65.6	79.2	96.4	82.8
Middle-income countries	8.0	12.5	17.1	64.0
Low-income countries	1.0	3.6	5.9	27.8
East Asia and the Pacific	0.5	4.5	5.5	11.1
South Asia	0.4	2.5	4.2	12.0
Middle East and North Africa	−0.8	−0.6	0.1	−133.3
Sub-Saharan Africa	0.3	0.4	1.2	75.0
Latin America and the Caribbean	8.1	7.9	9.2	102.5

Scenario definitions:

Scenario 1 assumes cuts of 45 to 75 percent in agricultural tariffs for rich countries and 35 to 60 percent for developing countries, with higher tariffs being cut more than lower ones.

Scenario 7 is the same as scenario 1 for agriculture, plus 50 percent cuts in nonagricultural tariffs for developed countries and 33 percent cuts for developing countries.

Note: The scenariio numbers are the same as those in the World Bank study. All scenarios assume elimination of export subsidies, cuts from actual levels of agricultural domestic subsidies in developed countries, and no commitments by least developed countries.

Source: Anderson, Martin, and van der Mensbrugghe (2006, 360, 370–71).

assuming average tariff cuts of 40 to 50 percent in agriculture and manufacturing by developed countries, smaller reductions by most developing countries, and no reductions at all by the least developed countries produces about a third of the overall potential gains from global free trade—$96 billion versus $287 billion (column 2; see table notes for details).

As in the free trade scenario, the majority of gains are from agricultural liberalization, but the regional breakdown shows interesting variation, and developing countries reap only about 20 percent of the potential gains they could accrue from full free trade.[9] Among developing countries, middle-income countries gain the most in the agriculture-only scenario, with most of the gains, not surprisingly, being captured by competitive Latin American exporters. Among low-income countries, agriculture is not the major source of gains, with the important exception of sub-Saharan Africa. The Middle East and North Africa region is a net loser in several of the World Bank's scenarios because many of the countries in this area are net food importers. In the scenario with broader and deeper liberalization by developing countries, however, all regions reap overall net gains (column 3).

Thus, even in a world of high trade barriers and subsidies, several middle-income developing countries have become important agricultural exporters, and these countries have the most to gain in the short run from further liberalization. But not all developing countries would gain equally from agricultural liberalization by wealthy countries, and there are significant challenges in many countries in translating such liberalization into meaningful opportunities for poor farmers.

Still, even countries that might lose in the short run would gain in broad terms from a deal that affirmed the utility and preserved the credibility of the multilateral trade system. A failure in this negotiation would have the potential to undermine the commitment to the WTO of the large, powerful countries that have alternative means of protecting their interests. A likely outcome would be further proliferation of bilateral and regional trade agreements that typically exclude the most vulnerable.

Why Is a Doha Agreement on Agricultural Liberalization Not Enough?

More than trade liberalization is needed to ensure that developing countries and the poor gain from globalization. Trade creates losers as well as winners, and policymakers interested in reducing poverty need to find

---

9. Anderson, Martin, and van der Mensbrugghe's (2006) central Doha scenario (the second column of table 1.3) shows middle-income and low-income countries gaining $16.1 billion, compared with the $86 billion that can be calculated from Anderson, Martin, and van der Mensbrugghe's global free trade scenario in table 1.2 (30 percent of $287 billion).

ways to compensate the losers or help them adjust. Many countries also lack the capacity to respond effectively to changing conditions in global markets and will need assistance if they are to take advantage of these changes.

As noted, many countries are net food importers that could lose from increased world prices for subsidized commodities; other countries might experience the erosion of their preferential access to markets in rich countries. In the poorest countries, the challenges are even greater. Many rural poor are subsistence farmers with potentially little to gain in the short run if the costs of getting their crops to market outweigh any price gain (Hertel and Winters 2006). But much analysis also suggests that these losses are not likely to be as great as feared (e.g., Badiane 2004). Moreover, gains in other developing countries that do not enjoy preferential access would counterbalance some of these losses. It is far better to compensate the losses and provide assistance to overcome obstacles to exporting than to forgo the potential gains.

In addition, there is a need to look beyond the traditional trade barriers and subsidies that are at the center of the negotiation. Many developing countries have responded to the distortions created by rich-country farm policies by focusing on exports of products that are relatively less protected and that exploit comparative advantage, such as tropical products (other than sugar) and fruits and vegetables. In these areas, it is also important to ensure that developing-country exporters can meet the quality and food safety standards that consumers increasingly demand.

Rich-country liberalization is thus only part of the answer because it may not trigger a significant supply response in countries where farmers lack infrastructure (transportation links, storage facilities), access to inputs including credit, and sensible national policies. Even substantial trade policy changes in rich countries are likely to produce disappointing results for the poorest unless the need for complementary domestic policy reforms and investments is also addressed. If both sets of challenges are addressed—market access in rich countries and supply constraints in poor ones—the World Bank (Hertel and Winters 2006) and Cline (2004) calculate that the long-term and dynamic gains from global free trade could lift 100 million to as many as 400 million people out of poverty by the middle of the next decade.

Plan of the Book

A successful Doha Round would open new opportunities for many poor countries, but grasping those opportunities and ensuring that poor people in those countries also benefit will require far more. The present volume organizes the discussion of these issues around three questions: First, what are the obstacles to a successful agreement in the agricultural area? Second, what are the likely distributional consequences of such an agreement?

Third, what would a good deal look like from the perspective of developing countries?

Chapters 2 and 3 address the problems posed by how rich countries support their agricultural sectors. Chapter 2 considers which products are supported by particular countries and examines the mechanisms they use. Chapter 3 focuses on the evolution of policies in the United States and the European Union in order to explore why agricultural protection in rich countries and so resistant to reform.

Chapter 4 explores the potential distributional effects of an agricultural agreement by examining current trade patterns involving developing countries and agriculture. The data highlight the opportunities that offer the greatest potential gain to developing countries, as well as the challenges some of these countries face in exploiting those opportunities.

Chapters 5 and 6 explore the elements of a potential deal. Chapter 5 examines the "devil in the details" of the Doha Round and suggests what rich countries need to do to ensure that meaningful agricultural liberalization occurs. Chapter 6 concludes with recommendations for the broad package that is needed to deliver on the promise to make Doha truly a development round.

2

The Problem: Rich Countries Supporting Rich Farmers

Oxfam International's "Make Trade Fair" campaign lambastes rich countries for spending "$1 billion a day on agricultural subsidies."[1] Other critics use the metaphor of cows in rich countries living in luxury, supported by subsidies that exceed the incomes of more than a billion people living in extreme poverty on $1 a day (Sharma n.d.). Pascal Lamy, now head of the WTO, rejected this criticism when he was the EU commissioner for trade, arguing that the true figure for total subsidies is a third of what advocacy groups claim. Who is right?

The first step in crafting a meaningful agreement to reduce agricultural support is to understand the mechanisms rich countries use to support their farmers, what these mechanisms cost, and who pays. This chapter begins with a summary of the main policy tools available to support farmers in wealthy countries. It then summarizes how the WTO organizes and addresses the various forms of agricultural support. The last two sections examine the pattern of support across countries and commodities as measured by the Organization for Economic Cooperation and Development (OECD).

Mechanisms for Supporting Farmers

Policymakers from different countries offer different justifications at different times for supporting agriculture, from food security, to supporting

---

1. See "The Issues: Rigged Rules" at the Make Trade Fair Campaign Web site, www. maketradefair.com (accessed April 24, 2006).

family farms, to preserving cultural or environmental amenities in rural areas. In practice, whatever the initial motivation, most policies evolve into programs that raise farm incomes and do so in ways that encourage increased production. Most governments also face a budget constraint that, along with structural characteristics of the agricultural sector, influence the specific policy mix chosen.

There are two basic approaches to supporting farmers:

- propping up market prices by controlling supplies through import restrictions (tariffs, quotas, or variable import levies or price bands), domestic supply controls (production quotas, public stockholding, land set-asides), or export subsidies; and

- propping up farm incomes through various types of subsidy payments, which can be, to varying degrees, linked to production, prices, or input use, or "decoupled" from production decisions.

The key to distinguishing between these two approaches is the price received by farmers when they sell in the domestic market. If that price is above world prices because of government policies, it is referred to here as market price support (MPS). If the domestic price is roughly the world price (adjusted for transportation and other distribution costs), with farmers receiving payments for any difference between that price and government targets, it is referred to as a subsidy.

The most common approach in much of the world is MPS, mainly through trade restrictions. Most of the costs of MPS are borne by consumers, while taxpayers foot the bill in the case of subsidies. But taxpayers also pay some of the costs of MPS when governments end up holding surplus stocks or must use export subsidies to help dispose of them on world markets. In some cases, domestic subsidies and price supports can be combined, as when farmers are paid to forgo production on a portion of their land. The policymakers of rich countries are gradually moving toward decoupled income support payments, but most support today still promotes production and distorts trade.

The degree of distortion depends on the gap between world prices and the domestic prices that policymakers want to achieve. Depending on domestic conditions and the desired level of support, MPS is sometimes provided primarily through import restrictions, as in Japan and South Korea. In other cases, such as for many commodities in the European Union, domestic supply controls and export subsidies are also required to prevent or to dispose of surpluses resulting from above-market prices.

In the United States, policymakers no longer make extensive use of supply controls for the major "program commodities," mostly grains, oilseeds, and cotton, because supporting prices above world levels discourages exports. Instead, farmers receive a variety of direct payments based on the difference between world prices and legislated price floors or targets, and sell at world prices (see chapter 3). In the more import-sensitive dairy and sugar sectors, MPS by means of import restrictions and domestic supply controls remains the instruments of choice.[2]

The result of these policies at home is that domestic producers gain at the expense of taxpayers, consumers, and producers in nonfavored sectors. Internationally, the opposite is true: Foreign producers and exporters lose as a result of lost sales and lower world prices, but consumers may gain (subject to their own country's trade policies).

Decoupled subsidies avoid these distortions because they are based on past levels of production or payment and have no link to current prices or production. This income support is paid for by taxpayers, rather than consumers and foreign producers, and, in theory, should not influence production decisions. In practice, large decoupled subsidies can reduce risk, discourage exit, and keep production at levels higher than would be expected in an undistorted market.[3]

Moreover, few subsidies are completely decoupled, and most commodities are supported with a combination of more and less distorting policies. For example, US Department of Agriculture (USDA) data show that upland cotton growers in the United States received, on average, a little more than $7 billion in income in crop years 2003 and 2004. Of that, roughly a third, $2.3 billion, was in government payments, but only a bit more than a quarter of that, $680 million, was decoupled from current production or prices.[4] It seems likely that under such a system, decoupled income payments marginally increase the incentive to produce. The extent to which US and EU agricultural subsidies are effectively decoupled is discussed in more detail in chapter 3.

In choosing between price supports and various subsidies, governments typically base their decisions on a particular commodity's relationship to international markets and on policymakers' willingness to bear the costs nationally. With decoupled subsidies, whatever level of support is desired must be paid for entirely through tax collections and transfers. In this case, if policymakers want to reduce the cost of subsidies, they can do so only by reducing the level of support that farmers receive.

Alternatively, if policymakers want to reduce the budget costs associated with production-linked subsidies, they have two options: They can,

---

2. Domestic production quotas for peanuts and tobacco have recently been eliminated and quota holders have been compensated with lump sum payments (distributed over a number of years), but import restrictions remain in place.

3. See Baffes and de Gorter (2005) for a discussion of issues related to decoupling, including recent experience in various countries.

4. Data on commodity payments and producer income by source are available under CCC Budget Essentials on the budget page of the USDA's Farm Services Agency, www.fsa.usda.gov (accessed April 25, 2006).

again, lower the level of support or combine supply controls and subsidies, which shifts some of the cost from taxpayers to consumers. In an autarkic economy, this can be achieved through direct production controls or acreage reductions that reduce supplies and raise commodity prices. With trade, sectors that are globally uncompetitive will also need protection from imports, which will transfer some of the cost of the policy to foreign exporters. But commodities with export potential can lose international competitiveness if supply controls raise domestic prices above world levels. Policymakers in this case can offset higher domestic prices with export subsidies, but this again raises budget costs, in addition to imposing costs on international competitors.

MPS usually requires import restrictions to be effective, and consumers pay the bulk of the costs. The specific methods policymakers employ are typically more costly and distorting when governments have official price targets that require them to intervene in markets to store or dispose of surpluses that threaten to breach the price floor, including through the use of export subsidies. The requirement to maintain a given price level typically leads policymakers to choose import restrictions that offer as much insulation from global markets as possible. For example, ad valorem tariffs, which are set as a percentage of the value of the imported product, provide some price support, but the level fluctuates with world prices, making it difficult to maintain domestic price targets. Specific tariffs, by contrast, are calculated as so many dollars, yen, or euros per unit of a product, and they provide relatively more protection when prices are low. For example, a specific tariff of 10 cents per pound of sugar is equivalent to an ad valorem tariff of 100 percent when the import price is 10 cents per pound, but only 50 percent when the price is 20 cents per pound. Not surprisingly, specific and compound tariffs (which combine specific and ad valorem tariffs) are far more commonly imposed on agricultural goods than on manufactured goods.

Import quotas provide an even greater level of certainty and domestic price stability by preventing import surges when world prices dip, which also makes quotas more costly than tariffs. Tariff-rate quotas (TRQs) are a hybrid tool, with lower tariffs up to a quantitative ceiling and higher tariffs over that amount. They are potentially more flexible than simple quotas because imports theoretically can enter at the higher tariff level when import prices fall. But if the tariff on imports in excess of the quota amount is prohibitively high, as it is in many cases involving agricultural products, then the TRQ functions like an import quota.

A second problem is that governments usually distribute the in-quota import quantity among potential exporters by administrative means, with the right to export allocated to various countries on the basis of historical ties or recent trade levels. This prevents imports from adjusting to changing competitive conditions in supplying countries and distorts production and trade patterns in exporting countries as well. For example, some Caribbean sugar exporters no longer fill their quotas in the US market, where the domestic price has averaged roughly twice the world level over the past two decades, because the EU sugar price is usually three times the world level and these countries do not produce enough sugar to fill both quotas.

To sum up, the costs of agricultural policies are paid principally by the consumers and taxpayers whose governments choose to support farmers, and those governments' citizens will be the primary beneficiaries of any policy reform. But governments also shift some of the costs to foreign suppliers through the use of trade measures, and these costs can be severe for developing countries with large numbers of poor farmers who suffer from depressed prices, even though consumers in such countries may benefit from lower food prices. Developing-country exporters lose access in markets protected by trade barriers, but they also suffer from production-related support and export subsidies that increase volatility and lower average world prices in other export markets.

The WTO Framework for Negotiating on Agriculture

During the Uruguay Round (1986–93), negotiators developed a broad framework for addressing agricultural distortions for the first time since the postwar trade system was created in 1948. In addition to trade barriers, negotiators recognized that production-linked subsidies distorted trade and needed to be addressed as well. The objective was not to force countries to eliminate all support for farmers or rural areas but to reduce the negative effects on the rest of the world.

The Uruguay Round negotiators initially planned to use a scheme based on a traffic signal metaphor, with red for prohibited (export) subsidies, amber for restricted domestic programs that should be reduced, and green for decoupled subsidies that would be permitted. But this organizing principle had to be dropped when the European Community refused to eliminate export subsidies, insisting that they be addressed separately. At this point, the negotiations coalesced around three "pillars" of agricultural support: market access, export subsidies, and domestic support.

Under the last pillar, domestic support, negotiators kept the amber and green boxes and, in a further departure from the traffic light metaphor, agreed to create a "blue box" to accommodate farm payments that, while recognized as trade distorting, were considered less so than amber box subsidies because they were tied to production limits. Figure 2.1 summarizes the domestic support approach the negotiators adopted.

Under the revised system of boxes, developed-country members agreed to reduce export subsidies by 36 percent in value and the volume of subsidized exports by 21 percent over six years. (The rates of reduction were set at 24 and 14 percent, respectively, for developing countries.) The most trade-distorting domestic subsidies were placed in the amber box, but

Figure 2.1 Uruguay Round agreement for reducing domestic support

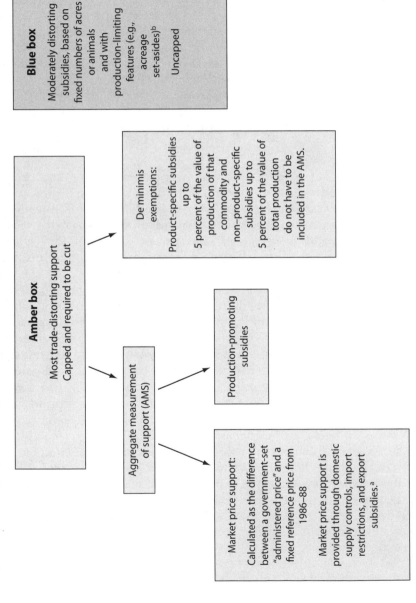

Amber box

Most trade-distorting support
Capped and required to be cut

De minimis exemptions:

Product-specific subsidies up to 5 percent of production of that commodity and non–product-specific subsidies up to 5 percent of the value of total production do not have to be included in the AMS.

Aggregate measurement of support (AMS)

Production-promoting subsidies

Market price support:

Calculated as the difference between a government-set "administered price" and a fixed reference price from 1986–88

Market price support is provided through domestic supply controls, import restrictions, and export subsidies.[a]

Blue box

Moderately distorting subsidies, based on fixed numbers of acres or animals and with production-limiting features (e.g., acreage set-asides)[b]

Uncapped

Green box

Minimally or non–trade-distorting policies, including direct payments to farmers that are "decoupled" from production; environmental programs; research and development; and domestic food aid (e.g., US food stamps)

Uncapped

a. Import restrictions on commodities without an administered price are not included in the AMS.
b. The United States proposes to change this definition to allow payments linked to prices but with a fixed base and no requirement to produce.

payments that would otherwise have been counted in this category were exempted as long as they did not exceed de minimis levels set at 5 percent of the value of production of specific commodities or 5 percent of the value of total agricultural production for non–product-specific subsidies (10 percent in each case for developing countries). The aggregate measurement of support (AMS) in the amber box included trade-distorting support above these limits and was made subject to 20 percent cuts over six years (13 percent for developing countries).

In addition to subsidies, the AMS includes a measure of MPS for commodities that have an "administered price." The MPS measure is calculated as the difference between the administered price and a measure of average world prices in 1986–88, multiplied by the volume of production of the commodity in question. Commodities whose prices are supported purely through import protection, without a guaranteed price floor or target, are covered only in the market access talks. The inclusion of some MPS in the amber box is unfortunate because it makes domestic subsidy measures less transparent and potentially more difficult to control. Japan, for example, eliminated the administered price for rice in the late 1990s but kept strict import controls. This allowed Japan to reduce its reported AMS by 80 percent, by eliminating the MPS portion while maintaining high levels of protection for rice.

Another blow to creating meaningful international discipline on domestic support was the choice of 1986–88 as the period on which the required cuts would be based. By 1995, when implementation began, both the European Union and United States were well under their Uruguay Round targets as a result of budget-driven domestic reforms adopted in the early 1990s and cyclical reductions in payments due to higher commodity prices. Little additional reform was required of either to fulfill their URAA commitments.

Minimally or nondistorting payments can be allocated to the green box with no limit. These include "decoupled" subsidies, which provide income support that is not linked to current production and prices, payments for environmentally motivated land set-asides, research and development support, and domestic food aid, such as the US food stamp program. The blue box, for partially decoupled subsidies that are still moderately distorting, also was not capped because it was regarded as a step toward reform.

The Uruguay Round agreement also required an average tariff cut of 36 percent but allowed cuts of as little as 15 percent for some tariff lines, as long as the overall average was achieved (an average 24 percent cut, with a minimum of 10 percent was required of developing countries). The agreement also required that import quotas be converted to tariffs with an equivalent effect, but countries manipulated the process and many tariffs were set at extremely high levels. In addition, TRQs were permitted for some sensitive products to ensure a minimum level of market access, with lower tariffs on imports up to at least 5 percent of domestic consumption and generally prohibitive tariffs for overquota imports. The net result of all this flexibility was very little additional market access for agricultural products. Under all three pillars of agricultural support, least developed countries were exempt from reduction commitments, and other developing countries only had to make cuts equal to two-thirds of those undertaken by the rich countries (as indicated in the discussion above by the figures in parentheses). In other respects, however, most developing countries were relatively more constrained than the rich ones. In effect, countries not providing export or domestic subsidies to agriculture at the time the agreement was reached had to "bind" their subsidies at zero. That is, under the agreement, only countries that committed to reducing these subsidies were allowed to have them, with two exceptions: First, developing countries were permitted a temporary exemption to provide subsidies to offset marketing, transportation, and certain other costs related to agricultural exports. Second, all developing countries got access to the 10 percent of production de minimis categories. Beyond that, only about a dozen mostly middle-income countries currently have the right to use export and trade-distorting domestic subsidies for agriculture (WTO 2004).

In a bid to facilitate monitoring, the agreement also required WTO members to periodically report on the application of TRQs and domestic and export subsidies. These notifications are a potentially important source of information on levels of support among WTO members. Unfortunately, members have been lax in following the rules, and the most recent data available in spring 2006 for most major countries were for 2000 or 2001. These data also do not allow for comparison to the prereform period since they have only been collected since 1995. Fortunately, the OECD has been publishing comparable estimates of the value of member governments' support for farmers, by country and commodity, since 1986.

Patterns of Support Across Countries

In its 2005 biennial report on the subject, the OECD estimated that member governments (i.e., taxpayers) and consumers supported agriculture with various policies whose total cost averaged nearly $350 billion annually from 2002 to 2004, a figure closer to Oxfam's assertion in the opening paragraph of the present chapter than Pascal Lamy's (OECD 2005a, 12).[5] But Lamy was correct in asserting that OECD government *payments* to farmers are much smaller. A common mistake is to confuse total support with subsidies. The difference between the two has two sources. The first is the MPS resulting from import restrictions, export subsidies, and domestic supply

---

5. This discussion of OECD policies focuses on the traditional and richest members, as shown in the tables and charts. Depending on the year, the OECD average also includes the Czech Republic, Hungary, South Korea, Mexico, Poland, Slovakia, and Turkey.

controls. The second is general government support for agriculture that does not directly affect production or corrects for market failures (e.g., subsidies for research and development or infrastructure). The OECD figure of roughly $350 billion is the "total support estimate," reflecting the gross value of transfers from consumers and taxpayers resulting from all policies in support of agriculture.

This figure that should be of concern in international trade negotiations is somewhere between Lamy's $100 billion and Oxfam's $350 billion. The starting point is the OECD's producer support estimate (PSE), which is a calculation of "the annual monetary transfers to *farmers* from policy measures" (emphasis in the original) that either maintain prices above world market levels or provide government payments to farmers (OECD 2004b, 2). Expressed as a percentage, the PSE is the value of producer support as a share of gross farm receipts, which are defined as the "value of total production (at supported farm-gate prices), plus budgetary support" (OECD 2003, 292). In other words, a PSE of 50 percent means that the value of producer support received by farmers equals the value of what they would receive from the market without support. On average, farmers in OECD member states receive transfers from consumers and taxpayers equal to roughly a third of gross receipts, though there is relatively wide dispersion, as shown in figure 2.2 and table 2.1.

Within the PSE, the OECD also calculates the most trade-distorting forms of support to farmers. These categories can be compared with the amber, blue, and green boxes under the WTO framework, though differences in definition and measurement mean they do not exactly match up. The principal difference comes in the measurement of MPS, which accounts for 80 percent of the OECD's classification of the most trade-distorting forms of support and 61 percent of the total (table 2.1). The OECD measures MPS using the gap between the price producers receive and a reference price based on world prices. In contrast to the WTO measure of MPS that is included in the amber box, the OECD measure includes all forms of MPS, not just those with administered prices. The OECD reference price in each report is also updated, while the WTO uses a 1986–88 reference period to calculate the price gap. In 2000, for example, members notified $51 billion in MPS to the WTO, while the OECD estimated such support was three times as high, at $153 billion (OECD 2005a and WTO Agricultural Trade Policy Commitments Database at www.ers.usda.gov).

The other forms of most trade-distorting support included in the OECD analysis are government payments that are linked to output that subsidize inputs, all of which are also included in the WTO's amber box. The OECD has estimated that from 2002 to 2004, the value of these forms of support across all OECD members averaged $190 billion annually. The balance of the PSE figures consist of less-distorting forms of support, including both decoupled, green box payments and, more often, blue box payments that have production-limiting elements.

Figure 2.2 Producer support estimate as percent of gross farm receipts , 1986–2004

percent

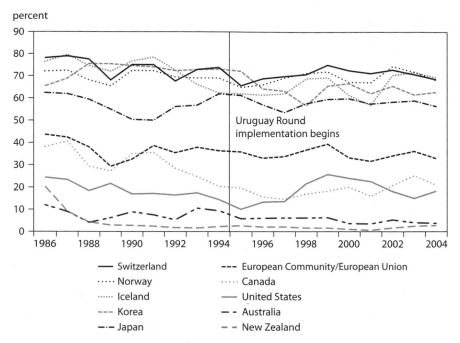

Note: EU-12 for 1986–94, EU-15 from 1995, European Union includes ex-East Germany from 1990. Austria, Finland, and Sweden are included in the OECD totals for all years and in the European Union from 1995.

Source: Producer and Consumer Support Estimates, OECD database, 1986–2004.

Among the high-income countries, four broad groups, corresponding roughly to negotiating positions in the Doha Round, can be identified in figure 2.2. At the top, providing the highest levels of support, are Switzerland, Norway, Iceland, South Korea, and Japan, all members of the Group of 10 (G-10), which opposes significant liberalization. (The other G-10 members are Bulgaria, Israel, Liechtenstein, Mauritius, and Taiwan.)

Providing the lowest levels of support are Australia and New Zealand, leaders of the Cairns Group of agricultural exporting countries, which has been pushing for deep reforms since the Uruguay Round. Between are the United States and Canada, which are below the OECD average of 30 percent, and the European Union, which is slightly above it.

In dollar terms, the United States and the European Union account for 60 percent of total OECD producer support (table 2.1), and these two remain key players in agricultural trade negotiations. However, the dynamics have changed since the Uruguay Round when they negotiated major components of the URAA bilaterally and then presented the results as a fait accompli to other negotiators. The developing countries that make up the Group

Table 2.1 OECD estimates of support to agricultural procedures, average 2002–04

Country	PSE (millions of US dollars)	PSE as percent of gross farm receipts	Percent of PSE that is:			PSE per hectare[b] (US dollars)	TSE as percent of GDP
			Most trade-distorting		Less distorting[a]		
			Market price support	Output and input subsidies			
Australia	1,068	4.3	0.8	76.0	23.2	2.4	0.3
Canada	5,521	22.3	47.8	9.6	42.6	81.8	0.8
European Union[c]	114,274	34.3	54.6	11.7	33.7	810.5	1.2
Iceland	195	70.3	45.2	42.0	12.8	85.5	2.1
Japan	46,924	57.7	90.1	6.5	3.5	9,041.3	1.4
Korea	18,253	63.1	92.6	2.6	4.9	9,442.6	3.5
New Zealand	186	2.3	82.2	17.2	0.6	10.8	0.4
Norway	2,902	71.3	47.1	25.3	27.6	2,808.8	1.4
Switzerland	5,343	70.5	55.7	9.3	35.1	3,503.4	1.8
United States	40,409	17.0	35.3	27.6	37.1	98.1	0.9
OECD total/average	254,244	30.3	61.3	13.3	25.4	231.9	1.2

PSE = producer support estimate
TSE = total support estimate

a. These subsidies include partially decoupled blue box payments as well as decoupled green box payments.
b. Agricultural land.
c. EU-15 (countries that were EU members as of January 1995); Austria, Finland, and Sweden are included in the OECD and EU totals for all years.

Source: Producer and Consumer Support Estimates, OECD database, 1986–2004.

Figure 2.3   Most trade-distorting support as share of total producer support, 1986–2004

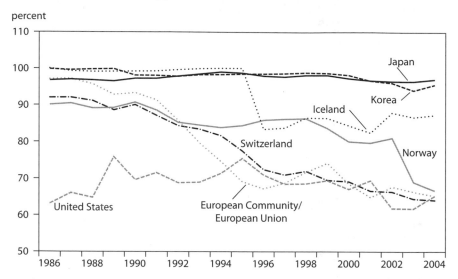

percent

Notes: The most trade-distorting support includes market price support, payments based on output, and payments based on input use. EU-12 for 1986–94, EU-15 from 1995, European Union includes ex–East Germany from 1990. Austria, Finland, and Sweden are included in the OECD total for all years and in the European Union from 1995. The OECD total does not include the six non-OECD EU member states.

Source: Producer and Consumer Support Estimates, OECD database, 1986–2004.

of 20 (G-20) demonstrated in Cancún in September 2003 that they expect to have their interests considered, and are insisting that the United States and European Union make real and substantial cuts in subsidies and trade restrictions.

Figures 2.2 and 2.3 illustrate the modest gains from the Uruguay Round agreement. Figure 2.2 underscores the fact that there has been relatively little change in overall levels of OECD farm support in most countries and that most of the decline occurred prior to implementation of the agreement. Figure 2.3 indicates that there has been more progress in reducing the most trade-distorting forms of support. The European Union, Switzerland, and Norway have made the most progress by this measure, but trade-distorting support, like support in general, remains at very high levels, particularly in the cases of Switzerland and Norway. Policies in Japan and South Korea have changed very little since the mid-1980s (when the OECD began quantifying them), and they remain both far more costly and more trade distorting than the OECD average.

US farm policy fluctuates more than most. The overall US PSE shows a downward trend in the first half of the 1990s but an upturn after that. The most trade-distorting forms of US support decreased in the second half of

Figure 2.4 Subsidies and prices, 1986–2004

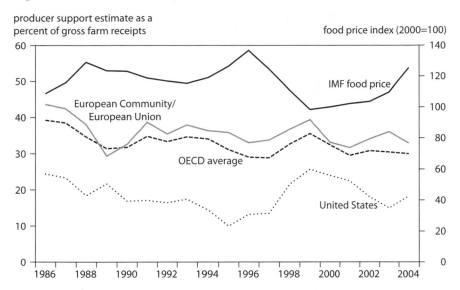

producer support estimate as a
percent of gross farm receipts

food price index (2000=100)

Notes: EU-12 for 1986–94, EU-15 from 1995, including ex–East Germany from 1990. Austria, Finland, and Sweden are included in the OECD total for all years and in the EU from 1995. The OECD total, does not include the six non-OECD European Union member states.

Source: Producer and Consumer Support Estimates, OECD database 1986–2004; IMF's *International Financial Statistics* 2005.

the decade, but Congress soon stepped in with emergency payments when prices dropped. Countercyclical payments, linked to prices but not production, were incorporated into the Farm Security and Rural Investment Act of 2002 as a statutory safety net to replace these ad hoc payments (neither reflected in figure 2.3). Not surprisingly, figure 2.4 shows that even with the reforms that have taken place, US and EU support to farmers has continued to move countercyclically with global prices.

Table 2.2, which shows average agricultural tariffs imposed by OECD countries, illustrates several additional things about OECD protection of member states' farmers. The broad patterns are the same as those reflected in the OECD data, with the G-10 countries having the highest tariffs, Australia and New Zealand the lowest, and the European Union and Canada in between. In this case, average US tariffs place it closer to the Cairns Group exporters, reflecting relatively heavier US reliance on subsidy payments than in the European Union or Canada.

Table 2.2 also highlights two other problems that need to be addressed in the trade negotiations: the use of specific tariffs and tariff escalation. Specific tariffs are less transparent than ad valorem tariffs, and because the protective effect varies inversely with world prices, they also contribute

Table 2.2 Average agricultural tariffs in selected rich countries

| Country | Ad valorem tariffs | | Ad valorem equivalent of all other duties[a] | Average tariff on raw products | Average tariff on final products | Average tariffs on developing-country exports[b] |
	Average (percent)	Percent of tariff lines covered				
Australia	1.2	99	5.0	0.3	2.3	0.8
Canada	3.8	76	n.a.	1.4	6.5	10.8
European Union	10.6	56	35.2	13.2	24.3	34.4
Japan	10.3	86	n.a.	4.2	15.9	158.1
Korea	42.2	98	n.a.	47.8	34.7	n.a.
Norway	8.6	46	n.a.	12.8	2.2	89.4
United States	8.1	60	11.7	5.5	12.6	5.0

n.a. = not available

a. Includes specific, compound, and all other types of duties on imports if countries report ad valorem equivalents of these tariffs.
b. Production-weighted average tariffs applied to developing-country exports.

Note: The first five columns are from data compiled by the World Bank and are applied most favored nation tariffs that do not reflect all tariff-rate quota duties. The last column is compiled by the Center for Global Development from data that include ad valorem equivalents of specific tariffs, efforts to estimate ad valorem equivalents of tariff-rate quotas, and various preference programs.

Sources: Aksoy and Beghin, supplementary CD (2005), and Roodman (2005).

Table 2.3 Tariff escalation on selected products (percent)

Country	Cocoa and chocolate		Coffee	
	Raw product	Final product	Raw product	Final product
European Union	0.5	30.6	7.3	12.1
Japan	0	21.7	6.0	18.8
United States	0	15.3	0.1	10.1

Source: Aksoy and Beghin, supplementary CD (2005).

relatively more to volatility in world prices. According to the limited data available, the ad valorem equivalents of specific tariffs also tend to be higher on average, markedly so in the European Union. The United States and Norway are also particularly heavy users of non–ad valorem tariffs, with 40 to 60 percent of agricultural tariff lines being specific or compound (i.e., combining ad valorem and specific components).

When duties are higher on more heavily processed products than on the inputs, this tariff escalation prevents developing-country exporters from being able to develop processing activities themselves. Adding value to primary commodities would create jobs and help to reduce the volatility associated with trade in raw commodities. The US, EU, Canadian, and Japanese tariff structures all show signs of escalation from the raw stage to the processed stage. Table 2.3 illustrates this problem with respect to tropical products that are of particular interest to many low-income countries. The treatment of cocoa is particularly striking because chocolate and other confectionaries with cocoa usually incorporate sugar, which is itself heavily protected.

Finally, the last column in table 2.2 shows average agricultural tariffs against developing countries as calculated by David Roodman for the Center for Global Development's Commitment to Development Index (Roodman 2005). These data are from a different source, are weighted differently than the World Bank data in the rest of the table, and incorporate TRQ duties more fully. With the exception of those for the United States and Australia, the Roodman estimates are substantially higher, but it is not clear that this is primarily the result of discrimination against developing countries. Overall average tariffs applied by industrialized countries to developing-country exports tend to be higher than those applied against other industrialized countries because of the concentration of developing-country exports in the relatively more protected agricultural and textile sectors. Within agriculture, however, industrialized countries provide high levels of protection to dairy, meat, and grains that are exported by other industrialized countries. Thus, the differences shown in the table are more likely the result of the different weights and more effective inclusion of the ad valorem equivalent impact of TRQs than of implicit discrimination against developing countries.

Patterns of Support Across Commodities

Not surprisingly, government support for farmers varies widely across commodities, as well as countries (table 2.4). Overall, among the commodities analyzed by the OECD, rice and sugar are the most highly supported, but support for these products is concentrated in the European Union, Japan, the United States, and, in the case of rice, South Korea. Dairy products are generously supported by all the rich countries except New Zealand and Australia.[6] "Other grains," beef, and wheat are also both generously and broadly supported by OECD governments, while poultry, eggs, pork, oilseeds, and "other products" are supported by several of these countries, but generally at more modest levels.

US cotton subsidies have received much attention in recent years, but unfortunately the OECD does not provide estimates for this product. Because the OECD publishes the methodology it uses, it is possible to approximate a PSE for cotton growers. The calculations in appendix 2A suggest that cotton receives generous public support—less than sugar, but about as much as dairy and much more than other commodities. In the peak subsidy year of 2001–02, US cotton growers received government price support and subsidies that was roughly equal in value to what an undistorted market would have provided, leading to a PSE equal to 52 percent of gross farm receipts (including the value of government support).

Table 2.5 provides a variety of evidence on protection in the three largest markets and suggests which products each country is likely to try to shelter from deep cuts in the Doha Round. The bottom row shows overall averages for agriculture. The production-weighted averages are *applied* tariffs against developing countries, while the mean and median figures are unweighted simple averages of all *bound* tariff lines. The median tariff for all three markets suggests that most agricultural tariffs are relatively low and that the high means are explained by a relatively small number of very high tariffs. The differences between these estimates and the higher average applied tariffs are, again, most likely due to the use of production weights and more effective inclusion of TRQs.

The rest of table 2.5 shows the production-weighted average and the incidence of TRQs by commodity. These show the same basic pattern as the OECD data for all producer support. Sugar and dairy products are pro-

---

6. Although to a far lesser degree than most other countries since it undertook reforms several years ago, Australia still provides support to dairy at a level nearly four times its overall producer support average.

Table 2.4 Producer support estimates by country and commodity, average 2002–04
(percent of farm receipts, including budget support)

Commodity	OECD average	Australia	Canada	EU-15[a]	Iceland	Japan	Korea	New Zealand	Norway	Switzerland	United States
Rice	76	6	n.a.	35	n.a.	83	77	n.a.	n.a.	n.a.	33
Sugar	55	11	n.a.	60	n.a.	64	n.a.	n.a.	n.a.	77	57
Milk	42	15	58	40	80	73	61	1	76	73	40
Other grains	42	3	16	50	n.a.	81	78	0	71	67	34
Beef, veal	35	4	21	73	47	32	63	1	82	74	4
Wheat	35	4	17	43	n.a.	85	n.a.	0	68	59	30
Sheepmeat	38	4	n.a.	53	57	n.a.	n.a.	0	68	54	15
Other	25	2	24	21	n.a.	51	n.a.	2	63	66	16
Pork	21	3	9	24	39	47	33	0	61	68	4
Maize	25	n.a.	15	39	n.a.	n.a.	n.a.	0	n.a.	67	20
Oilseeds	23	3	15	37	n.a.	57	89	n.a.	n.a.	84	18
Poultry	18	3	5	40	86	11	38	48	73	85	4
Eggs	7	3	11	2	70	16	19	31	43	75	4
Wool	6	4	n.a.	n.a.	45	n.a.	n.a.	0	83	n.a.	24
Average	30	4	21	33	69	56	63	3	68	68	18

n.a. = not applicable

a. EU-15 (countries that were EU members as of January 1995); Austria, Finland, and Sweden are included in the OECD totals for all years and in the European Union from 1995.

Source: Producer and consumer support estimates, OECD database, 1986–2004.

Table 2.5 Average applied tariffs, tariff peaks, and tariff-rate quotas (TRQs), 2001

Commodity	European Union			Japan			United States		
	Weighted average applied tariff	Number of TRQs	Number of tariff lines under TRQ	Weighted average applied tariff	Number of TRQs	Number of tariff lines under TRQ	Weighted average applied tariff	Number of TRQs	Number of tariff lines under TRQ
Sugar	90.4	3	7	227.0	0	0	24.2	6	16
Dairy	38.0	12	51	82.4	10	56	16.7	24	97
Beef, sheepmeat	75.8	15	51	38.2	0	0	2.6	1	1
Pork, poultry, other meat	15.2	13	66	36.5	0	0	3.3	0	0
Rice	110.8	3	3	886.7	1	17	5.2	0	0
Wheat	0.7	2	2	214.4	1	23	3.2	0	0
Corn, other grains	17.2	10	12	53.2	1	12	0.9	1	0
Fruits, vegetables, nuts	19.1	15	33	21.4	3	9	5.0	5	6
		Mean bound tariff (unweighted)	Median bound tariff		Mean bound tariff (unweighted)	Median bound tariff		Mean bound tariff (unweighted)	Median bound tariff
All agricultural	34.4	30.0	13.0	158.1	58.0	10.0	5.0	12.0	3.0

Sources: Roodman (2005) and Gibson et al. (2001).

tected by high tariffs and, in the United States and the European Union, by TRQs. Negotiators representing rich countries are likely to seek more lenient treatment for these sectors, as well as beef in the European Union, and rice and other grains in Japan. An important question is whether the European Union will also try to shield fruits and vegetables, which are subject to moderate average tariffs but are also protected by TRQs.

Implications for the Doha Round

The United States and the European Union account for 60 percent of the dollar value of OECD agricultural support, but Switzerland, Norway, Iceland, South Korea, and Japan provide by far the most support relative to farm receipts (see table 2.1). Japan and South Korea also provide by far the most support per hectare of farmland, while Switzerland and Norway far surpass most other OECD countries on this measure. Thus, the G-10 countries have primarily defensive interests in the Doha Round agriculture negotiations. Australia and New Zealand are at the other end of the spectrum, with PSEs under 5 percent. Along with other members of the Cairns Group and the G-20, they are pushing an offensive agenda on agriculture.

The European Union and the United States, however, are the two big players in the negotiations. In addition to providing 60 percent of overall producer support, they account for more than 80 percent of subsidies because most other rich countries provide support primarily through border measures (OECD 2005a). They are also among the heaviest users of specific tariffs and impose escalating tariffs on products of interest to low-income countries. Like those representing the G-10, the EU negotiators have primarily defensive interests. But they also realize that the Doha Round will fail unless they make concessions on agriculture, and they also have internal reasons to undertake Common Agricultural Policy reform (see chapter 3). US negotiators have mixed interests in the agriculture negotiations: While they wish to increase access for competitive US exporters (including in the larger middle-income developing countries), they also face political pressure to maintain subsidies and protection for less competitive sectors such as sugar. As in the Uruguay Round, concessions by the two biggest players will be the key to a successful negotiation on agriculture. Brazil, India, and the other members of the G-20 group of developing-country exporters will insist on it.

Appendix 2A
Producer Support Estimate for US Cotton

According to *Methodology for the Measurement of Support and Use in Policy Evaluation* (OECD 2002), the producer support estimate (PSE) can be calculated as the sum of

- market price support (MPS);
- payments based on output;
- payments based on area planted or animal numbers;
- payments based on historical entitlements;
- payments based on input use;
- payments based on input constraints;
- payments based on overall farming income; and
- miscellaneous payments.

Using the information provided in a World Bank report (Baffes 2005), it is possible to use this method to obtain an estimate of the PSE for US cotton producers.

Three important assumptions underlie the calculation using these data:

- Step-2 payments are used as a proxy for MPS. These are subsidies paid to exporters and domestic end users of cotton to compensate them for higher US cotton prices when they exceed a Northern European reference price. If the latter is similar to the world price, Step-2 payments would be similar to total production times the difference between domestic and world prices (the definition of MPS).
- The data contain all forms of direct support to cotton producers in the United States.
- Though CCPs do not fit exactly in the categories used regularly by the OECD, its current approach is to include them in the payments based on area planted.

These estimates can then be used to calculate the percentage PSE (%PSE) and the nominal assistance coefficient (NAC). These measures are defined by

$$\%PSE = PSE / (Q.Pp + PP) \times 100$$

$$NAC = [100 \times 1 / (100 - \%PSE)]$$

Where

$$PP = \text{Payments to producers} = PSE - MPS,$$

and

$$(Q.Pp = \text{value of production at producer prices}$$
$$(\text{not including output payments}).$$

Table 2A.1 Government assistance to US cotton producers, 1995–2003 (millions of US dollars)

Policy instrument	PSE category	1995–96	1996–97	1997–98	1998–99	1999–2000	2000–2001	2001–02	2002–03
Coupled payments	B, E	3	0	28	535	1,613	536	2,507	248
PFC/DP	D	0	599	597	637	614	575	474	914
Emergency/CCP	C	0	0	0	316	613	613	524	1,264
Insurance	C	180	157	148	151	170	162	236	194
Step-2	A	34	3	390	308	422	236	196	455
PSE[a]		**217**	**759**	**1,163**	**1,947**	**3,432**	**2,122**	**3,937**	**3,075**

PFC/DP = production flexibility contracts/direct payments

CCP = countercyclical payments

PSE = producer support estimate

a. Except for 2002–03, where I added data for the Step-2 program, it is unclear why the total payments are not the same as reported in Baffes (2005).

Sources: Baffes (2005, 265) and US Department of Agriculture.

Table 2A.2 Percentage PSE and NAC calculation, 1995–2003

	1995–96	1996–97	1997–98	1998–99	1999–2000	2000–2001	2001–02	2002–03
Farm price (cents per pound)	70.5	66.2	61.7	46.8	51.6	32.0	45.7	63.2
Production (millions of pounds)	9,092.0	9,021.0	6,681.0	8,145.0	8,250.0	9,745.0	8,260.0	8,762.0
Q.Pp (millions of US dollars)	6,410.0	5,972.0	4,122.0	3,812.0	4,257.0	3,119.0	3,775.0	5,538.0
PP (millions of US dollars)	183.0	756.0	773.0	1,639.0	3,010.0	1,886.0	3,741.0	2,620.0
%PSE	3.3	11.3	23.8	35.7	47.2	42.4	52.4	37.7
NAC	1.0	1.1	1.3	1.6	1.9	1.7	2.1	1.6

Q.Pp = value of production at producer prices (not including output payments)
PP = payments to producers (PSE–MPS)
PSE = producer support estimate
NAC = nominal assistance coefficient
MPS = market price support

Source: Table 2A.1 and US Department of Agriculture.

3

Prospects for Reform: Lessons from US and European Experience

A successful Doha Round on agriculture depends on US and European policymakers having the political will to reform their domestic programs. Other members of the Organization for Economic Cooperation and Development (OECD) provide higher levels of support, but most of them are too small for their reforms to have much effect on global markets. Opening the Japanese and South Korean markets for rice would offer potentially large gains to Asian exporters, but if even a little flexibility is permitted for sensitive products, Japan and South Korea will exempt rice to the maximum extent permitted. These and the other Group of 10 (G-10) countries will fight to minimize their concessions on agriculture, but US and European negotiators, along with those from Brazil and other exporting states, will largely determine the parameters of the agreement. Thus, it is particularly important to understand the pressures for and constraints on reform in the United States and the European Union.

Given the high costs to consumers and taxpayers, as well as the highly inequitable distribution of subsidies among farmers, it is something of a mystery why reform should be so difficult. But political economy theories of rent seeking tell us that smaller groups with concentrated gains or losses have an advantage over larger groups with more diffuse interests when it comes to influencing policy. Smaller groups find it relatively easier to organize and engage in collective action in lobbying Congress, and the benefits from subsidies and trade protection give them both the means and the incentive to do so (Moyer and Josling 1990, chapter 1; Paarlberg 1999). Much larger groups with more diffuse costs or benefits arising from government policy—in this case, consumers and taxpayers—care less intensely and typically fail to organize to protect their interests. Moreover, food is a small and declining share of the consumption basket in rich countries, and farm subsidies are a relatively small share of overall government budgets. But government support can be an important part of a farmer's income, and it contributes significantly to wealth by raising land values.

As long as key legislators receive large campaign contributions and other support from pro-subsidy agricultural interests and face little or no tangible opposition from other constituents or offsetting lobbying from other campaign contributors, this political equilibrium likely will remain stable. But one can imagine at least two scenarios that could upset the equilibrium. First, budget pressures often force legislators to choose among constituents and have contributed to reductions in the level of agricultural support in the past. Budget pressures have been a particularly important force for reform in Europe, and the legislators who rewrite the US farm bill in 2007 will confront such pressures as well. In addition, if inadequate movement on agriculture continues to impede progress on nonagricultural market access and services liberalization in the Doha Round, key political constituencies in those sectors will have an incentive to lobby in favor of agricultural reform in order to break the logjam.

This chapter reviews the recent history of European and US agricultural policies and the pressures for and against reform. It then explores the political economy of agricultural policy, particularly in the United States, and analyzes internal and external pressures for reform.

The Evolution of US and European Agricultural Policy

Reviewing the evolution of European and US farm policy provides valuable information on the nature of current subsidies and protection, as well as insights into what has and has not worked in past reform battles. The European Economic Community (EEC; later the European Community and now the European Union) launched the Common Agricultural Policy (CAP) in 1962, when memories of food shortages during and after World War II were still fresh and the region was a large net importer of most agricultural products. Thanks to the CAP, European farmers who otherwise would have had to compete with imports were insulated form global markets. But high target prices eventually resulted in surpluses that had to be disposed of on world markets with the help of large export subsidies. US policymakers first provided support to US farmers during the Great Depression, when they were not much concerned about exports because of the collapse in international trade. US policies subsequently fluctuated more than those of Europe, depending in part on the degree of engagement with global markets and the effects of price supports and other policies on export competitiveness.

By the mid-1980s the costs of support had reached unsustainable levels, and the EC and US governments began to explore options for reform.

Box 3.1 Policy reform options

In broad terms, agricultural policy reforms can be either fast or slow, and farmers may or may not be compensated. Orden, Paarlberg, and Roe (1999, 7–11) identify four combinations of these two choices that suggest four possible strategies for reducing agricultural support:

- The least radical is a "cash-out" that involves gradually replacing supply controls with direct payments that may be used to compensate farmers when market prices fall below targeted levels or when support prices are reduced by policy-makers. These payments may either continue to be coupled to prices or be based on historical payment levels and decoupled from current production decisions.

- The most radical and least likely option is a "cut-out" that quickly ends farm supports with no compensation.

- A "squeeze-out" works by raising the costs or reducing the benefits of farm program participation, thereby encouraging farmers to withdraw gradually.

- "Buyouts" promise a quick end to subsidies by compensating farmers for asset value losses linked to the loss of subsidies. Buyouts have been used in the United States in recent years to reduce price supports for peanuts and eliminate them for tobacco.

As a guide to assessing the relative merits and feasibility of various proposals, Orden, Paarlberg, and Roe (1999, 8–10) identify four alternative reform strategies, whose distinguishing characteristics are speed of implementation and whether farmers are compensated for reductions in support (see box 3.1). The revealed preference of policymakers in both the United States and Europe has been for a gradual and partial "cash-out," which provides direct income support, often as compensation for lower levels of price support.

The Uruguay Round approach of encouraging a shift from trade-distorting amber box supports to minimally distorting "green box" measures (see chapter 2, especially figure 2.1) was also aimed at reducing the global spillovers from farm policies. But the Uruguay Round agreement, delayed three years over agriculture, was shaped more by US and EU reforms than the reverse. Even though the Uruguay Round helped to lock in those reforms and constrained backsliding to a degree, agricultural reform in the United States and the European Union in subsequent years continued to be driven primarily by domestic concerns. With the emergence of the Group of 20 (G-20), an informal association of developing countries with a strong interest in liberalizing agricultural exports, the hope is that the Doha Round will create a more positive two-way interaction between domestic reforms and trade negotiations than its predecessor.

European Farm Policy: From Net Importer to Net Exporter to Incremental Reformer

The 12 countries making up the European Community in the mid-1980s had only a quarter the arable land of the United States, but they had three times as many farms (Newman, Fulton, and Glaser 1987). When the CAP was created in the early 1960s, the EEC was a net importer of most commodities, and import restrictions were a necessary condition for supporting domestic prices above world levels. In addition, policymakers tilted in the direction of raising farm incomes indirectly, through price supports, rather than with direct payments, because the EEC lacked the tax power of a state. Because EC policymakers did have authority over trade policy, they chose as their principal tool a "variable levy" on imports that was adjusted as necessary to maintain internal prices.

Over time, because of high price targets, called intervention prices, and technological progress, production increased, consumption was dampened, and surpluses accumulated. As a result, EC expenditures for storage costs and export subsidies to dispose of surpluses increased sharply. Trade conflicts also multiplied as the European Community moved from being a large net importer to a net exporter of sugar, beef, butter, and wheat in the 1970s and 1980s (Newman, Fulton, and Glaser 1987). As figure 3.1 shows, imports fluctuated but exports grew steadily, and by the early 1990s the agricultural trade deficit had closed.[1] By that time, the European Community was under intense pressure, both from its budget and its trading partners, to find a way to reduce the costs of supporting its farmers.

A key problem was that, for most products, the CAP initially controlled supplies primarily through trade measures: the variable levy on imports and export subsidies for surplus disposal. Not until chronic surpluses threatened to break the budget in the 1980s did policymakers resort to modest production controls, beginning with dairy products in 1984. At the same time, they modestly lowered intervention prices for cereals and, in 1988, began paying farmers to take land out of production. But these limited reforms did little to rein in surpluses, and budget outlays hit record levels (Moyer and Josling 1990, chapter 4). In addition, subsidized wheat exports and conflicts over oilseeds, beef, and other imports were roiling trade relations, particularly with the United States.[2] Finally, the United States and the proliberalization Cairns Group of agricultural exporters (including Australia, New Zealand,

---

1. The data underlying the charts are in nominal dollars, which accounts for some of the fluctuation.

2. Bayard and Elliott (1994) document and analyze the numerous US-EC disputes over agricultural market access in the 1970s and 1980s.

Figure 3.1   EC-10 agricultural trade (excluding intra-EC trade), 1970–2003

billions of dollars

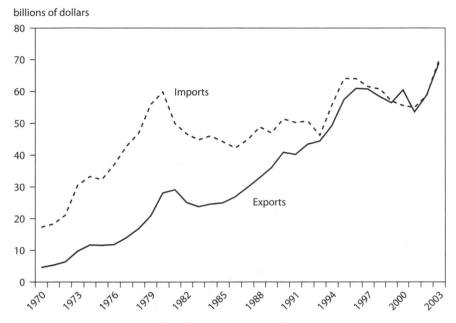

Note: After 1985, the EC-12 includes Greece, Portugal, and Spain.

Source: UN Food and Agriculture Organization, FAOSTAT database.

Argentina, Brazil, and several other states) insisted that the new round of trade negotiations, launched in Punta del Este, Uruguay, in September 1986, address trade-distorting *domestic* subsidies to agriculture, as well as traditional trade barriers.

But member-state policymakers could not agree among themselves on further reforms, and the Uruguay Round negotiations were extended beyond the scheduled 1990 end date. After another three years of negotiation, European policymakers agreed on CAP reforms proposed by EC Agriculture Commissioner Ray MacSharry that modestly lowered levels of support, continued the move toward paying farmers to set aside some land, and introduced the idea of decoupling some payments from production, though this provision was weakened in the end (Swinbank and Tanner 1996, chapter 5). With this accomplished, EC negotiators concluded a deal with the United States to resolve an escalating bilateral conflict over oilseeds and, at the same time, to set the parameters for a multilateral agreement that would essentially ratify the reforms the European Community had undertaken unilaterally.

According to OECD figures, these reforms and the Uruguay Round agreement had relatively little effect on the overall level of EU producer support, which has actually increased in value terms and declined only modestly in percentage terms since the 1986–88 period, from 41 percent of gross farm receipts to 34 percent for the 2002–04 period. But at the same time, the most trade-distorting elements of that support have declined from nearly 100 percent of the total to 65 percent (figure 2.3). Market price support also declined by more than a third, to 55 percent.

In preparation for the accession of 10 new members to the European Union and to determine the parameters of an agreement they could live with in the Doha Round, EU policymakers undertook additional reforms in 2000 and 2003. The 2000 reform, which lowered intervention prices for dairy products for the first time, also further lowered intervention prices for cereal and beef. Under this and earlier reforms, producers received compensatory payments for the price cuts that were linked to production limits and allocated to the blue box category of moderately distorting subsidies under WTO rules. The 2003 reform went further, introducing a "single farm payment" that is based on historical support levels and non–commodity specific (OECD 2004a, 7). Because the new payment is decoupled from current production, the European Union plans to allocate it to the WTO green box.[3]

The initial EU plan proposed converting almost all commodity-linked payments to the decoupled single farm payment beginning in 2005. Under the final compromise, however, member countries were given flexibility to delay adoption of the single payment. Several decided to wait until 2006 and to permit designated shares of the payments for various commodities to remain "coupled." According to the most recent OECD review of agricultural policies, the United Kingdom, Ireland, Germany, and several others will maximize use of the single farm payment while France will minimize it, meaning that many of its farm payments will remain trade distorting (OECD 2005a, 8). More important, the single farm payment does not affect market price support provided through trade measures, which still accounts for more than half of total EU support to farmers. In addition, while farmers do not have to produce particular products in order to collect the single farm payment, they are prohibited from shifting production to fruits, vegetables, or table potatoes, and they are required to keep their land in "good agricultural or environmental" condition.[4] Continued price support for most commodities and these constraints on land use are likely, at the margin, to encourage farmers to continue producing what they have traditionally produced. The evolution of the CAP is summarized in figure 3.2.

---

3. Analyses of the 2003 reform may be found in Jotzo et al. (2003) and Kelch and Normile (2004).

4. Although not binding on any other country, a WTO dispute settlement panel decision that affirmed Brazil's challenge to US subsidies on cotton raises questions about the green box eligibility of decoupled payments that include *any* restrictions on what can be planted. This issue is addressed in greater depth later in this chapter and in chapter 5.

Figure 3.2 Evolution of the European Common Agricultural Policy (CAP), 1960–2005

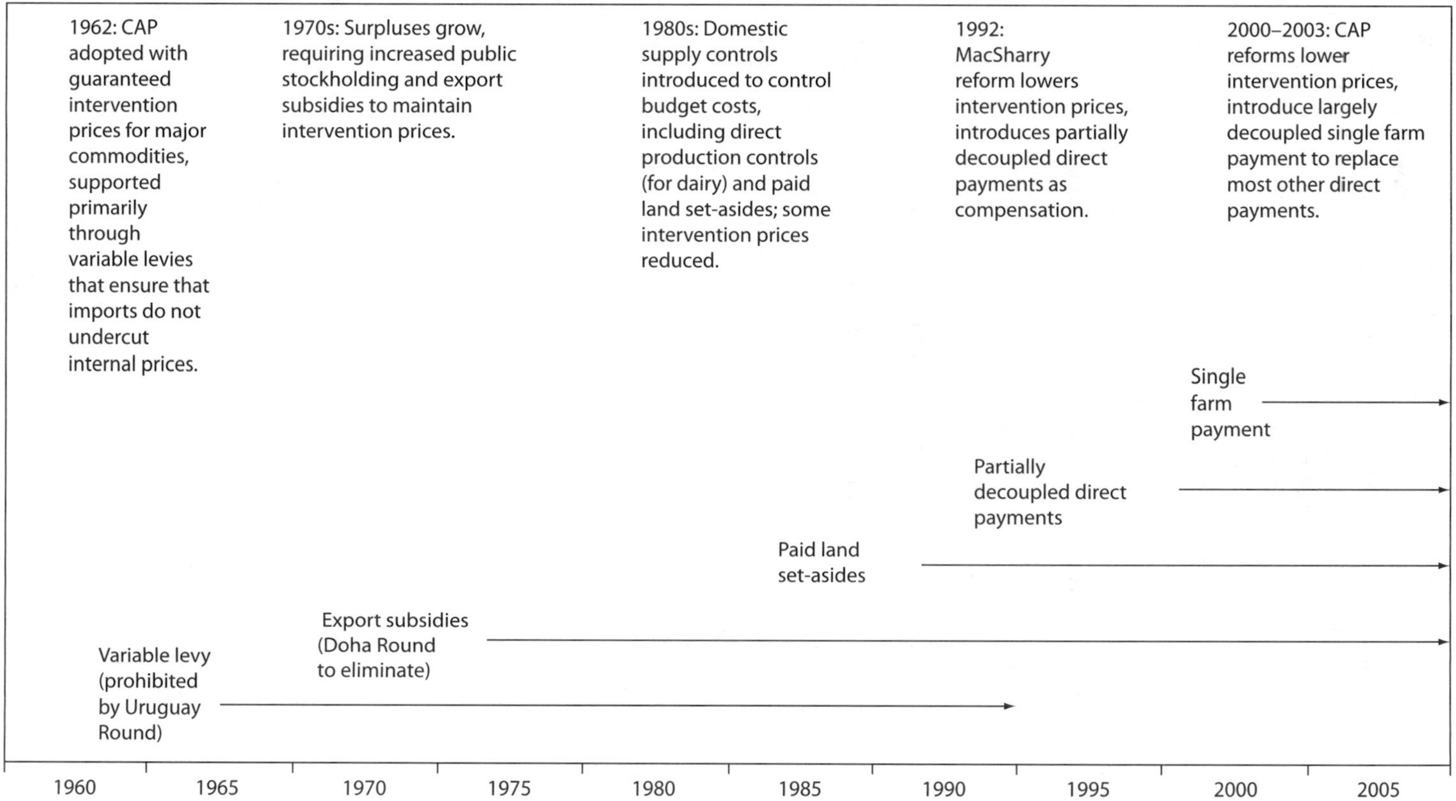

1962: CAP adopted with guaranteed intervention prices for major commodities, supported primarily through variable levies that ensure that imports do not undercut internal prices.

1970s: Surpluses grow, requiring increased public stockholding and export subsidies to maintain intervention prices.

1980s: Domestic supply controls introduced to control budget costs, including direct production controls (for dairy) and paid land set-asides; some intervention prices reduced.

1992: MacSharry reform lowers intervention prices, introduces partially decoupled direct payments as compensation.

2000–2003: CAP reforms lower intervention prices, introduce largely decoupled single farm payment to replace most other direct payments.

Single farm payment

Partially decoupled direct payments

Paid land set-asides

Export subsidies (Doha Round to eliminate)

Variable levy (prohibited by Uruguay Round)

| 1960 | 1965 | 1970 | 1975 | 1980 | 1985 | 1990 | 1995 | 2000 | 2005 |

Note: This is a summary of broad changes in agricultural support policies that does not apply to all commodities at all times. Arrows cover period over which tools were used.

OECD projections of the effects of the 2003 CAP reform also suggest a continuation of recent trends, with little change in the overall level of support and a modest further reduction in the *most* trade-distorting elements to 64 percent by 2008 (OECD 2004a). The latter development is due to the fact that the single farm payment will mostly replace blue box payments, which are less distorting than amber box payments and are not included in the OECD's most trade-distorting category. In WTO terms, however, maximum decoupling could allow the European Union to move more than $20 billion dollars in these partially decoupled blue box subsidies to the green box, thereby giving EU representatives more room to negotiate subsidy reductions in the Doha Round. The major problem for the European Union is that its relatively heavy reliance on off-budget trade measures means that further moves toward decoupled subsidies will require either additional budget resources or lower levels of support.[5]

US Farm Policies: Earlier Reforms but Recent Setbacks

The United States, with its abundant endowment of land, emerged in the 19th century as a net exporter of bulk commodities, such as feed grains, oilseeds, and cotton. And as in many developing countries a century later, policymakers protected manufacturing at the expense of agriculture for decades. After World War I, global markets for US farm products shrank markedly, and pressures for subsidies or protection grew until they became irresistible during the Great Depression of the 1930s. With the collapse of global markets and the drought-created "Dust Bowl" threatening farmers' livelihood, and with few alternative jobs available elsewhere in the economy, the US government stepped in to encourage farmers to stay on the land.

Since trade had collapsed, and because the new policy was intended to be temporary, the government's response was developed with little regard to the international effects, including export competitiveness. The Agricultural Adjustment Act of 1933 sought to raise prices by paying farmers to reduce the acreage planted in most major commodities.[6] Section 22 of the act also authorized the use of tariffs and quotas if imports threatened to undermine these domestic supply control programs. Dairy products were protected from imports from the beginning, while beef (at relatively low levels), sugar, peanuts, and tobacco (at much higher levels) were added later.

As an interim measure to keep farmers in business until the supply controls took effect, the government introduced commodity loans. These

---

5. The budgetary consequences of moving to decoupled subsidies will be even greater in countries such as South Korea and Japan that rely even more heavily on import restrictions to maintain prices and farm incomes.

6. This discussion of the history draws on Orden, Paarlberg, and Roe (1999, 18–24).

allowed farmers to take out loans using their crops as collateral, which they could either sell to repay the loans if prices rose or forfeit to the government as payment in full if prices dropped below the level specified as the "loan rate." Like so much else in agricultural policy, commodity loans did not remain temporary. Instead, Congress took over the setting of loan rates, and they became another mechanism for providing a floor under prices.

Though there were fluctuations related to changes in control of Congress, with Republicans generally favoring lower loan rates and Democrats favoring higher ones, the policies forged in the 1930s remained more or less intact until the 1960s. During the recovery following World War II, US farm exports were mostly in the form of food aid. But as global commercial markets revived, high loan rates were increasingly seen as impeding US exports (Gardner 1990), as well as causing the government to hold large surplus stocks. At this point, US policy moved toward what Orden, Paarlberg, and Roe (1999, 61–67) call a "partial cash-out" of price supports (box 3.1). Congress lowered the loan rate to near world prices, allowing farmers to increase exports. Also, those willing to withdraw a portion of their acreage from cultivation, in order to reduce surpluses, could receive direct payments from the government to compensate for the lower loan rate on domestic sales. From this point on, US farmers were relatively more exposed to global market conditions than those in Europe, and US policy fluctuated more in response to changes in export markets and budget costs.

High prices during the 1970s commodities boom could have been used to ease farmers off public support through a "squeeze-out," by keeping the loan rate constant in nominal terms and allowing inflation to erode the real value of supports. Instead, fears of food shortages and the low immediate budget impact lulled both US and EC policymakers into excessive generosity in raising nominal support prices to make up for inflation. Congress also introduced target prices and deficiency payments, which compensated farmers for any difference between the higher of the loan rate or the market price and the target price, albeit only on a base level, rather than all production.

These policies helped to set the stage for the US farm crisis and proliferating trade conflicts in the 1980s when inflation eased. High prices in the 1970s had stimulated production and exports, but the US trade balance soon turned sharply downward, driven by a confluence of events in the early 1980s (figure 3.3):

- overvaluation of the dollar;

- declining demand in developing countries because of the debt crisis; and

- increasing competition in export markets from the EC and emerging competitive exporters, such as Brazil and Argentina.

Figure 3.3   US agricultural trade, 1970–2003

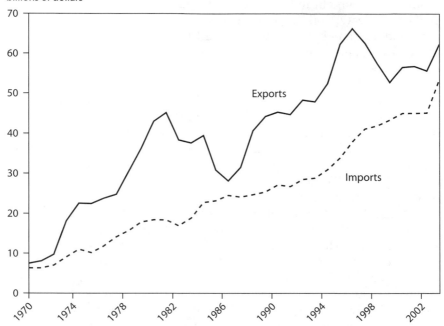

billions of dollars

Source: UN Food and Agriculture organization, FAOSTAT database.

US policymakers responded to the farm crisis of the mid-1980s, like their counterparts in Europe, with modest, incremental changes. The Food Security Act of 1985 resorted to extensive paid acreage set-asides to bolster prices. But it also lowered loan rates to encourage exports and, in response to European policies, added the Export Enhancement Program to provide export subsidies for commodities, especially wheat, that were competing with subsidized exports. Congress also linked environmental concerns to farm policy with a "conservation reserve" acreage set-aside program to take environmentally sensitive cropland out of production.[7] The Conservation Reserve Program (CRP) differed from traditional acreage reduction and diversion programs in requiring participants to retire land for 10 to 15 years at a time (with the possibility of renewal), rather than the much shorter periods explicitly geared to supply concerns. Still, the CRP did not

---

7. The 1985 farm bill also conditioned eligibility for programs on farmers' protection of "highly erodible" land and their willingness not to convert wetlands to cropland. These two provisions were referred to as "Sodbuster" and "Swampbuster," respectively.

retire land permanently and still had the effect of bolstering prices by reducing output, at least in the short run.

In order to reduce budget outlays for storage costs and to further promote exports, without regard for the beggar-thy-neighbor effects on other exporters, US policymakers shifted from traditional "nonrecourse" loans to "marketing loan" payments for cotton and rice. The secretary of agriculture was given the option to authorize marketing loans for other commodities as well. Nonrecourse loans led to government stockpiling when prices dropped below the loan rate because the government had to accept the commodities held by farmers as collateral. With forfeitures and storage costs escalating rapidly in the first half of the 1980s, Congress shifted to marketing loans to give farmers the option of exporting commodities held as collateral when market prices were below the loan rate. The government covered the difference with a "loan deficiency payment," an important move in the trend away from market price support and supply controls and toward direct payments to support incomes. Target prices and deficiency payments were also retained in the 1985 farm bill.

"Freedom to Farm"

After following the path of incremental reform for more than a decade, US policy took a sudden and dramatic turn in 1996 at a time of high commodity prices and with Republicans in control of the House of Representatives for the first time in more than 40 years. Orden, Paarlberg, and Roe (1999) argue that these two factors were both necessary and together sufficient to trigger a major shift in US farm policy. Still, the shift was less radical than it appeared, and important elements were reversed within two years when conditions changed and prices declined sharply. While some elements of the reform were retained, important reversals, including a move back toward linking payments to prices, were institutionalized when a new farm bill was written in 2002.

The chief innovation of the 1996 farm bill, initially called the Freedom to Farm Act, was to free farmers from having to produce particular crops in order to receive payments and, in times of low prices, refrain from producing as much as they otherwise might. Instead, farmers could, at their option, sign production flexibility contracts that would allow them to plant what they wanted in response to market signals (with a few exceptions) and would no longer link payments to current prices or production. Rather, the new decoupled payments would be based on historical acreage enrolled in subsidy programs, and would be reduced over time. The bill eliminated the long-standing acreage reduction program, though it continued the authority for compensated set-asides under the CRP.

Thus, the 1996 farm bill, which ultimately became law as the Federal Agriculture Improvement and Reform (FAIR) Act of 1996, marked a decisive break with the past practice of trying to prop up prices by controlling supplies of the major commodities. Target prices and deficiency payments were also eliminated under the reform, but the concept of a price floor was retained through marketing loans and loan deficiency payments. It is important to note, however, that even this relatively radical reform, trumpeted in some news media stories as "ending farm subsidies," applied *only* to the traditional program commodities that are exported (wheat, corn, other grains, cotton, rice, and oilseeds). Despite efforts to reduce market price supports for sugar, dairy, peanuts, and tobacco, the final compromise made minimal changes to programs for the more heavily protected, import-competing sectors.

The shift to Republican control of Congress made "Freedom to Farm" possible because the party was more ideologically opposed to market interventions in general and to mechanisms such as production controls in particular. Although there were regional differences, many Republicans also represented areas dominated by the larger-scale, more commercially oriented and competitive farming operations that chafed at supply controls and would suffer relatively less from reductions in price supports. Democratic Party concerns focused on smaller-scale farmers, whom they feared would not survive without supply controls to prop up prices (Orden, Paarlberg, and Roe 1999).

But the Republican takeover of Congress likely would not have been sufficient had there not also been a surge in agricultural commodity prices during 1994–96. Some skeptical farmers were sold on the radical shift to decoupled payments because sticking with the old system of deficiency payments would have meant that they received *less* from the government than under the system of historically based fixed payments under "Freedom to Farm" (Orden, Paarlberg, and Roe 1999). In other words, decoupled payments at a time of high market prices offered the opportunity for a windfall for farmers in affected sectors. Moreover, if traditional payments were authorized at low levels because of high prices and pressures to balance the budget, that would limit the baseline for farm spending for years to come.

Congressional Democrats argued against this reform on the basis that farmers would be trading away their permanent safety net for a short-term windfall. But, when prices collapsed following the Asian financial crisis of the late 1990s, and farmers in some regions were hit by severe flooding and others by drought, Congress quickly intervened with an ad hoc safety net by providing large emergency payments called "marketing loss assistance."

While the next farm bill was being written, in 2002, Democrats regained control of the Senate by the slimmest of margins. Prices had recovered a bit but were still well below mid-1990s levels, and the appetite for radical farm policy reform had waned. Congress retained decoupled payments, but it renamed them "direct payments" and dropped the production flexibility contract concept. Legislators also undermined the reform element of these decoupled payments by allowing farmers to update the supposedly "fixed" acreage that would be eligible and by making new commodities eligible. Although the payments remain non–commodity specific, and therefore less distorting than otherwise, the expectation of similar changes in future farm bills could encourage farmers to produce at higher levels than they otherwise would.

In addition to that retreat, Congress took a much larger step back from decoupling by introducing countercyclical payments. These are similar to the disbursements under the old target price/deficiency payment program and were intended to codify the ad hoc marketing loss assistance provided by Congress in previous years. The countercyclical payments are partially decoupled because they are paid based on 85 percent of base acreage and do not require that farmers currently produce the commodity in question. Still, the payments are based on the difference between the higher of the loan rate or market price and the target price, and that is likely to influence production decisions. The broad changes in US farm policy since 1960 are summarized in figure 3.4.

The net result of the farm policy changes since 1996 is that the overall level of US support for agriculture, as measured by the OECD's producer support estimate, was down about a fifth during 2002–04 from its peak during 1986–88 (17 percent of the value of farm production versus 22 percent earlier). But as figure 2.3 shows, the share of the most trade-distorting forms of support, after declining steadily under the 1996 farm bill, has gone back up, with the overall level of distorting payments (including those in the blue box) during 2005–06 approaching the 1999–2001 level. Moreover, while the United States' trade-distorting share started from a lower level than that of the European Union, the shares are now similar, though the overall level of European support remains higher (figures 2.2 and 2.3).

Decoupled EU, US Subsidies: Implications for the Doha Round

The goal of the Doha Round of negotiations on agricultural subsidies, like that of the Uruguay Round before it, is *not* to eliminate these subsidies, but to reduce them and encourage their conversion to less trade-distorting forms. To decouple subsidies, as the WTO seeks to do, requires governments to move from supporting farm incomes indirectly, by supporting the prices farmers receive, to providing support directly through payments pegged to historical production or payment levels or some other base that does not distort production and trade patterns. This approach is based on the US and European reforms described earlier in this chapter.

Although substantial differences in the details of reform and in other aspects of farm policy remain, European and US policymakers have moved to cut price targets and floors for most crops and to compensate farmers with direct payments based on fixed numbers of acres or animals, or production in a base period. Under the Uruguay Round framework, US deficiency payments and European compensatory payments could be allocated to the blue box for moderately distorting subsidies (see figure 2.1) because

Figure 3.4 Evolution of US agricultural policies, 1960–2005

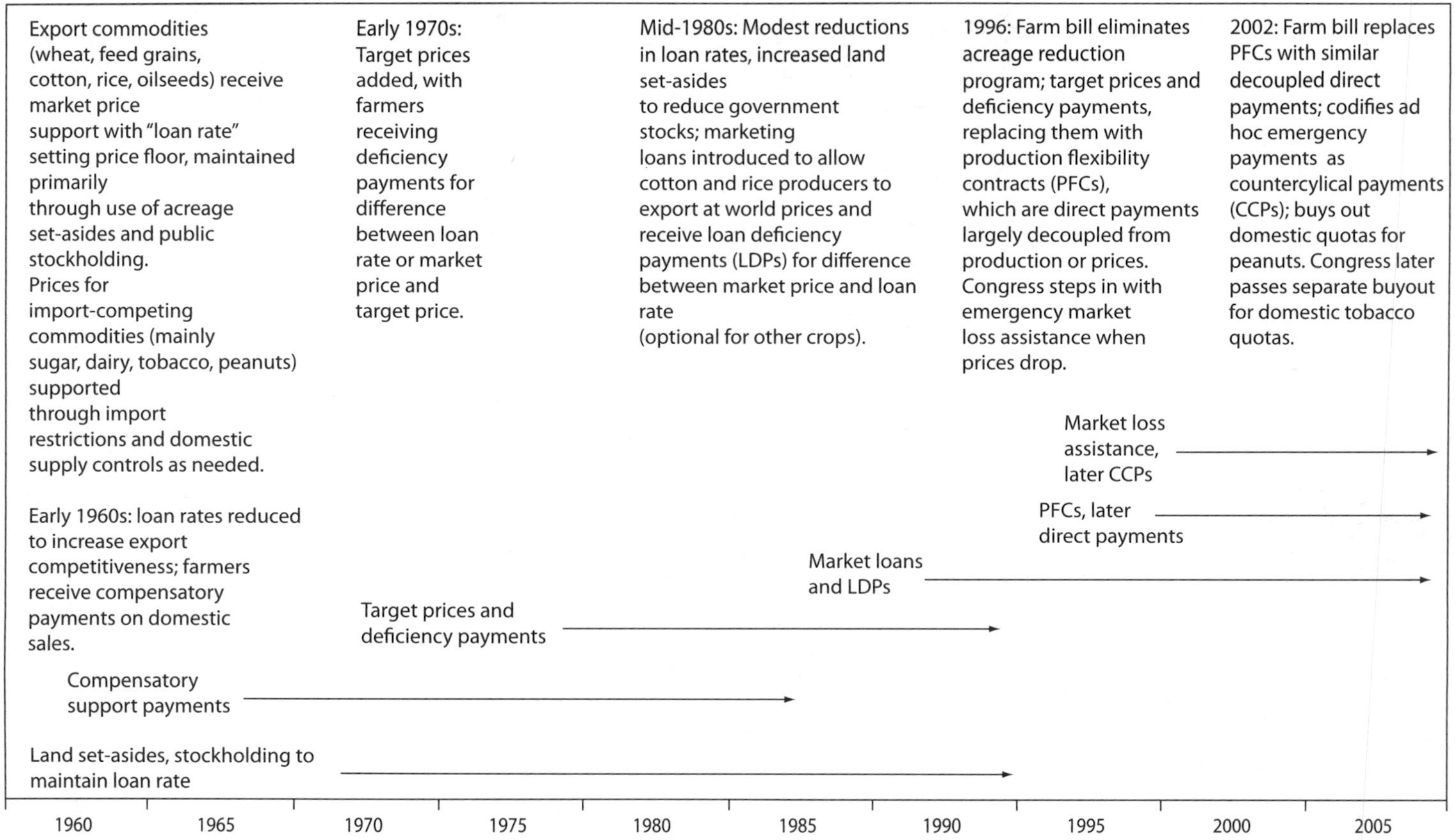

Export commodities (wheat, feed grains, cotton, rice, oilseeds) receive market price support with "loan rate" setting price floor, maintained primarily through use of acreage set-asides and public stockholding. Prices for import-competing commodities (mainly sugar, dairy, tobacco, peanuts) supported through import restrictions and domestic supply controls as needed.

Early 1960s: loan rates reduced to increase export competitiveness; farmers receive compensatory payments on domestic sales.

Early 1970s: Target prices added, with farmers receiving deficiency payments for difference between loan rate or market price and target price.

Mid-1980s: Modest reductions in loan rates, increased land set-asides to reduce government stocks; marketing loans introduced to allow cotton and rice producers to export at world prices and receive loan deficiency payments (LDPs) for difference between market price and loan rate (optional for other crops).

1996: Farm bill eliminates acreage reduction program; target prices and deficiency payments, replacing them with production flexibility contracts (PFCs), which are direct payments largely decoupled from production or prices. Congress steps in with emergency market loss assistance when prices drop.

2002: Farm bill replaces PFCs with similar decoupled direct payments; codifies ad hoc emergency payments as countercylical payments (CCPs); buys out domestic quotas for peanuts. Congress later passes separate buyout for domestic tobacco quotas.

Compensatory support payments

Land set-asides, stockholding to maintain loan rate

Target prices and deficiency payments

Market loans and LDPs

Market loss assistance, later CCPs

PFCs, later direct payments

1960   1965   1970   1975   1980   1985   1990   1995   2000   2005

Note: This is a summary of broad changes in agricultural support policies that does not apply to all commodities at all times. Arrows cover period over which tools were used.

Figure 3.5 Partially or mostly decoupled subsidies as a share of producer support, 1986–2001

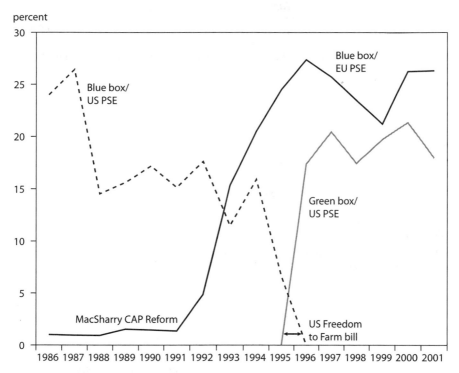

percent

Blue box/
EU PSE

Blue box/
US PSE

Green box/
US PSE

MacSharry CAP Reform

US Freedom
to Farm bill

1986 1987 1988 1989 1990 1991 1992 1993 1994 1995 1996 1997 1998 1999 2000 2001

CAP = Common Agricultural Policy
PSE = producer support estimate

Note: The US Freedom to Farm bill zeroed out the blue box/US PSE and added the green box/US PSE.

Sources: OECD (2005a) and US Department of Agriculture.

they were paid only on a fixed base and had production-limiting elements (for example, land set-asides).

But after the 1996 US farm bill abolished deficiency payments and created the mostly decoupled production flexibility contracts, the United States no longer had anything to allocate to the blue box and reported the new payments in the green box for minimally or nondistorting subsidies. As measured and categorized by the OECD, these blue box and, later, green box payments averaged 15 to 20 percent of total US producer support (figure 3.5). The 2002 farm bill retained decoupled direct payments, but the creation of countercyclical payments and the decision to allow farmers to update the base acreage on which the decoupled payments would be calculated are creating problems for US negotiators in the Doha Round.

Under current rules, the countercyclical payments will have to be in the amber box, either under the aggregate measurement of support ceiling or

Table 3.1 US and EU agricultural subsidies (millions of dollars)

| | Amber box | | | | Green box (decoupled payments only) |
| | AMS | | | | |
	MPS	Subsidies	De minimis	Blue box	
United States					
1998	5,776	4,774	4,762	0	5,659
1999	5,921	10,970	7,435	0	5,471
2000	5,840	11,025	7,341	0	5,068
European Union					
1998	38,382	13,949	142	23,012	144
1999	35,316	14,364	57	20,638	998
2000	27,945	11,512	678	20,239	449

AMS = aggregate measurement of support
MPS = market price support

Source: US Department of Agriculture, WTO Agricultural Trade Policy Commitments Database, available at www.ers.usda.gov/db/wto (accessed on April 14, 2000).

as non-product-specific de minimis. Keeping them there in the current round would make it difficult for US negotiators to agree to substantial cuts, so they are seeking to redefine the blue box to accommodate them. Other negotiators, however, are resisting and are also seeking additional clarification of the rules for allocating subsidies to the blue and green boxes to ensure that they are less or minimally distorting, in part by ensuring that "fixed" bases for payments remain fixed.

In the European Union, blue box payments went from negligible to somewhere between 20 and 25 percent of producer support in the latter half of the 1990s. With the 2003 CAP reform, the European Union is now essentially trying to replicate what US policymakers did in the 1996 farm bill and shift most of its blue box payments to the green box. The single farm payment is intended to replace most other subsidies, but only partially for some commodities and not at all for others. Moreover, this reform also does nothing to affect the still-high levels of EU market price support.

Table 3.1 shows US and EU notifications of amber box and blue box supports to the WTO, as well as the portion of the green box that is allocated to decoupled direct payments.[8] Although members are required to report these figures regularly, in practice there are long lags for most countries,

---

8. The bulk of US green box subsidies are for food stamps and general services; only about 10 percent are for decoupled payments to farmers. In the European Union, the bulk of green box subsidies are general services, environmental programs, regional assistance, and "structural adjustment through investment aids."

not just the United States, and the latest data available in the US Department of Agriculture's WTO commitments database is for 2000. The US share of producer support that is attributable to decoupled payments during 1999–2000 is just under 20 percent. At this point, and until the 2003 reform is implemented, EU decoupled payments are negligible, but blue box payments were roughly a third of total producer support during 1999–2000. If maximum decoupling occurs under the CAP reform, most of these payments would become eligible for the green box. In both cases, the share of at least partially decoupled subsidies is higher than when the OECD data are used because the WTO measure of market price support in the denominator is smaller.

Keeping US direct payments and EU single farm payments in the green box, however, will require either further reforms of both programs, or renegotiation of the green box. A WTO dispute settlement panel ruled in 2004 in a complaint brought by Brazil that US direct payments were not fully decoupled and could not be allocated to the green box. The panel found that the payments were not decoupled because, while farmers were not required to plant any particular crop, or to plant anything at all, they had to refrain from planting fruits and vegetables in order to remain eligible for the payments.[9] The panel ruled that this would tend to encourage farmers to continue to plant what they traditionally had, or to plant another program crop that received subsidies.

The dispute settlement panel's finding, though not binding in any other case, suggests that the European Union's single farm payment could not pass the decoupling test either because it has a similar prohibition on planting fruits and vegetables (as well as a few other commodities). In addition, the meaning of the EU requirement that eligible farmers keep their land in "good agricultural and environmental condition" is not clear. The 2002 US farm bill explicitly states that land may be allowed to remain fallow and that farmers do not have to produce anything on it to remain eligible. With respect to the CAP reform language, a US Department of Agriculture analysis concludes that "in practice, this means that [European farmers] must continue producing something and most likely will continue producing what they have historically produced, given that their other options are limited" (USDA 2003, 2).

Finally, for most commodities these partially decoupled payments are not the only form of support, and other forms are still linked to production or prices. Under the CAP reform, intervention prices were lowered for some EU commodities but not others, and market price support remains significant for most. The OECD estimates that maximum implementation

---

9. The fruit and vegetable sectors do not receive the subsidies that other crops do, and the authors of the 2002 farm bill wanted to keep producers in these sectors from having to compete with subsidized producers.

of the single farm payment would still leave more than 60 percent of EU producer support in the most trade-distorting categories. In the United States, the program crops that are eligible to receive direct payments are also eligible for marketing loans, which are not decoupled at all, and countercyclical payments, which are only partially decoupled.

In sum, going into the final stages of the Doha Round, roughly a fifth of US support to farmers is in decoupled green box payments. The EU situation is less certain because the single farm payment is just now being implemented and because countries are allowed flexibility in deciding how far to go in decoupling payments for some commodities. With full implementation of the CAP reform and the single farm payment, most EU *subsidies* might be eligible for the green box, but this would account for a third or less of total producer support. Moreover, the updating of base acreage in the 2002 US farm bill and the restrictions on planting certain crops in both the United States and the European Union suggest that these payments are not completely decoupled and could continue to influence planting decisions. Finally, sugar and dairy products, among the most protected commodities, remain largely unreformed.[10]

Reform Obstacles and Opportunities in 2006

A variety of political economy theories explain the origin and, especially, the persistence of agricultural subsidies, most pointing to rent-seeking behavior and collective action problems to explain why support is so much more entrenched in agriculture than other sectors in most rich countries.[11] What seems obvious from a brief review of the past few decades is that when pressure for reform became irresistible, it was because policymakers were concerned about competitiveness (primarily in the United States) or the need to contain the budget costs of agricultural support. Minimizing the negative impact of agricultural supports on other countries was rarely if ever a driving force. This conclusion is supported by the limited gains produced by the Uruguay Round of multilateral trade negotiations, which mostly affirmed rather than led agricultural reform in OECD countries in the 1980s and 1990s.

Eventually, ongoing structural changes would be expected to make prospects brighter for agricultural policy reform. The number of farmers in the industrialized countries continues to decline while their average age

---

10. In response to a Brazilian challenge in the WTO of the EU sugar program, the European Commission announced a plan to reduce internal prices by a third, but this will still leave EU prices at roughly twice the world level.

11. Moyer and Josling (1990) and Paarlberg (1999) review some of the more prominent and compelling theories.

continues to increase, as does the concentration of payments to larger, richer farmers. Both the United States and the European Union are also facing renewed budget pressures that will again highlight the costs of farm subsidies. And perhaps most important, developing countries that are competitive agricultural exporters are demonstrating themselves to be better organized and more effective than they were during the Uruguay Round. In addition, with the end of the Multi-Fiber Arrangement of quotas restricting the textile and apparel trade, the rich countries have little left to offer in reciprocal negotiations outside agriculture. These factors, combined with the mobilization of nongovernmental organizations (NGOs) on behalf of poor developing countries, are contributing to a different dynamic in these trade talks, though the ultimate outcome remained highly uncertain in the spring of 2006.

Internal Pressures for Reform

Of the various potential sources of reform pressure, structural economic change—the declining importance of agriculture in economies as they industrialize—has long seemed the most likely to eventually have an impact. But the question remains, when? Two decades ago, Honma and Hayami (1986) hypothesized that government support for agriculture would peak with the proportion of farmers in the total population between 5 and 10 percent, then begin to decline once it dropped below 5 percent. Perhaps it is just too early, but the trends in figure 3.6 do not appear to support this hypothesis. The share of the US population in farming dropped below the 5 percent threshold 30 years ago, but subsidies have fluctuated with world prices and the value of the dollar and have shown no consistent decline (figures 2.2 and 2.3). The share of the EU population in farming dropped below 5 percent much more recently, but budget pressures to reduce subsidy levels began before that. The Japanese farming population also recently dropped below the 5 percent threshold, but thus far Japan shows no sign of significantly reducing support for its farmers. Moreover, there has been little impact on policy from the facts that the farming populations of the United States and Europe are getting older— roughly half of US and EU farmers are at least 55 years of age—and that 50 percent of US farmers and more than 70 percent of EU farmers are, in effect, part-timers, earning significant shares of household income from nonfarm sources (USDA 2004).

Rather, the reverse appears to be true: The structural economic changes that remove common rationales for agricultural subsidies simultaneously make it harder to reform them. With industrialization and urbanization, the manufacturing and service sectors draw labor away from agriculture. Along with technological change and the substitution of capital for relatively more expensive labor, these structural changes contribute to consolidation of

Figure 3.6   Share of population dependent on agriculture, 1960–2003

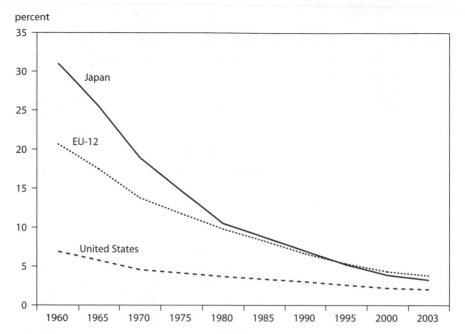

percent

Note: Agricultural population is defined as persons dependent on farming, fishing, hunting, or forestry for their livelihood, including nonworking dependents.

Source: UN Food and Agriculture Organization, FAOSTAT database.

agricultural operations. One consequence of declining numbers of farmers and the consolidation of farm operations is the accompanying concentration of subsidy payments. Because coupled subsidies tend to be based on levels of production and decoupled subsidies on historical levels of payments or acreage, most subsidies end up going to the largest operations. And with fewer farmers, it is easier and more profitable to organize and to lobby Congress for policies that raise prices and incomes, which, in turn, give those farmers both the means and the incentive to continue lobbying.

The concentration of payments in the United States and the European Union is striking. According to a database of payments compiled by the Environmental Working Group (n.d.), the top 10 percent of recipients of US agricultural subsidies from 1995 to 2003 got 72 percent of total payments, an average of more than $300,000 per recipient over that period, while the bottom 80 percent got only 13 percent of the total and an average payment of under $7,000 (table 3.2). According to the US Department of Agriculture (USDA 2000), 64 percent of farms receive no subsidies at all, and only 40 percent of those that do have sales under $50,000 annually. Similar comprehensive data are not available for the European Union, but a recent

Table 3.2 Concentration of US farm subsidy payments, 1995–2003

Category of all recipients	Percent of payments	Number of recipients	Total payments, 1995–2003 (billions of dollars)	Payment per recipient (dollars)
Top 1 percent	23	30,502	30.5	1,001,416
Top 10 percent	72	305,023	94.5	309,823
Bottom 80 percent	13	2,440,184	16.9	6,918
Subsidies received by top 10 percent of recipients, by commodity				
Corn	68	144,272	25.5	176,415
Wheat	74	122,420	13.8	113,004
Cotton	80	22,095	11.3	512,005
Soybeans	60	88,780	7.2	81,295
Rice[a]	65	5,848	6.1	1,044,507
Sorghum	75	54,017	2.5	47,034
Livestock	55	74,561	1.4	19,209
Barley	75	31,569	1.1	35,389

a. Rice subsidies are often paid to cooperatives representing a number of farm operations, and information on individual recipients is not available.

Source: Environmental Working Group (n.d.).

study estimated that 80 percent of CAP subsidies go to only 20 percent of farm operations, with large agribusinesses receiving the most.[12]

Although one might think that outrage over the inequitable distribution of subsidies would lead to calls for reform, most consumers and taxpayers simply do not care enough about this issue to become actively engaged. Moreover, the farm lobby and its congressional supporters have cleverly expanded the coalition backing farm bills by bringing in other issues that would attract supporters who would not otherwise vote for agricultural subsidies (Orden, Paarlberg, and Roe 1999, chapter 2). Food stamps and other nutrition programs were wrapped into farm bills in the 1970s to attract the support of urban legislators; in 1985, environmentalists were attracted by the CRP, which pays farmers not to produce in wetlands or areas prone to soil erosion. Whatever their views of agricultural subsidies, these groups may be

---

12. "CAP Reforms Fail to Diminish Gap Between Rich, Poor Farmers: Study," *Bridges Weekly Trade News Digest* 9, no. 29 (September 7, 2005). A few countries release data similar to the Environmental Working Group's on the distribution of farm subsidies, and a British NGO recently won a court case to force the disclosure of similar information in the United Kingdom. In late 2005, a group of European NGOs, journalists, and others banded together to create a Web site, www.farmsubsidy.org, that brings together the available data. They acted in the hope that these efforts would create pressure for greater transparency on recalcitrant countries.

inclined to lobby against overall cuts in the agricultural budget because they know that the agricultural committees on Capitol Hill will be more inclined to take the cuts out of these programs than out of traditional subsidies. There are signs, however, that this dynamic may be changing, with a number of environmental and antihunger NGOs arguing for fundamental reforms in the 2007 farm bill (e.g., American Farmland Trust 2006).

Americans tell pollsters that they do not favor subsidies to large operations and do not favor subsidies at all except in "bad years," but very few of them vote on this issue or bother to lobby their representatives. In contrast, US farm interests lobby vociferously and contribute lavishly; in the 2004 federal election cycle, they gave roughly $36 million to political campaigns (Center for Responsive Politics 2006). Advocacy groups for poor countries have also stepped up lobbying for reductions in OECD farm support on grounds of *international* equity, but thus far Americans appear unconvinced by these arguments. A 2004 poll on globalization by the Program on International Policy Attitudes (www.pipa.org) showed that a slim majority of Americans (53 to 56 percent, depending on the question) thought that US subsidies to farmers were justified by the need to compete with farmers in poor countries with lower returns, and that it was "not our responsibility to take care of farmers in other countries" (Kull 2004, 24).

Sugar is one of the most striking examples of both the inequities of agricultural policy and the power of farm lobbies. It is a product that some developing countries can produce far more cheaply than US or European farmers, yet it is one of the most heavily protected, with domestic prices in both markets supported at two to three times world prices, and one of the least reformed. Those guaranteed prices create a mighty incentive to lobby for continued support as well as, in the United States, the means to get access to the key congressional players (see box 3.2 and Elliott 2005b).

Budget pressures have the potential to be more effective in stimulating agricultural policy reform because they force policymakers to make choices among competing priorities and constituents. Over the past two decades at least, reductions in farm subsidies are correlated with budget debates, especially in periods when markets turned down and the costs of support prices set in good times soared. In the 1980s, escalating farm subsidy costs coincided with large budget deficits in the United States and a budget crunch in the European Community that increased interest in reforms. Conversely, a likely reason that Japan and South Korea have reformed so little is that almost all support is provided through trade barriers that require few budget outlays. (Unlike the United States, both countries export very few farm products and have no competitive concerns about using supply controls to prop up prices.) But with coupled subsidies, outlays tend to be high in times of low prices, and it is politically difficult to cut subsidies when farmers are suffering losses.

The result of the tension between containing costs and helping farmers in bad times, when public support also tends to be highest, is that most

Box 3.2 The political economy of US sugar policy

Support for sugar producers today has no connection to the original motivation, born of the Great Depression, to keep farmers on the land by supporting their incomes. Rather, the policy transfers hundreds of millions of dollars to a handful of farmers and processors at the expense of American consumers, workers, and firms of the US food processing industry and more efficient developing-country exporters. Despite changing rationales, however, the principal mechanism for supporting US sugar prices remains much the same, a system of country-by-country quotas that sharply restrict imports (see also chapter 4, box 4.1). Since the restoration of import quotas in 1982, US sugar prices have typically been two to three times higher than world prices, and imports' share of US consumption has decreased from nearly half to less than a fifth.

The distortions created by US sugar policy are many. As a result of artificially high prices, the United States produces more sugar than it otherwise would, and more efficient producers such as Brazil and Thailand, export—and earn—less. The costs to American consumers depend on the size of the gap between world and US prices at any given time, but several studies over the past decade calculate them at roughly $1.5 billion annually, and the US Government Accountability Office (formerly the General Accounting Office) estimates that producers collect $1 billion of the total (GAO 1993, 2000; see also Hufbauer and Elliott 1994, Tokarick 2003). As shown in table 2.4, estimates of the relative level of support for sugar are higher than for any other major product. Other costs of US sugar policy include degradation of the Florida Everglades, a national park that was designated a United Nations World Heritage Site in 1979.

Sugar is somehow able to maintain its protection despite being a relatively minor crop in the United States. In 2000, acreage planted in sugarcane and sugar beets represented 0.8 percent of total harvested cropland, compared with 23 percent each for corn and soybeans, 17 percent for wheat, and 4 percent for cotton. Sugar's share of gross farm receipts in 2000 was 1.1 percent, versus 3 percent for wheat, 8 percent for corn, and 6.5 percent for soybeans.

But the sugar industry has more political clout than its relative size would suggest. According to the database compiled by the Center for Responsive Politics (2006), 3 of the top 10 agribusiness contributors in the 2004 election cycle were sugar producers. In the narrower crop production and basic processing sector, sugar's share of total 2004 contributions was 23 percent, and sugar producers were in 7 of the top 10 slots. To put this in perspective, the sugar and dairy sectors contributed roughly $3 million each to federal candidates in the 2004 cycle, while farm receipts were just over $2 billion for sugar and $23 billion for dairy products.

reforms have been modest and incremental. Indeed, the most far-reaching attempt to reform US farm policy came during 1995–96, when commodity prices were high, subsidy payments low, and pressures in Washington to cut the federal budget deficit intense. As explained above (and in detail in Orden, Paarlberg, and Roe 1999), the 1996 farm bill departed sharply from past practice, introducing payments to farmers that were largely decoupled from production and prices. In this environment, however, the desire to preserve a high budget baseline for future subsidies was at least as important in gaining congressional approval as the desire in some quarters to reform US agricultural policy.

In the European Union, long-standing budgetary pressures have been exacerbated by the accession of 10 Eastern European countries in 2004. Absorbing all of the farmers in these countries (and they are proportionately more numerous than in the 15 countries that previously constituted the European Union), confronts member states with a stark choice of either large increases in the CAP budget or lower levels of support. The European Union is dealing with this in the short run by phasing in the proportion of direct payments for which farmers in the accession countries are eligible: From a starting point of 25 percent it will rise to 100 percent only in 2013. But farmers in the new member states are immediately eligible for export subsidies and other "intervention mechanisms." As all these costs rise, pressures to lower the level of support farmers receive will also increase.

In addition, discussions in mid-2005 on the EU budget revived long-simmering tensions between the United Kingdom, which provides relatively low levels of support to its farmers, and France, which is the largest recipient of CAP payments. A resolution of this tension in the 1980s had provided for a partial rebate of British contributions to the EC budget because of its low CAP expenditures. With the 2004 expansion, France wanted a reduction in the British rebate to provide additional resources for the accession countries. But British Prime Minister Tony Blair linked any rebate reduction to reform of the CAP, which France rejected.[13]

In the United States, a sharply deteriorating fiscal picture resulting from tax cuts and increased spending, particularly on the military, has revived the debate over budget deficits and is contributing to pressures to reduce agricultural spending in the next farm bill. In the 2006 and 2007 budgets submitted to Congress, President George W. Bush proposed modestly cutting the agriculture budget, in part by capping payments to individuals at $250,000 (down from $360,000). In addition, the president's budgets proposed reducing the total value of all payments to supported crop and dairy oper-

---

13. The dispute was resolved at the end of 2005 with the United Kingdom agreeing to give up roughly 20 percent of its rebate in return for France agreeing to a budget review during 2008–09 that could result in further subsidy cuts, five years earlier than previously agreed (BBC News, "EU Leaders Agree on New Budget Plan," December 17, 2005, at www.bbc.com, accessed on January 4, 2006).

ations by 5 percent. No details were provided, but the 2006 budget also proposed partially decoupling market loan payments and basing them on historical production levels.

But Congress rejected these proposals. With the House of Representatives intent on protecting commodity programs and cutting food stamps, and the Senate strongly supporting protection for food stamps, the two bodies compromised, first by cutting the 2006 agriculture budget by less than half of the president's request ($2.7 billion versus the proposed $6 billion), then by making no more than minimal reductions in subsidy programs and food stamps and making most of the cuts in conservation and research and development. In policy terms, all of this was directly contrary to the objectives of reform-minded WTO negotiators (*Inside U.S. Trade*, January 6, 2006, 1). In general, budget pressures have frequently triggered concern about agricultural subsidies in the United States, but to less effect than in Europe, perhaps because the European Commission lacks the power to independently raise revenues.

External Pressures for Reform

The increased role played by developing countries in pushing for agricultural reforms was underscored by the contrast between the outcome of the Doha Round's mid-term ministerial meeting in Cancún in September 2003 and the endgame of the Uruguay Round. During 1992–93, US and EC negotiators concluded an agreement that resolved a bilateral dispute over oilseeds and set the parameters of the Uruguay Round agreement on agriculture. They then presented it as a fait accompli to the other negotiators, many of whom found it grossly deficient in the level of liberalization achieved. In hopes of avoiding the delays and disruptions associated with sharply divergent US and EU positions on agriculture through most of the Uruguay Round, other WTO members asked US and EU negotiators to work out a compromise prior to the Cancún meeting. But when the US and European negotiators came out with a proposal that appeared designed to protect their own policies, including retention and expansion of the blue box, the response was quite different from that of a decade earlier: The major agricultural developing countries organized themselves into the G-20 and rejected the proposal.

As of early 2006, Brazil, India, and other key developing countries continue to be reluctant to put forward their own offers on nonagricultural market access and services until they determine whether US, EU and other rich-country negotiators are serious about reducing agricultural support. Without that, a meaningful liberalization package simply will not be possible. But the battle is not just North-South. While the West African cotton-exporting states, Brazil, Argentina, and the other competitive agricultural exporters want significant reductions in US subsidies, US farmers will not acquiesce to large subsidy cuts unless they get increased market access for their exports, including the large European and Asian markets.

In addition, Brazil's success in challenging US cotton subsidies and European sugar subsidies under the WTO's dispute settlement system creates another incentive to negotiate reforms. Recent studies suggest that the alternative in many sectors could be making reforms under the threat of WTO-authorized retaliation, without getting something in return in the form of increased access for manufacturing and services (Oxfam International 2005, Sumner 2005).

In addition to responding to WTO pressure on agricultural policies, the United States, the European Union, and Japan are also all engaged in bilateral and regional trade negotiations that are increasing the pressure for reform. For example, US negotiators overturned the principle of no exclusions in free trade agreements when it rejected increased access for sugar in the agreement with Australia. The Central American countries and the Dominican Republic will be permitted to increase sugar exports modestly, but US import barriers will not be eliminated, even though trade barriers will be coming down for all other sensitive products (albeit after long phaseouts). Several proposed partners in free trade agreements are even larger sugar exporters, and US negotiators will find it increasingly difficult to reconcile the existing provisions of the sugar program and the US trade agenda.

But there is a tension between the internal and external pressures for reform. In the European Union, and even more in Japan and South Korea, where trade measures are a major component of farm support, the budget impact of moving to decoupled subsidies would be high in the short run. Similarly, buying out the sugar and dairy quotas in the United States, as has been done recently for peanuts and tobacco, would require increased budget outlays (Orden 2005). Unless policymakers are willing to reduce support levels, this could make reforms involving decoupling more difficult in the short run. In the longer run, however, decoupling limits outlays by basing them on past production or acreage rather than on current prices. And whether announced as a buyout or not, moving from border measures to decoupled subsidies makes farm support more transparent and improves the chances that it will be reduced over time.

Unfortunately, events in spring 2006 suggested that policymakers in key countries had not yet summoned the political will to take on agricultural interests. In France, the government revoked labor market reform legislation in the face of street protests and dropped other legislation to reduce smoking in public places, suggesting that *any* economic reform is unlikely until after the presidential election in April 2007. In the United States, President Bush nominated the popular and effective US trade representative, Robert Portman, to become his director of the Office of Management and Budget just prior to a key April 30 deadline in the Doha Round agricultural negotiations. Many observers at home and abroad interpreted the move as indicating that the president expected little from the round and had decided to devote his limited political capital to other priorities. Not suprisingly, the April deadline for agreeing on key elements of the agricultural negotiating framework was missed.

Political weakness and policy drift in France and the United States make it increasingly unlikely that the Doha Round can be completed in late 2006 or early 2007. That, in turn, means that the US Congress will likely have to vote on whether to renew so-called trade promotion authority, which authorizes the president to negotiate trade agreements that the Congress commits to vote up or down, without amendment. The current authority expires in mid-2007 and was passed in the House of Representatives by a slim 3-vote margin in 2002. There is no guarantee that Congress will approve an extension of trade promotion authority, especially if there is little progress in the negotiations before they have to vote. The risks of dithering are high.

4

Opportunities and Challenges for Developing Countries

The structural transformation that occurs as countries develop economically involves large numbers of people moving over time from subsistence farming and other low-productivity agricultural activities to higher-productivity activities in the manufacturing and service sectors. Because governments often focus on industrialization as the path to development, many discriminated against agriculture until recently, taxing that sector in order to subsidize urban consumers and manufacturing activities. But many governments have come to realize that rural development can also contribute to economic growth during the transition, especially to pro-poor growth that causes the poverty rate to decline faster than it otherwise might at a particular rate of growth.[1]

Moreover, many developing countries have a comparative advantage in agriculture, and increased agricultural exports can help them address balance of payments problems, reduce debt burdens, and import the capital goods and technologies they need to move up the development ladder. Increased exports to liberalized rich-country markets—and reduced competition with subsidized exports—are, therefore, components of a pro-poor growth strategy.

But developing countries also have to adopt policy reforms and investment strategies that help the rural poor connect to markets and take advantage of any trade opportunities that arise. Most developing countries that previously taxed agriculture in order to subsidize the urban poor have moved to more neutral or even promotional agricultural policies. But most

---

1. Issues related to rural development and pro-poor growth are addressed in more detail in Timmer (2002, 2005).

Table 4.1 Agricultural indicators for developing countries
(simple average unless otherwise noted)

Indicator	Low-income countries	Lower-middle-income countries	Upper-middle-income countries	All developing countries
Percent of population in rural areas, 2003[a] (132)	70	50	22	57
Percent of economically active population in agriculture[b] (120)	69	33	23	48
Percent of poor in rural areas (52)	74	72	37	73
Percent of agricultural value added in GDP, 2004 (107)	31	13	7	20
Average cereal yields (kg/hectare), 1997–2004 (124)	1,543	2,331	2,741	2,070
Agricultural value added per worker, 2002 (2000 US dollars) (123)	424	1,971	6,734	2,234

a. Population weighted.
b. Most recent for which data available, generally early 1990s.
Note: Number of countries for which data is available is in parentheses.
Source: World Bank, World Development Indicators.

also still have a long way to go to provide the infrastructure, investments in human capital, and access to credit markets that must also be part of pro-poor growth strategies.

Agricultural Trade and Developing Economies

Agriculture provides a much larger share of income and employment in poor countries than in rich ones. Overall, almost half the population across all developing countries lives in rural areas and works in agricultural activities, but the sector generates an average of only 20 percent of developing-country GDP. The percentages are even higher in low-income countries, where 7 of 10 people work in agriculture, accounting for almost a third of GDP (table 4.1). As indicators of productivity, average cereal yields and agricultural value added per worker are both far lower in low-income

Table 4.2 Distribution of developing-country exports (percent)

Category	Agriculture[a]	Textiles and apparel	Electronic, computer, telecommunications equipment (SITC 75–77)[b]
Low-income countries	14	22.3	1.5
Lower-middle-income countries	8.1	13.9	18.2
Upper-middle-income countries	8.3	4.6	25.5
All developing countries	8.7	11.8	18.9

SITC = Standard International Trade Classification

a. Agriculture excludes fish (SITC 03) and cut flowers (SITC 29), includes SITC categories 00–12, 21–22, 26, 41–43.

b. SITC categories 75–77 (electronics, computers and other office equipment, and telecommunications equipment)

Source: UN Conference on Trade and Development, Trade Analysis and Information System (TRAINS) database.

countries than in middle-income countries. One consequence of this low productivity is that poor people in poor countries are more likely to be rural dwellers. In a sample of 52 countries compiled by the World Bank, 73 percent of the poor lived in rural areas (Aksoy 2005, 18).

While agriculture has a much bigger share of the economy in poorer countries, low productivity and the role of subsistence farming in these countries mean that they are not necessarily major exporters of agricultural products. Indeed, developing countries as a group are not much more dependent on agricultural exports than the industrialized countries, and most are net agricultural importers. Nearly 9 percent of total developing-country merchandise exports derive from agriculture (excluding fishing and forestry), compared with just over 7 percent for industrialized countries as a group. Among 115 developing countries for which data are available, 39 are net exporters of agricultural products and 76 are net importers. Thirty-seven of the latter group have an overall net deficit in agriculture but are net exporters in at least one of three broad subcategories (cereals, other food, or agricultural raw materials).

As shown in table 4.2, however, broad averages again mask wide variance in the level of dependence on agricultural exports, with low-income countries as a group more dependent on agricultural exports than middle-income countries. For low-income countries, the share of agricultural products among all exports is nearly twice that for middle-income countries. Also, textiles and apparel make up a little more than a fifth of the poorer countries' exports. Middle-income developing countries are much less dependent on

Table 4.3 Developing countries most dependent on agricultural exports

Country	Income level	Agriculture as a share of total exports (percent)	Top agricultural exports as percent of total agricultural exports	Top agricultural exports
Malawi	Low	89.5	74.5	Tobacco
Ethiopia (excludes Eritrea)	Low	83	75.8	Coffee, tea, cocoa, spices
Burundi	Low	82.4	97.6	Coffee, tea, cocoa, spices
Chad	Low	81.5	96.3	Cotton
Benin	Low	78.6	79.9	Cotton
Paraguay	Lower-middle	77.4	52.3	Oilseeds
Burkina Faso	Low	76.1	68.2	Cotton
Mali	Low	75	92.9	Cotton
Uganda	Low	73	80.2	Coffee, tea, cocoa, spices
Côte d'Ivoire	Low	68.9	79.3	Coffee, tea, cocoa, spices
Tonga	Lower-middle	67.4	81.5	Fruits, vegetables
Afghanistan	Low	63.5	35.7	Textile fibers other than cotton
Swaziland	Lower-middle	60.9	67.4	Sugar
St. Lucia	Upper-middle	60.2	86.1	Fruits, vegetables
Comoros	Low	56.2	97.9	Coffee, tea, cocoa, spices
Uzbekistan	Low	55.3	86.5	Cotton
Cuba	Lower-middle	53.4	33.6	Sugar
Zimbabwe	Low	52.9	61.2	Tobacco
Kenya	Low	51.3	61.5	Coffee, tea, cocoa, spices
Rwanda	Low	50.5	95.2	Coffee, tea, cocoa, spices

Sources: World Bank, *World Development Indicators;* UN Conference on Trade and Development, Trade Analysis and Information System (TRAINS) database.

both agriculture and textiles and have moved into electronic, telecommunications, and information products.

For certain countries, however, dependence on agricultural exports is quite high and often revolves around just one commodity. There are 20 developing countries, 14 in sub-Saharan Africa, where agriculture accounts for more than half of total merchandise exports (table 4.3), and 45 countries where the share is over a quarter. Of the latter group, 25 are characterized as low-income and 12 as low-middle-income. Among the 20 most agriculture-dependent exporters, more than half of the agricultural exports of all but two are concentrated in just a single two-digit Standard International

Table 4.4 Agricultural trade positions in developing countries
(number of countries by category)

Category	Low-income countries (44)	Lower-middle-income countries (45)	Upper-middle-income countries (26)
Net importers			
Cereals	40	38	24
Other food[a]	26	25	15
Total food	28	27	19
Agricultural raw materials	21	34	21
All agricultural categories	24	32	20
Net exporters			
Cereals	4	7	2
Other food[a]	18	20	11
Total food	16	18	7
Agricultural raw materials	23	11	5
All agricultural categories	20	13	6

a. Excludes fish and other seafood.

Source: UN Conference on Trade and Development, Trade Analysis and Information System (TRAINS) database.

Trade Classification (SITC) category. This group includes the four West African cotton exporters that put that product on the Doha Round agenda, as well as several others dependent on traditional tropical products such as coffee, tea, cocoa, spices, sugar, and tobacco.

Table 4.4 further underscores the relatively greater dependence of the poorest countries on agricultural trade. Nearly half of the low-income countries in the sample are net agricultural exporters (20 of 44), compared with less than a third of middle-income countries (19 of 71). Overall, half of the developing countries with net agricultural exports are in the lowest income category. But nearly two-thirds of these 115 developing countries are net importers of food and almost all of them import cereals, which are typically the major source of calories in poor countries. The potential impact of agricultural reform on net food-importing countries is taken up later in this chapter.

The Opportunities:
What Do Developing Countries Export?

Clearly, agricultural policies in rich countries affect global trade patterns and influence what developing countries are able to profitably produce and export. But developing-country patterns of agricultural production and trade are also affected by climate, geography, the allocation of natural resources, including land and water, and their own policies. Because most rich countries have relatively temperate climates, their agricultural output commonly includes grains, oilseeds, dairy products, and meat, while many developing countries are located in tropical latitudes that are appropriate for a variety of goods that are not produced at all or only in very small quantities further north.

In a recent World Bank analysis (Aksoy 2005, 30), agricultural production and exports were categorized in four broad groups:

- tropical products, including coffee, tea, cocoa, spices, and nuts (which are grouped together in SITC category 07), sugar, and textile fibers (mostly cotton, wool, and silk);

- temperate products, which most countries of the Organization for Economic Cooperation and Development (OECD) support, including meat, dairy products, grains, animal feed, and oilseeds and edible oils;

- nontraditional, dynamic products, including seafood, fruits, vegetables, and cut flowers; and

- "other processed products," including beverages, tobacco and tobacco products, and "other processed foods."

According to World Bank figures, the nontraditional, dynamic products make up the largest share of developing-country agricultural exports, more than 40 percent, and were the fastest growing in the 1990s, at an average annual rate of nearly 7 percent. For the purposes of this analysis, however, fish and other seafood and cut flowers are dropped from consideration because these products typically are not covered by rich countries' agricultural programs or in the Doha Round agricultural negotiations. However, sanitary and phytosanitary (SPS) standards, which are important in these sectors, are discussed later in this chapter. Domestic subsidies are also an important problem for trade in fish and fish products, but these issues are being addressed in the negotiations on nonagricultural subsidies.

If the focus is on the products that are covered in the agricultural negotiations, then the protected temperate products make up more than a third of developing-country exports, while traditional tropical products and fruits and vegetables each make up roughly a quarter. But fruits and vegetables remain one of the fastest-growing product sectors, behind only "other processed foods" and oilseeds and edible oils, both of which start from much lower bases (Aksoy 2005). This is important because fruits and vegetables are relatively less protected and subsidized in the industrialized countries, at least through traditional means, and thus could represent an important opportunity for developing-country exporters.

But these broad trends again mask important differences among developing countries. As shown in figures 4.1 and 4.2, middle-income countries have been more successful than low-income countries in diversifying away from traditional tropical products, with temperate products and fruits and vegetables accounting for larger shares. In the middle-income countries, the share of traditional tropical products has fallen by more than half, from 35 to 40 percent in the 1970s to about the same level accounted for by processed foods, beverages, and tobacco products. Despite high levels of OECD protection for grains, meat, dairy, and other temperate products, these products now make up nearly 40 percent of the exports of middle-income countries. Low-income countries have also managed to increase exports of some of the temperate products while reducing the share of traditional tropical products by nearly half. Low-income countries have had less success in developing exports in the fast-growing fruit, vegetable, and processed product categories.

The bottom halves of the two figures, showing commodity-specific data at the two-digit SITC level, present both a potentially more promising picture for the middle-income countries and a more challenging one for low-income countries. Middle-income countries have moved strongly into the dynamic fruits and vegetables sector, while the volatile coffee, tea, cocoa, and spices category still dominates for low-income countries. For both groups of countries, cereals are the second most important category, though most developing countries are net importers of cereals, with vegetable oils another of the temperate products that developing countries export. In the case of the low-income countries, however, these exports are relatively concentrated and often not in direct competition with those of rich countries. The cereal exports are largely accounted for by rice exports from India, Pakistan, and Vietnam to other developing countries, while the vegetable oil exports are mostly palm and coconut oil from Indonesia. Figure 4.1b also indicates that meat is relatively important for middle-income countries, but three-quarters of total meat exports from developing countries are accounted for by Brazil, China, Thailand, and Argentina. Moreover, pork and poultry, which the rich countries support less than beef, are important for all these countries except Argentina.

The importance to individual countries of tropical products, fruits and vegetables, cotton, and cereals is underscored in table 4.5, which shows the number of countries for which each product category is one of its top three agricultural exports. Coffee, tea, cocoa, and spices are a top export for 34 of 55 low-income countries and 25 of 80 middle-income countries. Fruits and vegetables are in the top three for 32 low-income and 55 middle-income countries. Again, what is notable is that these are commodities that the rich countries tend not to protect as heavily as sugar, dairy products, meat, rice, and other grains.

For tropical products tariff escalation is a problem, but, with the exception of sugar, the basic commodities typically do not face trade barriers in rich

Figure 4.1   Shares of middle-income country agricultural exports, 1970–2002

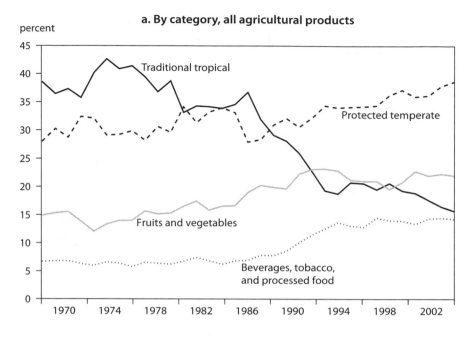

a. By category, all agricultural products

percent

Traditional tropical

Protected temperate

Fruits and vegetables

Beverages, tobacco, and processed food

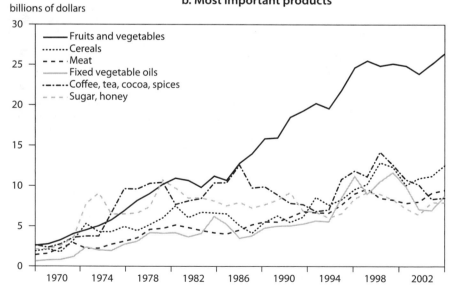

b. Most important products

billions of dollars

— Fruits and vegetables
······· Cereals
– – – Meat
—— Fixed vegetable oils
·–··–·· Coffee, tea, cocoa, spices
– – – Sugar, honey

Source: UN Food and Agriculture Organization, FAOSTAT database.

Figure 4.2   Shares of low-income country agricultural exports, 1970–2002

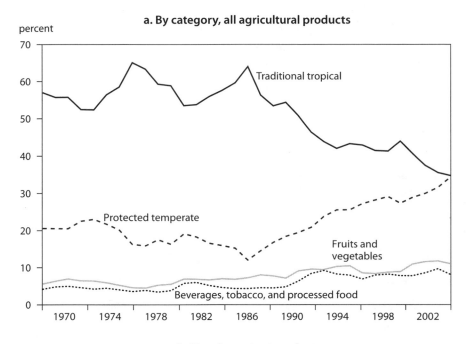

a. By category, all agricultural products

percent

Traditional tropical

Protected temperate

Fruits and vegetables

Beverages, tobacco, and processed food

b. Most important products

billions of US dollars

——— Fruits and vegetables   ——— Fixed vegetable oils
·············· Cereals   ·—·—· Coffee, tea, cocoa, spices
– – – Cotton   – – – Sugar, honey
·—··—· Tobacco

Table 4.5 Most important commodities among developing-country agricultural exports

Low-income countries (44)		Middle-income countries (71)	
Commodity	Number of countries[a]	Commodity	Number of countries[a]
Coffee, tea, cocoa, spices	34	Fruits and vegetables	55
Fruits and vegetables	32	Cereals	27
Cotton	25	Coffee, tea, cocoa, spices	25
Tobacco	17	Beverages	23
Oilseeds	11	Sugar	20
Sugar	9	Animal feed	17
Animal feed	8	Fixed vegetable oils, fats	13
Vegetable oils, fats	8	Tobacco	12
Cereals	7	Oilseeds	12
Beverages	5	Cotton	10
Meat	3	Meat	10
Dairy products	3	Miscellaneous food	9
Wool	3	Wool	4
Miscellaneous food	0	Dairy products	3

a. Number of countries for which each commodity is one of the top three agricultural exports.

Source: UN Conference on Trade and Development, Trade Analysis and Information System (TRAINS) database.

countries. Rather, the problems with export dependence on these products lie in other areas, including price volatility (indicated in figure 4.2b, in nominal dollars) and the tendency of many developing countries to be relatively dependent on just one or a few commodities, such as coffee. Sugarcane is a tropical product in which many developing countries have a comparative advantage but limited export opportunities because the United States, the European Union, and Japan protect their sugar producers from competition. But the effects of sugar liberalization would not benefit all the countries that currently export sugar to the United States and the European Union because of preference erosion (see box 4.1).

In sum, for a combination of reasons, including both comparative advantage and the deterrent effects of trade barriers, key developing-country exports are not those that rich countries support most generously. OECD liberalization of temperate products could help to encourage export diversification, especially among low-income countries that continue to be dependent on traditional tropical products. Substantial reductions in US cotton subsidies are also important to many very poor countries. But reduced intervention in other highly distorted commodity markets, including dairy products, meat, and sugar, might have fewer short-run benefits

Box 4.1 Sugar preferences in the United States and the European Union

The triangular trade In manufactured goods, human beings, and sugar and other tropical products that developed between Europe, western Africa, and the Caribbean in the 17th and 18th centuries was incredibly lucrative and morally repulsive. But sugar shipments to Europe were disrupted as a result of slave rebellions and trade embargoes accompanying the Napoleonic wars. About the same time, the process of producing sugar from beets was discovered in Germany, and the governments of France and other countries encouraged farmers to increase production of beets to replace Caribbean sugar. In 2005, with the help of export subsidies, the European Union was the world's second largest exporter of sugar. Adding to the distortions, the small amount of foreign sugar that is allowed into the EU market under the Sugar Protocol is mostly from former colonies in Africa and the Caribbean that have preferential access because of historical ties and not because they are the most efficient—or poorest—suppliers (Mitchell 2005).

The pattern of US trade is also influenced by historical events and has little connection to efficiency or comparative advantage. Like Europe, the United States initially relied on imports from the Caribbean. In 1898, however, the US government annexed Hawaii, partly as the result of demands from American investors in sugar and other forms of plantation agriculture who wanted to ensure tariff-free access to the US market. That same year, the treaty settling the Spanish-American War was signed, with Spain recognizing Cuban independence and agreeing to sell the Philippines to the United States for $20 million. Until 1960, almost all US imports came from Cuba and the Philippines, and imports accounted for one-half to three-quarters of US sugar consumption. In 1960, Hawaii accounted for 23 percent of domestic sugar production and 60 percent of sugar from cane; today it contributes under 5 percent of total domestic production (Mitchell 2005). But the Philippines remains the third-largest supplier of US sugar imports, while Cuba's quota was revoked following Fidel Castro's nationalization of the sugar industry. Unlike the European Union, the United States is a net sugar importer and does not subsidize significant sugar exports. But like the European Union, the United States strictly controls imports in order to support domestic prices while minimizing the budget costs.

One consequence of these historically rooted distortions is that in the short run there will be losers as well as winners among developing-country exporters with preferential access to the EU and US markets. Liberalization of the American and European markets would lower prices in Europe and the United States, but because it would eliminate subsidized EU exports and increase demand for imported sugar, liberalization would raise prices on the world market.

(box continues next page)

**Box 4.1 Sugar preferences in the United States
and the European Union**   (*continued*)

The most likely winners from reform are the low-cost, globally competitive exporters that currently gain relatively little from preferential access to the US and EU markets. On average in 2001–03, eight countries had significant shares of the global sugar market but shipped only a small fraction to the protected American and European markets. Brazil and Thailand alone accounted for 40 percent of global sugar exports, while Australia, Cuba, South Africa, Colombia, and Guatemala collectively accounted for another 20 percent. For most of these countries, the US and EU markets accounted for less than 3 percent of total sugar exports, the exceptions being Colombia (9 percent) and Guatemala (16 percent). India is also one of the world's top three producers of sugar and was a large net exporter of sugar in this period (2001–03). But these were unusually good years. Over a longer period, India is only a sporadic exporter, but its producers would still benefit from higher world prices.

The most likely losers from sugar trade liberalization are countries that continue to export to the United States and the European Union only because they hold quota rights, but which are overall net importers of sugar (the lower right quadrant of table 4.9). Some of these countries import and then reexport sugar in order to sell in these markets at prices that are on average two to three times the world price. Others export as much as their quotas permit while importing to meet domestic consumption needs. These countries would lose the protection-induced transfers from US and EU consumers, but these could be replaced with equivalent transfers from taxpayers through increased aid flows. Thus far, the compensation levels proposed by EU policymakers have been criticized as grossly inadequate. But these countries would nevertheless gain from reallocating resources wasted on rent seeking to areas where they are competitive.

In the middle, with uncertain futures, are smaller net exporters of sugar. Whether these countries gain or lose from US and EU policy reform depends on whether they can increase their global market share to the point that higher world prices make up for lower prices in the previously protected markets. Certain exporters would likely gain from liberalization because they currently sell at least twice as much on world markets as they do in the United States and European Union (those in the upper left quadrant of the table), and would therefore receive a higher price for most of their exports. But several other countries send a third or more of their sugar exports, and some as much as 100 percent, to these protected markets (upper right quadrant of table 4.9). They would lose a larger share of export revenues. Countries that could be hit particularly hard are producers for which sugar accounts for a significant share of total export revenues, such as Mauritius, Fiji, and Guyana.

than expected for developing countries *as a group,* particularly those at lower-income levels. Meat and dairy are high-value products because they are relatively capital-intensive and expensive to produce. These exports also face standards related to animal as well as human health and safety. For some countries, potential losses as a result of higher staple food prices or preference erosion could offset some or all of the benefits from increased market access that mostly accrue to others. And in the more dynamic fruits and vegetables sectors, the more important challenge is likely to be health and safety standards.

What Are the Challenges?

The premise behind the push to put agriculture at the center of the Doha Round is that significant agricultural liberalization by rich countries would provide increased opportunities for developing-country farmers to export, which would raise incomes in rural areas, where the bulk of the world's poor live. But developing countries are a diverse lot, and some could suffer losses as a result of higher food import bills or preference erosion. Thus, the effects on individual countries and on the poor who reside there would depend on which products each country traded and how those products were liberalized. The effects would also depend on whether the country had the infrastructure, credit markets, and domestic policies to enable farmers to respond to new trade opportunities.

Net Food Importers and the Distributional Effects of Agricultural Liberalization

Concerns about the potential impact of reductions in agricultural subsidies for poor countries that are net food importers were first raised in the Uruguay Round. These concerns proved to be premature because the limited reforms that were adopted had little, if any, impact on world food prices. With the Group of 20 developing countries insisting on significant reductions in agricultural support in the Doha Round, concerns about the impact on net food-importing countries have resurfaced. The problem arises because most analyses of OECD agricultural policy reform predict increases in the world price of affected commodities as domestic production and exports decline and demand for imports increases. Net food importers worry about both the potential impact on their balance of payments and the distributional consequences if the wages of low-skilled workers do not rise enough to make up for higher food prices. As shown in table 4.4, all but 13 of the 115 countries for which data are available are net importers of cereals, which along with locally grown root crops are usually staple food commodities for the poorest people.

While concerns about the effects of reduced subsidies on the poor are valid, a careful look at patterns of trade and agricultural support suggests that the impact of *feasible* reforms will not be as great as feared. Some net importers would likely become net exporters of some agricultural products if world prices rose and market access for their products increased. Cline (2004, chapter 3) also points out that most developing countries have even larger trade deficits in manufacturing than in agriculture, and thus should still gain overall from a broad liberalization package that lowers prices for their manufactured imports. However, that outcome is based on the assumption that developing countries, including the least developed, will undertake some liberalization of their own.

Even if national-level balance of payments problems are mitigated by offsetting export gains due to increased market access and reduced import prices from lowering of the importers' own barriers, there will still be distributional consequences within countries. Depending on what happens to low-skill jobs and wages in other sectors, poor consumers may suffer from rising food prices, even if prices for other goods drop, because food is such a significant part of the consumption basket. Moreover, much recent research using microlevel data based on household surveys shows that the rural poor, expected to be major beneficiaries of OECD agricultural reform, are often net buyers of food and could end up worse off, at least in the short run.

But the OECD estimates of producer support for agriculture described in chapter 2 showed that dairy products, sugar, and rice receive the highest levels of support. Of these, only rice is a staple commodity consumed regularly by the poor. According to data from the UN Food and Agriculture Organization, more than 60 percent of the daily calories consumed in most developing countries come from cereals and starchy roots and less than 10 percent from animal products (table 4.6). The exception is Latin America and the Caribbean, which has a higher average per capita income than other developing regions and a more diverse diet. In sub-Saharan Africa, half of daily calories are provided by products that are little traded, principally sorghum and millet, local varieties of maize, and cassava. Rice, which has one of the lowest ratios of trade to consumption of any commodity, is the dominant crop in Asia, accounting for a third of daily caloric intake in South Asia and half in East Asia and Southeast Asia. In South Asia, wheat is also important, but imports account for a small share of the supply.

Thus, the commodity of most concern in the context of trade liberalization would appear to be rice; the World Bank estimates that export prices could rise on a trade-weighted average basis by a third.[2] But most countries in Asia are largely self-sufficient in rice as a result of deliberate government

2. Projected export price increases for the different varieties of rice vary widely, from less than 10 percent for long-grain rice to as much as 91 percent on exports of medium-grain rice (Wailes 2005).

Table 4.6 Sources of daily calories in developing countries (percent)

Source	Sub-Saharan Africa		Latin America and the Caribbean		South Asia		East and Southeast Asia	
	Daily calories provided by:	Imports as share of domestic supply	Daily calories provided by:	Imports as share of domestic supply	Daily calories provided by:	Imports as share of domestic supply	Daily calories provided by:	Imports as share of domestic supply
Cereals, starchy roots	64	21	40	31	63	2	64	25
Wheat	7	77	13	62	21	3	6	105
Rice	8	42	9	16	35	negl.	49	5
Maize	15	9	14	18	2	2	5	38
Sorghum, millet	14	1	negl.	33	3	negl.	negl.	negl.
Starchy roots	20	negl.	4	2	2	negl.	4	6
Addendum:								
Other vegetable products	28		40		29		27	
Animal products	6		20		8		9	

negl. = neglible

Source: UN Food and Agriculture Organization, FAOSTAT database.

Table 4.7 Price effects of complete global trade liberalization, selected countries and commodities (change in the import price index)

Commodity	World	Bangladesh	Indonesia	Mozambique	Vietnam
Primary products	6.1	9.5	13.4	5.1	9.2
Paddy rice	22.2	3.0	9.4	14.4	9.2
Wheat	9.0	2.7	7.8	8.1	3.7
Cereal grains	12.2	5.3	8.2	4.8	5.0
Food	2.8	4.8	4.2	2.5	3.3
Beef	8.4	1.1	4.8	4.7	6.3
Other meat	3.4	3.8	−2.0	2.7	−0.6
Vegetable oils	3.4	4.7	−0.1	3.4	1.6
Dairy products	11.8	5.7	8.6	1.9	7.6
Processed rice	7.7	5.2	10.6	7.2	5.4

Source: Hertel and Ivanic (2006).

policies to stabilize domestic prices and promote food security (Timmer 2004). Moreover, a World Bank study shows that under a scenario of global free trade, in which developing countries would also reduce their tariffs on rice, average *import* prices for rice would fall by roughly 15 percent (Wailes 2005, 187). This study finds that the most likely losers from liberalization of rice markets would be net importers that already have low tariffs and limited ability to influence prices, such as Brazil, Turkey, the Middle Eastern countries, Hong Kong, and Singapore, all middle-income or higher-income countries.

Bangladesh is a very poor country and a net food importer that appears in many analyses as one of the potential net losers in some trade liberalization scenarios. But even Bangladesh is a large net importer of rice only in years when the local crop fails because of bad weather or other reasons (Wailes 2005, 182). Moreover, Bangladesh in recent years has chosen to impose a tariff on rice of more than 20 percent, which it could reduce in the face of global price increases. Potential losses for Bangladesh arise from a more complex interaction of various potential liberalization effects. In addition to higher food prices, Bangladesh could also face higher prices for cotton and cotton textiles, which would raise costs for its apparel export sector at the same time that preference erosion undermines the competitiveness of those exports in the European market. Table 4.7 summarizes World Bank estimates of the world price effects of moving to global free trade for selected commodities. The World Bank model predicts average price increases for primary products of 6 percent and for food products of less than 3 percent (Hertel and Ivanic 2006). Not surprisingly, since rice is one of the most distorted grain markets, rice prices could rise by about 22 percent on average, but the projections are lower in selected poor countries, including

Indonesia. Prices for wheat and for other grains are both projected to rise by around 10 percent on average. In four of the poorest countries selected for analysis, price effects for wheat and other grains range from a 2.7 percent increase for wheat (Bangladesh) to 8.2 percent for grains (Indonesia).

It should be noted that, according to commodity price statistics from the International Monetary Fund (IMF), the projected price increases are not much different from and are often lower than the "normal" fluctuations in prices of major commodities. The average annual price change (up and down) over the past 20 years for rice, wheat, and corn was around 15 percent (author's calculations). Moreover, no one expects the result of the Doha Round to be complete global liberalization, and whatever liberalization is achieved will likely be phased in over a number of years. Nor is the elimination of export subsidies likely to have much effect on the price of staples. In the two most recent years for which notifications to the WTO are available (2000 and 2001), export subsidies on wheat and other grains dropped sharply, and sugar, dairy, beef, and other processed products accounted for roughly 80 percent of all export subsidies.[3] Finally, the potential effects of OECD agricultural reforms on the rural poor are more complicated than is often assumed. The premise behind the push for liberalization as a key poverty reduction mechanism is that while poor urban consumers will lose from higher food prices, a greater number of poor rural producers will gain. Cline (2004, 129), for example, estimates that an average 10 percent increase in agricultural prices as a result of liberalization would lift 200 million people out of poverty in 72 developing countries for which data are available.

However, recent research derived from household surveys finds that the short-term effects of agricultural liberalization for the poorest people may be either neutral or negative. Liberalization-induced price effects may not trickle down to poor farmers at all if they are in remote areas with few roads and little or no access to markets. A World Bank study on the distributional effects of trade liberalization in Mexico found that the transmission of import price changes was less in rural areas than in urban areas, and was also less the further one got from the border (Nicita 2004). But to the extent that higher prices do trickle down to rural areas, other research shows they could have negative effects for the poorest people because they are often net buyers of food rather than net sellers.

The World Bank (2005a, 64) concludes, "In rural areas, the empirical finding that emerges consistently in most parts of the developing world is that a majority of households are net food buyers, while a relatively small minority of wealthier households are grain sellers. The poor, who are overwhelmingly net food purchasers, suffer disproportionately from high food prices." But it is important to remember that this is the short-run effect and

---

3. See WTO Agricultural Trade Policy Commitments Database at the USDA Economic Research Service Web site, www.ers.usda.gov (accessed on April 19, 2006).

that increased exports do offer the potential to raise incomes significantly among farmers able to switch from subsistence farming to agricultural production for the market. Research on Zambia provides evidence that such switching does occur but emphasizes that complementary domestic policies are necessary if the potential gains are to be fully realized (Balat and Porto 2005, Timmer 2002).[4]

Preference Erosion

Preference erosion is another problem raised by the Doha Round, though it is a more limited one in the agricultural area than the potential problems of net food importers. It is more limited both in terms of the countries affected, which are often not the poorest, and the commodities involved. This is contrary to what might be expected, since average tariffs are much higher on agricultural commodities than on manufactured goods. But most sensitive agricultural products are excluded from—or their import highly restricted under—the Generalized System of Preferences (GSP) as implemented by most rich countries. Many countries provide greater access to the *least* developed countries (LDCs), though the European Union's "Everything But Arms" program still delayed liberalization of sugar, rice, and bananas. And the United States has not yet committed to quota-free and duty-free access for all products from all LDCs.

Thus, as argued by Cline (2004) and others, preference erosion for the LDCs could be addressed in part by improving access for sensitive commodities where it remains restricted and by making rules of origin less restrictive and easier to meet. This could help to preserve access for the most vulnerable states even as most favored nation barriers are gradually reduced. But one might also expect the impact of preferences on low-income countries to be limited, given the still-heavy dependence on exports of tropical products that, with the exception of sugar in all major markets and bananas in the European Union, usually face low or no tariffs. Combined with the fact that poorer countries tend to have less administrative capacity and greater difficulties meeting the eligibility and rules of origin requirements for preferences, it is not surprising that a US Department of Agriculture study finds that LDCs "do not appear to benefit from incentives provided by preferential programs" (Wainio et al. 2005).

---

4. Additional research on the distribution of gains and losses from agricultural trade, focusing on Ethiopia and Mexico, may be found in Levinsohn and McMillan (2005) and Ashraf, McMillan, and Zwane (2005), respectively. These studies support the finding in the World Bank report that the poorest people in rural areas tend to be net buyers of food. Additional World Bank research on price transmission and the distributional effects of agricultural liberalization may be found in Hertel and Winters (2006).

Table 4.8 Indicators of trade preferences for agricultural products

Country/preference	Simple average tariff (percent)	Duty-free lines (as percent of total)
United States		
MFN	9.3	24
GSP	8	54
LDC, regional arrangements[a]	5.1–5.3	87–88
European Union		
MFN	21.9	14
GSP	19.7	18
Africa, Caribbean, and Pacific[b]	13.3	60
Everything But Arms	1.1	98
Japan		
MFN	15.6	20
GSP for non-LDCs	15.1	30
GSP for LDCs	14.2	35

GSP = Generalized System of Preferences
LDC = least developed country
MFN = most favored nation

a. Includes preferences under the Caribbean Basin Economic Recovery Act, the Andean Trade Preference Act, and the African Growth and Opportunity Act.
b. Lomé and Cotonou arrangements.

Source: Wainio et al. (2005).

Table 4.8 shows indicators of preference margins for developing countries in the US, European, and Japanese markets. The table shows that Japan largely excludes agriculture from its GSP program, even for LDCs. Neither the European Union nor the United States provides much additional access under its regular GSP programs, but both are more generous toward LDCs and certain regional partners. As noted in the opening paragraph of the present section, the European Union provides duty- and quota-free access for LDCs except for sugar, rice, and bananas. The preference margin for the African, Caribbean, and Pacific countries under the Cotonou arrangement (which replaced the Lomé Convention on June 23, 2000) is nearly nine percentage points, but the average tariff remains relatively high at 13.3 percent. Provisions for LDCs and eligible trading partners in the Caribbean, the Andean region, and sub-Saharan Africa reduce the average US agricultural tariff by almost half, to just over 5 percent, but that is still double the average tariff on manufactured exports (Wainio et al. 2005, 23).

Agricultural import barriers in the United States are relatively concentrated in a few sectors, and 62 percent of US agricultural imports entered duty free in 2002 without any preference at all. Preferences are more important in Europe both because the EU preference margin is larger and because only a third of the European Union's agricultural imports enter duty free without preferences. But excluding the tariff-rate quota (TRQ) commodities, preference margins in both the United States and the European Union are largest for fresh and prepared fruits and vegetables and other processed foods that are more likely to be exported by middle-income countries (Wainio et al. 2005). But 40 percent of the preference benefits received by 76 middle-income countries still come from sugar, and another 20 percent come from bananas (Gillson, Hewitt, and Page 2005). According to US Department of Agriculture calculations, the top 20 preference beneficiaries (for all products, not just agricultural products) in the US market account for nearly 90 percent of total preferential imports, and none of them are LDCs. In the European Union, the top 20 beneficiaries account for two-thirds of total preferential imports (not just agriculture), and only one of them, Madagascar, is an LDC (Wainio et al. 2005, 16–17).

Sensitive products protected by TRQs, primarily bananas in the European Union and sugar in both the European and US markets, present a particular problem because preferential access involves transfers of millions of dollars arising from the quota rents. In these cases, restricted market access is allocated on the basis of colonial or other historical ties, rather than either need or efficiency. Caribbean banana exporters have already been forced to undergo some adjustment because of WTO challenges to the EU banana regime by more efficient Latin American producers. In the sugar case, the desire of rich countries to continue protecting their sugar producers coincides with the desire of preferred exporters to maintain their quota rents (see box 4.1). Here again, however, WTO litigation, this time by Brazil, forced the European Union to reform its sugar program, cutting the support price by roughly a third so as to bring subsidized exports into line with prior commitments. This reform is not expected to lower the level of imports from preferred exporters, but they will receive lower revenues as a result of the internal EU price cut.

But again, in the cases of sugar and banana preferences, the beneficiaries are not typically the poorest countries. In the European Union, only two of the countries with preferential access for bananas and five with preferential access for sugar fall into the LDC category. Only four sugar quota holders in the US market are LDCs. A study by the British Overseas Development Institute has produced an estimate that preference erosion losses from complete liberalization of the EU banana and sugar markets would be $100 million and $500 million, respectively (Gillson, Hewitt, and Page 2005, 74). Eighty percent of the losses would be concentrated in five countries: Mauritius, Swaziland, Guyana, Jamaica, and Fiji. In regard to average external income (exports of goods and services plus gross aid flows) during 1999–2002, only 8 of the 22 countries that were studied had losses of 5 percent or greater: Belize, Dominica, Fiji, Guyana, Mauritius, St. Lucia, St. Vincent and the Grenadines, and Swaziland. Jamaica had estimated losses of 2 percent of external income, while the losses of the others were 1 percent or less (Gillson, Hewitt, and Page 2005, 74). The principal problem is that many of these countries are small island states with few alternative sources of employment.

With respect to bananas, the European Union is moving from a TRQ to a tariff-only system as a result of the WTO litigation. Unless the tariff is set at a very high level, most of the currently preferred high-cost Caribbean exporters will likely lose market share. The lower the new tariff, the more the low-cost Latin American exporters will gain. The sugar situation is discussed in more detail in box 4.1, and table 4.9 shows potential winners and likely losers from EU and US liberalization of sugar TRQs.

In sum, the preference erosion problem is primarily a bilateral one between the European Union and a small number of African, Caribbean, and Pacific countries exporting bananas and sugar.[5] While the problems for these countries are potentially serious, they do not appear to be widespread enough to justify sacrificing the potential gains for many other poor countries that would benefit from liberalization.

Domestic Obstacles to Grasping Trade Opportunities

Higher world prices resulting from agricultural liberalization by rich countries should stimulate increased production and exports by farmers in poor countries with comparative advantage in those products—if the price signal gets to those farmers. But as recent research at the World Bank indicates, border price changes do not always reach remote areas where the costs of getting goods to and from markets are high (Nicita 2004). Government policies, such as overvalued exchange rates or the maintenance of monopsonistic state trading companies, can also mute market signals. Unless these domestic challenges are also addressed, potential benefits from trade liberalization may go unrealized.

"Connecting the poor to markets" (Lucas and Timmer 2005) requires access to credit and inputs, storage facilities, telecommunications, roads, and ports. Processing facilities, which add value and create jobs for the rural poor, especially for products with higher value added such as meat and dairy and the more dynamic fruit and vegetable sectors, require reliable sources of electricity for refrigeration. In many areas with spotty rainfall, irrigation projects will also be necessary to expand production. Many parts of sub-Saharan Africa need improved seed varieties and methods for dealing with pests.

---

5. Preference erosion of a sort has been an issue in the textile and apparel sector since the Multi-Fiber Arrangement expired at the beginning of 2005 (Bhattacharya and Elliott 2005).

Table 4.9 Possible winners and likely losers from US and EU sugar policy reform (based on average data for 2001–03)

	US and EU share of exports is one-third or less	US and EU share of exports is one-half or more[a]
Net exporters	Argentina Bolivia Costa Rica Ecuador El Salvador Ethiopia Honduras Nicaragua Zambia	Barbados (9.1) Belize (19.1) Dominican Republic (1.6) Fiji (19.3) Guyana (20.3) Jamaica (5.9) Malawi (8.9) Mauritius (16.3) Mexico (0) Panama (1.6) Papua New Guinea (0.1) St. Kitts and Nevis (26.9) Swaziland (6.7) Zimbabwe (4.2)
Net importers	Kenya Sudan	Burkina Faso Congo Cote D'Ivoire[b] Madagascar Mozambique Nepal Paraguay[b] Peru Philippines Taiwan Tanzania Trinidad and Tobago Uruguay

a. The share of sugar in total exports is shown in parentheses. Countries such as Fiji, Guyana, and St. Kitts and Nevis that are relatively dependent on sugar for export revenues and ship a large share to protected markets are particularly vulnerable to disruptions from preference erosion.
b. FAOSTAT has these countries as net exporters but USDA data have them as net importers, and neither produces enough to meet domestic consumption needs, suggesting they must be re-exporting imports to fill their US and EU quotas and underreporting imports to the UN Food and Agriculture Organization.

Note: Potential winners are at the upper left and the most likely losers at lower right.

Some of the barriers to getting products to market in developing countries are suggested by the data in table 4.10. The road network in low-income countries is less than a quarter of that in upper-middle-income countries, and only a quarter of those roads are paved. Even in middle-income countries only half the roads are paved, compared with 95 percent in developed countries. Thirty of the 31 land-locked developing countries have low or

Table 4.10 Indicators of infrastructure quality and trade costs

Indicator	Low-income countries	Lower-middle-income countries	Upper-middle-income countries	Developed countries
Kilometers of roads per square kilometer of area, 1999 (127)	0.17	0.29	0.77	2.44
Percent of roads that are paved, 1999 (118)	25	50	50	95
Aircraft departures per million people per year (average 2000–2002)	285	1,250	4,120	16,780
Fixed line and mobile phone subscribers per 1,000 people (2002)	39	302	501	1,250
Number land-locked (134)	21	9	1	10
CIF-FOB factor for developing-country exports[a] (103)	1.18	1.14	1.13	1.07

a. The ratio of the value of imports with the cost of insurance and freight (CIF) included to the value free on board (FOB), without those costs.

Note: Number of countries for which data are available is indicated in parentheses.

Sources: World Bank's *World Development Indicators;* IMF's *Direction of Trade Statistics.*

lower-middle incomes, and most of them are in sub-Saharan Africa. Aircraft departures are much less frequent in lower-income countries, and only about 4 out of 100 people in low-income countries have phones, versus about 1 in 2 in upper-middle-income countries. Further indication of relative trade costs is provided by the costs of insurance and freight, which are on average twice as high for developing-country exports as for developed countries.

Other evidence of the obstacles faced by businesses may be found in the World Bank's investment climate surveys covering 28,000 firms in 58 developing countries. One of the questions on the survey asks respondents to rate the severity of various potential obstacles from minor to very severe. Table 4.11 shows the percentage of respondents in 53 developing countries that ranked the obstacles as "major" or "very severe." Regardless of income level, businesses in most countries complain that taxes are too high. But in developing countries, complaints about tax administration are relatively more common. Uncertainty about economic policy and macroeconomic instability are also frequently expressed concerns, as are access to finance

Table 4.11 Firm perceptions of major or severe obstacles to doing business (percent)

Obstacle	Low-income countries (18)	Low-middle-income countries (27)	Upper-middle-income countries (8)[a]
Economic policy uncertainty	36.8	48.4	35.8
Macroeconomic instability	34.3	46	29
Corruption	44.1	40.2	18.7
Crime, theft, and disorder	26.7	31.9	13.8
Anticompetitive practices	27.4	36	22.2
Legal system, conflict resolution	22.7	24	16.1
Telecommunications	14.1	10.6	3.1
Electricity	38.3	20.6	4.8
Transportation	15.8	13	4.4
Access to land	19	13.5	7.1
Tax rates	39.7	42.1	41
Tax administration	37	32.5	24.5
Customs and trade regulations	25.9	20.9	12.8
Labor regulations	12.6	20.8	11.8
Skills of available workers	15.8	21.2	14.6
Obtaining or renewing permits	14.6	18.7	11.2
Access to finance	33.2	32.5	24.4
Cost of finance	40.1	40.5	27.4

a. Eastern European countries.

Note: Percent of respondents indicating that a particular problem is a major or severe obstacle to doing business in that country.

Source: World Bank's *Investment Climate Survey* database.

and the cost of finance. Corruption and inadequate infrastructure, especially reliable electricity supplies, are far more severe in low-income countries than in the eight upper-middle-income countries included in the sample, but corruption is viewed as nearly as severe an obstacle in lower-middle-income countries as in poorer ones.

Some of the surveys also differentiate between exporters and non-exporters. In a subsample of 20 low-income and lower-middle-income countries, exporters in five countries generally find many obstacles to be *less* severe than other types of firms do in their country. Exporters in nine countries report facing *more* problems than other types of firms do in their country. Exporters in five more countries report mixed experiences relative to nonexporting firms, while in Senegal, exporters appear to be little different from other firms in assessing obstacles. In Bangladesh, Brazil, El Salvador, Honduras, and Pakistan, governments appear to have successfully reduced some burdens, with exporting firms reporting relatively fewer problems in some areas, particularly taxes, access to finance, corruption, and economic policy uncertainty and instability. In the nine countries where exporters are more likely than nonexporters to report that they face major obstacles (China, Ecuador, Ethiopia, Guatemala, Nicaragua, Philippines, Sri Lanka, Turkey, and Uganda), problems are cited in the areas of customs administration, corruption, infrastructure (especially telecommunications and transportation), and occasionally the cost of finance. In the five countries where firms' experience is mixed (Cambodia, Kenya, Mozambique, Tanzania, and Zambia), exporters report fewer problems with access to finance and land and some government policies but relatively greater problems with customs administration and infrastructure.

Sanitary and Phytosanitary Standards: Both a Challenge and an Opportunity

Many analysts are increasingly concerned that as tariffs and other traditional barriers to trade come down, they are being replaced by nontariff barriers, including standards that often discriminate against imports, sometimes intentionally and sometimes not. In the agricultural area, SPS standards, which are at least nominally aimed at protecting human, plant, and animal health, cause the greatest concern. There is no systematic method for measuring the scope or impact of SPS regulations, but many analysts believe that they have increased in both number and diversity over the past decade or so. A World Bank project on food safety and agricultural health standards attributes the trend to governments' reaction to consumer concerns over a series of "food safety events" over the past two decades, most notably the scare over beef from animals with a brain-wasting disease (bovine spongiform encephalopathy, or BSE) that could be transferred to humans (World Bank 2005b, 16).

Developing countries are particularly concerned about the spread of SPS standards because many lack the capacity to comply with rich countries' standards. Further, within specific countries there are concerns that stringent standards will particularly disadvantage smallholders. The Uruguay Round negotiators attempted to lower the costs associated with standards and to reduce the possibility of associated impediments to trade by providing guidelines for the establishment and implementation of standards in the Agreement on the Application of Sanitary and Phytosanitary Measures. The core principles of the agreement include harmonization of standards, science-based risk management, recognition of equivalence when standards differ, regionalization (recognizing that animal or plant diseases or pests may be restricted to particular regions within an exporting country), and transparency.

Adoption of the SPS agreement has led some countries to review and modify some standards to make them more efficient and effective, and there has been progress in loosening countrywide bans on products affected by plant or animal pests or diseases so as to allow imports from regions that are unaffected. The transparency of the standard-setting process has also been improved through the requirement that the WTO be notified of new or changed regulations. There has been far less progress in international harmonization of standards or in recognition of equivalence of different standards across countries.

A recent analysis by three prominent agricultural policy experts concluded that harmonization and recognition of equivalence, while conceptually appealing, might not be practical, cost-effective approaches to the problem of SPS standards (Josling, Roberts, and Orden 2004, 44–50). First, harmonization of standards is not always economically efficient because of differences from country to country in climate, income level, and food tastes and preferences. Thus, the SPS agreement allows countries to set standards that exceed internationally agreed levels as long as a science-based risk analysis can be cited in justification. In addition, national standards cannot be harmonized where no international standard exists. According to a World Bank study that examined the thousands of new or modified SPS standards submitted to the WTO, only 22 percent involved measures for which an international standard existed (World Bank 2005b, 22).

With respect to recognition of the equivalence of different standards, Josling, Roberts, and Orden (2004) note that the few cases in which this was attempted by developed countries involved a lengthy and expensive process of negotiation and investigation by the relevant regulatory authorities in each country. A US submission to the WTO on the issue suggested that the trade benefits from equivalence agreements may not justify the administrative burden involved in reaching them (Josling, Roberts, and Orden 2004, 50). They conclude that technical and financial assistance to developing countries might be better used to help them with conformity assessment and verification of compliance, rather than to encourage their participation in standards-setting processes (pp. 204–05).

SPS and other standards thus remain a challenge for most developing countries. But approaching the problem from a traditional trade policy perspective as a new form of protectionism, or as a set of rules under which developing countries need special and differential treatment, is not likely to be helpful, for several reasons. First, especially with respect to food safety, reputation matters. Challenging standards in other countries or taking advantage of special and differential provisions in the SPS agreement that allow developing countries to take longer to implement standards may simply make consumers suspicious of affected imports. Second, while protectionist abuses certainly exist, most food and agricultural safety regulations are aimed at market failures resulting from incomplete or faulty information or from collective action problems, including the inadequate provision of public goods. Even when standards have a protectionist element, they typically have some basis in science, and it can be difficult to disentangle the two. In addition, what limited evidence exists (notifications of new regulations, Dispute Settlement Understanding cases, rejections of products at the border), does not suggest that questionable SPS regulations are a *major* impediment to trade. Between 1995 and 2001, WTO members submitted more than 2,400 notifications of new standards to the SPS Committee, but over the same period only 187 complaints challenging the legitimacy of notified standards were filed with the committee (Josling, Roberts, and Orden 2004, 59–60). The World Bank study on SPS standards found that rejections of import shipments for health and safety reasons had increased in recent years, but that such rejections often occurred in the context of increasing market share by imports and that the rejections most often affected large middle-income and industrialized exporters such as Brazil, Mexico, Thailand, and Turkey. The study found relatively few rejections of shipments from low-income countries, in part because these countries tend to export less sensitive products, such as tropical beverages and sugar. But the authors also found that many low-income countries had managed to gain certification of compliance with some standards—for example, EU standards for fish—and were not subjected to high levels of border inspection. This study concluded that "border rejections are more of an irritant than a major problem for large exporters" (World Bank 2005b, 103).

But even legitimate standards can present daunting challenges for poorer countries, to the point that a strategy of contesting standards as too high or as unfair addresses only a fraction of the problem. Moreover, many quality and food product standards are increasingly being imposed on suppliers by *private-sector* buyers such as grocery stores and other retailers that are responding to consumer demand for improved quality and other product and process attributes, including environmental and social standards.

Thus, the World Bank study recommends looking at SPS and other standards as part of the broader competitiveness problem facing many developing countries in export markets. This wider perspective leads to a focus on policy priorities distinct from the traditional "standards as nontariff barriers" approach and downplays traditional special and differential treatment. The World Bank concludes that technical and financial assistance to developing countries should focus on helping them to develop a proactive and strategic approach to standards compliance that includes the possibility of exit from certain markets or products if the costs of compliance would outweigh the benefits. In some cases, producers may do better by shifting to supplying local or regional markets where standards are less demanding, though this is increasingly being challenged by the spread of supermarkets with standards of their own. Alternatively, standards for some products may be more achievable than others. Where compliance is feasible, standards may serve as a "catalyst" to improved competitiveness and product upgrading more broadly, including in poor countries, as indicated by Kenya's success in supplying European markets for fruits and vegetables (World Bank 2005b, 86–89).

In many cases, certification, rather than compliance per se, poses a significant problem for countries in export markets, as well as smallholder producers trying to sell either globally or to supermarket chains. In the case of Kenyan horticultural exports, for example, they have not been able to replicate their success in the European market in the United States, in part because of a shortage of US inspectors in East Africa. Producer organizations and public assistance in providing certification services or encouraging public-private partnerships can help to reduce these transactions costs (Timmer forthcoming). As part of the assistance package to help developing countries take advantage of increased market access resulting from any Doha Round agreement, US officials have reportedly been discussing the possibility of seeking EU cooperation in creating a mechanism of mutual recognition of one another's standards for certain imports from Africa.[6] While mutual recognition agreements have not gotten far to date, a pilot program as part of a broader Doha Round package might be more attractive.

Finally, assistance may be needed in some cases to enable developing countries with limited capacity to file WTO cases against standards that are not justified and that are truly protectionism in disguise. But low-income West African cotton-exporting countries were able to free ride on Brazil's efforts to challenge US cotton subsidies without having to expend resources themselves. More research on the degree to which free riding can address this problem would be helpful. Bown and Hoekman (2005) offer further ideas on how nongovernmental organizations and other groups might help low-income countries with legal assistance.

---

6. Greg Hitt, "Wanted: Rocker-Activist's Support," *The Wall Street Journal*, November 23, 2005, A4.

5

The Devil in the Doha Details

Beyond summoning the necessary political will, a successful Doha Round agreement on agriculture depends on learning the lessons of the past. On paper, the Uruguay Round required rich countries to cut agricultural tariffs by an average of 36 percent and other trade-distorting support by 20 percent. In practice, estimates by the Organization for Economic Cooperation and Development (OECD) show very little decline in the level of producer support provided by member countries. There have been modest moves in some countries away from the most trade-distorting forms of support, and the recent moves toward further decoupling subsidies from production in the European Union merit applause. But overall levels of support and, especially, the barriers to market access in most rich countries remain high.

Ensuring that the Doha Round does not go down the same path as the Uruguay Round requires looking underneath the overall figures at the details of how agreed-upon cuts in tariffs and subsidies will be implemented. Flexibility in the tariff-cutting formula and the choice of a base period that set high ceilings for subsidies undercut the nominal disciplines negotiated in the previous round. The course of the current negotiations suggests that they are in danger of repeating those mistakes.

The present chapter focuses on the commitments needed from the rich countries to ensure meaningful reform of agricultural policies. It looks at each of the three pillars in turn, beginning with export subsidies, going on to domestic support, and concluding with market access. The final chapter addresses how special and differential treatment for developing countries might be shaped to ensure a successful outcome in the Doha Round. It also includes discussion of the need for "aid for trade" to ensure that developing countries are able to take advantage of new market access opportunities and addresses the forms this aid should take. The final section of chapter 6 summarizes the recommendations from both chapters 5 and 6. The intent is to provide both recommendations and a standard against which to assess the final outcome.

Export Subsidies and the Role of Food Aid

A commitment to eliminate export subsidies by 2013 was the one concrete achievement of the Doha Round's agricultural negotiations as of early 2006. Many view this commitment as not all that important because of the relatively small size of direct export subsidies, less than $3 billion during 2000–2001. But its importance lies not in the dollar figures but in the signal it sends about the commitment to reform in Europe. The European Union is the main user of export subsidies, and its willingness to give them up is possible only because of agricultural reforms that have lowered supported prices and thereby reduced the problem of domestic surpluses. Thus, the value in eliminating export subsidies, especially if it is combined with expansion of market access, is that it forces policymakers to bear more of the costs of agricultural policies domestically, by either paying to store and dispose of surpluses or reducing supported prices and other incentives to overproduce.

EU negotiators, however, conditioned their willingness to eliminate direct export subsidies on other WTO members' amenability to addressing "parallel" forms of export subsidy. Thus, the communiqué from the Hong Kong ministerial meeting in December 2005, which set the 2013 date, emphasized the need to eliminate any subsidy element from public export credit and guarantee programs, state trading enterprises, and food aid. As of early 2006 some progress had been made on the other issues, and the most divisive remaining issue was the EU demand that in-kind food aid, used primarily by the United States, should be prohibited, except in "well-defined emergencies." EU negotiators have persisted in this demand, despite protests from UN food aid officials that overly stringent rules could reduce the availability of food aid (*International Trade Reporter*, May 12, 2005, 774).

It is true that the principal US food aid program, Public Law (PL) 480, (Title I of the Agricultural Trade Development and Assistance Act of 1954), was intended to promote US exports and was used for surplus disposal when it was first implemented. But with the move in US farm policy toward subsidies and away from supply control and price supports, the government is no longer forced to acquire large stocks in times of low prices and then dispose of them. Still, in-kind food aid clearly has the potential to disrupt local and regional markets, and, to the extent that it still occurs, dumping of surpluses on developing countries in the guise of food aid should be disciplined. A recent OECD report underscores how costly, inefficient, and slow in-kind food aid typically is, even when commercial displacement does not occur (OECD 2005b). This is particularly so in the United States because of the requirements to use US-flagged vessels to ship food aid that must be purchased and at least minimally processed (bagged) domestically. According to some estimates, shipping takes up half of the $1 billion budgeted for food aid, and a typical delivery takes four months (*New York Times*, September 23, 2005). But these inefficiencies may be the political price of maintaining current levels of food aid in the United States. In mid-2005, both the House and the Senate rejected a proposal by US Agency for International Development Administrator Andrew Natsios to allow up to a quarter of the US food aid budget to be spent in or near the area with the food crisis (*New York Times*, September 23, 2005). What surprised many was the opposition from some nongovernmental groups that receive in-kind food aid and then sell it in developing countries to raise money for their projects in those countries, a process called "monetization." These groups opposed the Natsios proposal out of concern both that their own budgets would take a hit and that congressional and business community support for food aid would decline.[1]

Recognizing the political constraints, the head of the World Food Programme (WFP) has repeatedly expressed concerns that already inadequate levels of food aid could fall further if the EU demand is accepted. Moreover, recent empirical research suggests that food aid in sub-Saharan Africa may not always have the negative effects shown in previous studies. Abdulai, Barrett, and Hoddinott (2005) find that when they control for household characteristics one would expect to be associated with recipients of food aid, the negative correlations with labor supply, agricultural investment, and production are no longer statistically significant. Thus, they conclude,

> National-level data from across sub-Saharan Africa suggest that whatever negative effects food aid may exert on food producer prices and on government incentives to invest in agricultural development must be at least offset by food aid's favorable effects on human nutrition, farmer seasonal liquidity, and food security. . . . If anything, food aid appears to have been mildly stimulative to, rather than a drag on, African agricultural productivity. (Abdulai, Barrett, and Hoddinott 2005, 23)

---

1. Subsequently, some of the NGOs benefiting from monetization, as well as others engaged in development in Africa and elsewhere, launched a review of food aid policies, their role in it, and how US food aid policy might be reformed to be more cost-effective, while not lowering the level of resources available. For background materials and a flavor of this debate, see the Web site of the Partnership to Cut Hunger and Poverty in Africa at www.africanhunger.org.

In other words, it appears that in sub-Saharan Africa, at least, food aid has been relatively well targeted to those who are unable to meet household needs through their own production or through purchases in local markets.

At a public event sponsored by the Center for Global Development just prior to the Hong Kong ministerial, experts from various perspectives, including USAID Administrator Natsios, agreed that US food aid should be reformed to make it more efficient and more flexible in responding to recipient countries' needs, by, among other means, allowing for a portion to be in cash and applied to local or regional purchases.[2] But all also agreed that the EU proposal to prohibit all in-kind aid except in narrowly designated emergencies would swing the pendulum too far in the other direction.

Food aid is tiny relative to global cereals exports and is typically provided to countries with limited financial wherewithal to purchase imports commercially, which suggests that any effects on trade would be small. Thus, the WTO is not the appropriate place to address fundamental problems associated with food aid. At the same time, the EU demands for parallel treatment of all forms of export subsidy provide rare leverage for disciplining the distortions created by inefficient US policy.

This suggests that food aid should be approached cautiously in the Doha negotiations, but that it would be helpful to agree on certain principles that would reduce clear distortions without threatening the supply of aid. In a 2005 analysis of the agricultural negotiations, the International Food and Agricultural Trade Policy Council (IPC 2005) made several useful recommendations for disciplining potential trade-distorting effects of food aid, including

- giving food aid only as grants, not on credit;

- prohibiting the use of food aid in market development programs; and

- when surpluses are disposed of as aid, channeling them through the WFP to minimize the chance of distorting local markets.

US food aid provision is already moving in this direction so these recommendations should not be difficult to accept.[3] A more far-reaching recommendation would be to require that *all* food aid be channeled through the WFP, but, as the IPC points out, that could undermine political support

---

2. A transcript and related materials may be found at www.cgdev.org.

3. Helpful materials on these issues may be found on the Web site of the Partnership to End Hunger and Poverty in Africa, in the section labeled Reconsidering Food Aid: Background Papers, under "Workshop Materials," www.africanhunger.org.

for food aid in the United States and lead to sharp reductions in the level. Restrictions in food aid clearly should not impinge on real needs, and, while other reforms may be needed, the WTO is not the best place to deal with broad food aid issues.

Domestic Support

Although difficult issues remain, negotiators had made enough progress as of early 2006 for the broad outlines of an agreement on domestic support to be discerned. The question is whether the underlying details will result in any cuts in actual levels of support. The negotiators are working within the framework developed in the Uruguay Round, which raises two challenges for those interested in genuine reform. First, the creation of different categories of subsidies, in combination with oddities in how subsidies are measured, creates a great deal of flexibility, which policymakers have proved adept at exploiting. Second, the base period chosen in the Uruguay Round for setting the ceiling from which subsidies would be cut was a time of low prices and high levels of support. Even after the required 20 percent cuts in trade-distorting support, the final bound ceiling was so high that most countries were left with a lot of wiggle room when prices rose.

Would-be reformers should draw two lessons from the flexibility in the Uruguay Round framework: First, they need to focus on reducing the flexibility that allows policymakers to shift subsidies among the various categories. Second, negotiations should be steered toward a base period and a target level of support that do not set the ceiling so high that it is meaningless. Thus far, the negotiating stances of the key players are, not surprisingly, focused on retaining their own policy flexibility while constraining other countries'. How the negotiations on these issues come out will determine how large the negotiated cuts in subsidies need to be to constrain policymakers in practice.

To briefly review, the domestic support pillar of the agriculture negotiations is divided into three categories according to the degree of trade distortion involved (see chapter 2, figure 2.1). The amber box contains the most trade-distorting forms of support, while the green box is for minimally distorting subsidies, including decoupled payments to farmers and general support, such as for research and development. The intermediate blue box is for payments regarded as less trade distorting than those in the amber box because production is limited. The amber box is further divided into two components. The first, aggregate measurement of support (AMS), was capped and then reduced in the Uruguay Round. But payments that would otherwise be included in the AMS can be deducted as long as they fall below a de minimis level, set at 5 percent of the value production of individual commodities or 5 percent of total production if they are not product-specific. Currently, no country makes much use of product-specific de minimis, and only the United States reports significant spending in the non-product-specific de minimis category. For that reason, product-specific de minimis is ignored in what follows, except for the recommendation that it be eliminated.

Although the domestic support pillar focuses on domestic subsidies, it is crucial to understand that the AMS also includes a measure of some but not all of the support provided by means of trade measures. Import restrictions bolster domestic prices by restricting supplies, but market price support (MPS) is included in the AMS only if there is an official administered price that requires additional government intervention in the market when the price floor is threatened. This form of MPS is more distorting than that provided purely through trade measures because it more effectively insulates producers from global price changes. With administered prices, governments must buy up and store or export surpluses that would otherwise push market prices below the target level. In the WTO, the value of this support is calculated as the difference between the administered price and an "external reference price" based on average world prices during 1986–88.

The role of MPS in the AMS is important to understand in assessing the potential impact of various reform proposals. Japan, for example, reduced its reported AMS nearly 80 percent in 1998 simply by eliminating the administered price for rice. But it maintained an equivalent level of protection for farmers through tight import restrictions. As figure 5.1 shows, the OECD estimate of Japan's MPS for farmers, which includes the effects of all trade measures, dropped very little from 1995 to 2000. Reducing support for commodities with administered prices that are included in the AMS thus requires reducing or eliminating the set price *and* lowering associated trade barriers. Almost all of the EU AMS consists of MPS, which is why the European Union's weak market access proposal was greeted with such disappointment. The US AMS is divided between MPS for sugar and dairy and price-linked subsidies for most grains, cotton, rice, and soybeans.[4]

Although the numbers remain to be filled in, the resolution of a few issues in Geneva in summer 2004 and in Hong Kong in December 2005 indicates progress toward curtailing some of the flexibility that undermined the Uruguay Round disciplines. First, there is apparently agreement that the AMS will include product-specific caps, that the de minimis exemptions

---

4. This can be confusing because the United States uses the phrase "loan rate" to refer to both the "administered prices" for sugar and dairy and the legislated price floors for wheat, corn, cotton, and other exportable commodities. In the latter case, however, the prices that farmers receive fluctuate in response to world prices, and any gap between the market price and the loan rate is closed with government payments.

Figure 5.1 Japanese farm support as measured by OECD and WTO

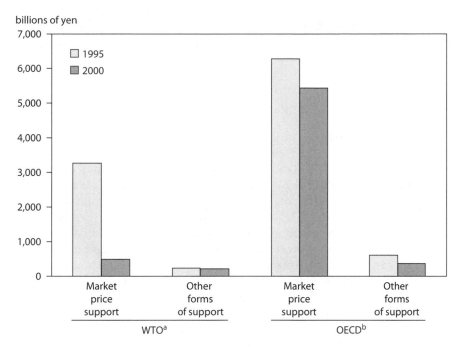

billions of yen

a. Value of amber box plus blue box notifications.
b. Producer support estimate.

Sources: OECD (2005a), US Department of Agriculture.

will be reduced, and that the blue box should be capped and then reduced. In Hong Kong, negotiators agreed that there will be three tiers for reductions in the AMS, with the European Union in the top tier, the United States and Japan in the second, and all other developed countries in the third. In addition to the size of the cuts in each box, the key outstanding issues are whether additional disciplines are needed for the blue and green boxes.

The tiered structure for reduction commitments is in response to the US demand for some harmonization of support levels, a sore point since the Uruguay Round permitted the European Union and Japan to maintain levels far above those of the United States. Even after those reductions were phased in, the European Union's final AMS ceiling of roughly $60 billion was three times as high as the $19 billion permitted the United States, while Japan's final $30 billion ceiling was 50 percent higher. Other OECD member states have higher subsidies as a percentage of farm receipts (see the percentage producer support estimates in chapter 2), but these states also have less impact on world markets because of their small size. Though the declaration following the Hong Kong meeting puts these countries in the third tier, with smaller reduction commitments, the declaration called on them to "make an additional effort in [AMS] reduction." Because the nature of those commitments is not yet known and because the top two tiers are most important in terms of global market effects, the analysis that follows focuses on those tiers, and in particular, on the United States and the European Union. As a result of the Japanese action on rice, Japan's reported AMS is only around $6 billion, sufficiently below its $30 billion ceiling that no feasible cut will do more than squeeze out the excess.

The Numbers Game

In early October 2005, US Trade Representative Robert Portman responded to an initial EU proposal by offering to cut the US AMS by 60 percent from the current *bound* ceiling if the European Union and Japan would cut their much higher bound levels by 83 percent. Portman further proposed reducing both types of de minimis payments by half and capping the blue box at 5 percent of production, with further cuts to 2.5 percent over several years. US negotiators also want to redefine the blue box to accommodate countercyclical payments (CCPs), which are likely to be allocated to the non–product specific de minimis category but which US officials argue are partially decoupled.[5] The chief EU negotiator, Peter Mandelson, countered with an offer to reduce the European Union's AMS ceiling by 70 percent, reduce de minimis (which the Europeans do not use) by 80 percent, and cap the blue box at 5 percent. Subsequently, EU negotiators indicated that they might be able to accept the 2.5 percent level for the blue box. Tables 5.1 and 5.2 show the implications of the proposals for EU and US farm programs.

Both the US and EU proposals would require large cuts in the applied, as well as the bound, AMS—from 50 to 70 percent for the European Union, depending on which proposal is analyzed, and 50 percent or more for the United States, depending on which year is chosen (see figure 5.2).

In response to individual member states' criticism that they had gone too far, EU negotiators have argued that their proposal for a 70 percent reduction in the European Union's bound AMS would be consistent with recent Common Agricultural Policy (CAP) reforms. US negotiators are also constrained by what Congress will accept, but they have somewhat more flexibility if the agreement is completed this year because the farm bill that

---

5. Countercyclical payments are based on acreage planted in particular crops in the past and do not require current production to be eligible, but their calculation involves a comparison of current market prices with a legislated target price. It is not actually known where in the amber box these payments will be allocated because, as of early 2006, the United States had not made the required WTO notifications since 2001.

Table 5.1 Potential impact of Doha domestic subsidy proposals on EU agricultural support (billions of euros)

	Permitted spending	Actual or projected spending	
		2001 WTO notification	Estimates of support after CAP reforms[a]
Amber box			
Current AMS	67.2	39.3	22
Market price support	n.a.	36.9	20
Subsidies	n.a.	2.4	2
Proposed AMS	11–20	n.a.	Based on 5 billion euros saved from reduced intervention prices for dairy, sugar, and minor cereals; assumes further 3 billion euros saved from proposed reforms to olive oil and tobacco. Up to 9 billion euros saved is from yet-to-be announced reforms of wine and fruits and vegetables and assumes that administered prices are eliminated but with no necessary increase in access unless tariffs are cut.
Current de minimis[b]	12.5	0.6	
Proposed de minimis[b]	3–6	n.a.	
Blue box			
Current	No cap	23.7	6–13
Proposed	6–12	n.a.	Based on OECD estimates; depends on the extent to which flexibility under the single farm payment is used to keep payments partially coupled.

AMS = aggregate measurement of support
CAP = Common Agricultural Policy
n.a. = not applicable

a. Based on best available information.
b. Product-specific de minimis, which is currently also capped at 5 percent of production for individual commodities, is ignored because it not used extensively by any country.

Table 5.2 Potential impact of Doha domestic subsidy proposals on US agricultural support (billions of dollars)

		Actual spending		
	Permitted spending	2001 WTO notification	Average 2003–04[a]	Average 2005–06[a]
Amber box				
Current/proposed AMS	19.1/7.6	14.4	9.9	15.2
Market price support	n.a.	5.8	5.5	5.5
Subsidies	n.a.	8.6	4.4	9.7
Current de minimis[b]	9.5	6.8	2.0[c]	2.0[c]
Proposed de minimis[b]	2–5	n.a.	n.a.	n.a.
Blue box				
Current	None	0	2.3[d]	3.5[d]
Proposed	5–10	n.a.		(5.1 projected for 2007)

AMS = aggregate measurement of support

n.a. = not applicable

a. Calculated from US Department of Agriculture data on price support loan and loan deficiency payments. The $5.5 billion in market price support (for dairy products and sugar) is based on the 2001 WTO notification, minus $0.3 billion for peanuts, which was partially reformed in the 2002 farm bill.

b. Product-specific de minimis, which is currently also capped at 5 percent of production for individual commodities, is ignored because it not used extensively by any country.

c. Estimated as average non–product specific de minimis payments reported to the WTO during 1999–2001, less reported ad hoc emergency payments, which were replaced with countercyclical payments in the 2002 farm bill and which US negotiators propose to move to the blue box.

d. Countercyclical payments are shown here, even though the United States is likely to report them as non–product specific de minimis, to suggest the potential impact of the US proposals to move these payments to the blue box and cap them after five years at 2.5 percent of production.

will determine future US policy has yet to be written. The US trade representative's challenge will be to preserve as much of that flexibility as possible and to fend off congressional criticisms that legislators' hands are being tied on the farm bill. Box 5.1 explicates the potential interactions between the Doha Round and the writing of the 2007 farm bill.

The rough estimates shown in table 5.1 seem to confirm EU negotiators' assertions regarding conformity between their proposal and CAP reforms, *as long as* proposed reforms of the olive oil and tobacco programs are approved and the administered prices for wine and fruits and vegetables are eliminated. In this scenario, most of the cuts come from the recent dairy and sugar reforms, as well as earlier cuts in intervention prices for cereals and beef, but the effects on trade would consist primarily of reductions in subsidized exports, not increased imports (OECD 2004a). The elimination of administered prices for fruits and vegetables would also have little impact on actual

**Figure 5.2   US aggregate measurement of support (AMS) with
and without market price support**

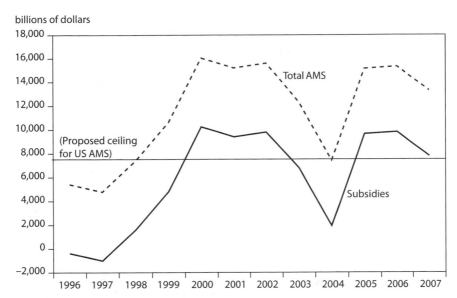

billions of dollars

Source: USDA Farm Services Agency, Budget Division Home page, table 35.

levels of support, unless significant reductions in tariffs are made in the market access negotiations. Finally, the US proposal for an 83 percent cut in the European Union's AMS ceiling would appear to require changes beyond the recent CAP reforms. EU negotiators indicated in early 2006 that they could go to 75 percent if the United States would go to 65 percent, but this proposal may have been more tactical than real.

Relative to other countries, the United States relies more heavily on subsidies than on MPS, but what happens to the MPS for sugar and dairy products has important implications for how much the subsidies for other commodities must be cut. The expected reduction in actual US spending is also harder to pin down because the subsidies are price based, which means that they fluctuate widely from year to year, as shown in figure 5.2 and table 5.2. The US proposal for a 60 percent cut in its AMS would lower the ceiling from $19 billion to just under $8 billion. That is roughly half the estimated AMS during 2005–06 or in 2001, the last year US officials submitted notification of support levels to the WTO. The proposed level is only 15 percent below the average level for 2003–04, however, and subsidies in those years would have been under the new ceiling without the $5.5 billion in MPS for sugar and dairy products (figure 5.2). Depending on what happens to the sugar and dairy programs, the new AMS ceiling could end up well above subsidy levels for other crops in good years and require only modest cuts in bad ones.

Box 5.1 Potential implications of the Doha Round for the 2007 US farm bill

The Farm Security and Rural Investment Act of 2002 weakened some of the decoupling reforms adopted in 1996, increased government spending on agriculture, and gave just the barest of nods to the constraints imposed by the Uruguay Round Agreement on Agriculture. Overall spending under the bill was difficult to project because many payments fluctuate from year to year with prices, but, in some years, it was expected to be perilously close to the overall $19 billion cap that the United States accepted in the Uruguay Round. As of April 2006, it remains difficult to assess the farm bill's conformity with US commitments because policymakers had filed none of the required WTO notifications since the farm bill passed.[1] The 2002 legislation expires in 2007, just after the hoped-for completion of the Doha Round. If the talks lag, Congress will have to pass a new farm bill without knowing exactly what the new constraints will be.

A Farm Bill after a Trade Deal

Enough is known from the proposals on domestic subsidies to identify some of the options that are likely to face Congress if it is writing the new farm bill after the deal is done. At one end of the spectrum, it is possible that Congress could decide to relieve American taxpayers and consumers of the costs associated with farm programs and adopt radical reforms. To borrow the terminology of Orden, Paarlberg, and Roe (1999; see box 3.1), Congress could simply "cut out" trade-distorting farm programs, eliminating them without compensation. Alternatively, they could buy out these programs, providing time-limited compensation to farmers for the value of the subsidies they currently receive. But neither option seems remotely likely.

In the real world, reform-oriented changes in the next farm bill are likely to range from tinkering at the margins to modest at best. The key to determining the nature and extent of reforms that might be required by a Doha Round agreement is what happens to the market price support programs for dairy products and sugar. Congress did choose to buy out domestic production quotas for peanuts and tobacco in recent years, so it is not out of the realm of possibility to do that for individual sectors. In each case, however, the buyout was possible in large part because producers themselves were dissatisfied with the operation of the support programs (Orden 2005). It is also notable that only tobacco involved a complete buyout of support, while peanuts were folded in with the other program crops and now receive marketing loan and countercyclical payments, albeit with a far lower price floor and target than previously. The dairy sector, which is characterized by regional and other tensions among larger and smaller producers, and which already receives

(box continues next page)

Box 5.1 (*continued*)

some direct payments in addition to market price support, seems a more likely candidate for this sort of reform than sugar.

Sugar producers claim to support negotiation of a multilateral deal that would eliminate barriers and subsidies globally. But they have been vociferous in opposing any opening of the US market under bilateral free trade agreements, and it is also unlikely that any conceivable Doha agreement will gain their approval. Thus, it is likely that USDA officials and Congress will have to decide what to do in the face of staunch opposition to changes in the sugar program. A plausible outcome in that case would be what Japan did with rice: eliminate the administered price for sugar but maintain a similar level of price support with the existing tariff-rate quota.

If Congress chooses either radical reform of sugar and dairy product supports or cosmetic reform by eliminating the administered prices while retaining import restrictions, the current subsidy proposals on the table in the Doha Round would require only modest changes in other US farm programs. Any combination of those options that removes the $5.5 billion in market price support for dairy products and sugar from the US aggregate measure of support will leave the entire $7.6 billion (under a 60 percent aggregate measurement of support cut) for wheat, corn and other feed grains, cotton, rice, soybeans, and other minor crops. That is about the level USDA estimates will be spent in 2005 and 2006, and well above subsidy levels in the first two years of the current farm bill. Similarly, few constraints would be imposed on countercyclical payments if the US proposal to cap the revised blue box at 2.5 percent of the value of production were adopted (table 5.3).

If Congress wanted to go beyond what a Doha Round might require, it could expand the gradual decoupling approach adopted in the 1996 farm bill and only partly reversed in the 2002 bill. It could again lower loan rates and compensate farmers with a larger decoupled direct payment.[2] It could also make countercyclical payments eligible for the green box by removing the link to current prices. Contrary to the approach in the House of Representatives during debate over the 2006 agricultural budget, Congress could increase funding for environmental purposes and acreage set-asides under the Conservation Reserve Program, as well as for research and development, both of which go into the green box.

A Farm Bill Without a Trade Deal

There are two broad alternatives for passing a new farm bill if the Doha Round is not completed by late 2006 or early 2007. Some in Congress have suggested that the 2002 farm legislation should be extended if the Doha Round is not completed before the bill expires, arguing that Congress will not want to redo farm legislation

(box continues next page)

**Box 5.1 Potential implications of the Doha Round
for the 2007 US farm bill** (*continued*)

before its regular expiration to accommodate a trade agreement. In addition, these representatives oppose giving up any leverage by making unilateral reductions in support levels.[3] This option would also make most farmers happy, at least those receiving subsidies, because they are quite satisfied with the current legislation.

Others, led by Secretary of Agriculture Mike Johanns and Senator Saxby Chambliss, chair of the Senate Agriculture, Nutrition, and Forestry Committee, argue that changes are needed to avoid further WTO litigation, regardless of the outcome of the Doha Round. The Brazilian complaint against US cotton subsidies revealed several vulnerabilities, and Uruguay has also threatened to bring a case against US rice subsidies. Economist Daniel Sumner (2005), who advised Brazil, has suggested that other commodity subsidies might also be open to challenge. Johanns argues that the potential for litigation increases uncertainty for farmers and that adjustments need to be made, regardless of whether a trade agreement is completed early next year. If this path were chosen, the options would be similar to those discussed in the previous section.

---

1. Sumner (2005) uses USDA data to update what the US notifications in recent years might look like. Given the conclusions of the WTO dispute settlement panel in the United States–Brazil cotton case, he concludes that the United States was in violation of its commitment in 2000 and 2001 and will be again in 2006.
2. Potential changes to the decoupled green box payments to bring them into compliance with the cotton ruling are discussed later in this chapter, in the section on clarifying the rules on decoupling.
3. Paarlberg (1997) analyzes the Uruguay Round negotiations as an example of the negative synergies that can arise between domestic politics and international bargaining when politicians deflect pressures for domestic reform by pointing to the need to preserve leverage in international trade talks.

The best way to avoid ending up with superficial cuts in the amber box would be to eliminate MPS from the AMS, but that is not on the table. Product-specific caps within the overall AMS ceiling, as have been proposed, would help to address the problem of changes in MPS undercutting pressures for subsidy reforms. Ensuring that these caps are meaningful, however, will require that negotiators avoid the Uruguay Round precedent of choosing a period of low prices and high subsidies as the base period for setting the ceiling. As figure 5.3 shows, the US proposal to adopt 1999–2001 as the base period for establishing product-specific caps would run the risk of a similar outcome in the Doha Round. Average annual payments were far lower during 1995–2000, the base period preferred by most other Doha

Figure 5.3   USDA payments for selected commodities

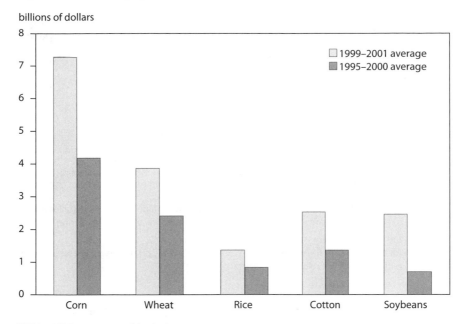

billions of dollars

USDA = US Department of Agriculture

Source: USDA Farm Services Agency, Budget Division Home page, table 35.

negotiators. An additional and useful discipline would be to have separate caps for MPS and subsidies within the AMS.

With respect to de minimis and the blue box, recent US Department of Agriculture (USDA) data suggest that the US proposal might constrain spending in bad years but do little more than that. Roughly $5 billion of the $7 billion in non–product specific de minimis spending reported to the WTO in 2001 resulted from emergency payments passed by Congress in response to low prices. The 2002 farm bill, the Farm Security and Rural Investment Act, created CCPs to replace this ad hoc safety net. If these payments are moved to the blue box, as US negotiators propose, average de minimis spending reported for 1999–2001 suggests that such spending generally would not exceed $2 billion, unless Congress adapted programs to take advantage of the flexibility that would result from moving CCPs to the blue box. The more ambitious EU proposal to cut de minimis (which it does not currently use) by 80 percent would remove that option.

Analysis of recent levels of spending on CCPs suggests that the US proposal eventually to cut the blue box to 2.5 percent of production would also not constrain these payments in most years but could cap them in low-price years. As of February 2006, the USDA was projecting that in fiscal year 2007 CCPs might slightly surpass the $5 billion proposed cap. Although other

Table 5.3 US countercyclical payments (millions of dollars)

Commodity	Average 2004–06	2007(e)	Peak-year payment	Average 2008–10(e)	Potential caps[a]
Corn	1,400	2,768	2,954 (2006e)	1,224	2,050
Other feed grains	112	189	234 (2006e)	96	150
Wheat	0	560	560 (2007e)	598	1,000
Cotton	889	1,229	1,421 (2005)	689	1,150
Rice	71	64	318 (2003)	43	100
Peanuts	151	180	191 (2005)	116	200
Soybeans	0	119	146 (2005)	191	300
Total	2,623	5,109	5,824	2,957	4,950

(e) = estimated

a. Assumed $5 billion total blue box cap (based on 2.5 percent of value of production) allocated according to each commodity's share of projected total countercyclical payments during 2008–09.

Source: USDA, Farm Services Agency, Budget Division Homepage, Commodity Estimates Book for FY 2007 President's Budget, table 50.

countries are very keen on constraining US CCPs, EU negotiators are hamstrung because it will be difficult for them to go beyond the 2.5 percent cap for the blue box under the current CAP reform. But the EU counterproposal, echoed by Brazil, to discipline US CCPs through rules that would specify a maximum price gap for calculating the payments is highly unpopular in Congress, which regards such proposals as impinging on its prerogatives in shaping the details of US farm policy.

One idea for further disciplining use of the blue box is to set product-specific caps in addition to the overall ceiling. Table 5.3 gives some indication of what these caps might look like. If they are based on the proposed overall cap of 2.5 percent of production, product-specific ceilings might constrain payments in bad years for some crops, mainly corn, but they would generally be well above recent average payments, as well as levels projected by the USDA for the first few years in which cuts would be implemented.

Clarifying the Rules on Decoupling

Two other important issues are ensuring that blue box payments are less trade distorting than amber box supports and that green box payments are minimally trade distorting. The Geneva framework from August 2004 indicates that blue box payments should be based on "fixed and unchanging" areas and yields, base production levels, or numbers of head of livestock. Strengthening this provision and applying it as well to decoupled payments based on historical subsidy levels in the green box is essential to ensure that expectations of future adjustments in the bases do not encourage farmers to maintain or increase production. The 2002 US farm bill allowed farmers to update the acreage base eligible for decoupled direct payments, a step back from decoupling that should not be permitted in the future.

A second issue facing negotiators will be how to handle the WTO decision in Brazil's dispute with the United States over US cotton subsidies that these direct payments are not sufficiently decoupled to be allocated to the green box. (Brazil also challenged the updating of base acreage as undermining the decoupling of the direct payments, but the panel did not rule on that particular issue.)

The 2002 farm bill prohibits US farmers from planting fruits and vegetables, with a few exceptions, if they are to remain eligible for these nominally decoupled payments. It also requires them to maintain their land in good agricultural or environmental condition. The WTO panel ruled that these restrictions would encourage producers to continue planting supported crops. While panel rulings do not set binding precedents, similar eligibility conditions related to the European Union's nominally decoupled single farm payment raise questions about those payments as well. In the US case, this condition was included in the farm bill because fruits and vegetables are not program crops that receive direct payments, though they do benefit from generally modest levels of traditional border protection and other green box programs (Thompson 2005). In the European Union, the situation is somewhat different, but horticultural crops there also benefit primarily from MPS rather than direct payments.

There are essentially two options for addressing the problem of ensuring that allegedly US and EU decoupled payments are eligible for the green box. One would be to negotiate changes to the green box to allow payments to be considered decoupled even if there were restrictions, such as those on planting fruits and vegetables, as long as the restricted sectors were not themselves eligible for amber box support. This would allow the United States to keep its current decoupled payment. But this option would likely still require the European Union to make changes to the single farm payment because fruits and vegetables currently receive a form of support that is included in its AMS. The single farm payment thus would not meet the revised standard unless the European Union eliminates administrative prices in these restricted sectors to meet amber box reduction commitments.

The preferable option in any case would be to lift the restriction on planting certain crops as a condition of eligibility for decoupled payments and use the opportunity to shift additional budget resources from traditional subsidy programs to other green box programs. In the United States, the impact on fruit and vegetable growers of allowing recipients of direct payments to move into the fruit and vegetable sectors would depend on location and a number of other variables. Thus far, reports suggest that these sectors are considering asking for an increased share of the agricultural budget in the next farm bill, but not in the form of traditional subsidy programs.[6] Rather, many suggestions focus on increasing demand to sop up any increase in supply if farmers receiving decoupled payments are allowed to plant fruits and vegetables. Examples include increased funding for domestic food aid and school lunch and snack programs that include fruits and vegetables as healthy options; increased access to environmental programs, such as the Conservation Reserve Program; and increased research and development spending, all of which would fall into the green box.

These programs should attract broad support from food aid and environmental advocacy groups, whose programs may otherwise face pressures for relatively deeper budget cuts to protect spending for traditional program crop subsidies. This approach would bring US fixed direct payments into compliance with the WTO cotton ruling while also promoting healthier eating habits and improved environmental conditions. If the increased demand for fruits and vegetables exceeds any increase in supply because of changes in the eligibility conditions for the decoupled payments, or if increased access by fruit and vegetable growers to conservation programs reduces their output, then the effects should be neutral to positive for developing-country exporters as well.

To more directly address the concerns of other exporters, however, the criteria for green box eligibility need to be more carefully defined, and perhaps some components should be capped. But an overall cap would be difficult to implement. Though there have been complaints about the sheer size of some green box allocations, the allocations among different types of payments vary widely among countries. The United States, for example, is by far the largest user of the green box, with $50 billion in payments in 2000. But more than 60 percent of that total was for food stamps and other nutrition programs. In Japan, the vast majority of green box support is allocated to "general services," particularly rural infrastructure. There clearly is a public goods aspect to many types of infrastructure, but such investments also increase production beyond what it would otherwise be. In the European Union, large payments for "structural adjustment through investment aids" and regional assistance programs could also cause concern if they are not aimed at encouraging diversification out of subsidized activities.

Market Access

The least progress in the Doha Round agricultural negotiations has been made on increasing market access. As shown in chapter 2, MPS still accounts for 60 percent of total producer support across the OECD, and it is half or more in most countries. There seems to be agreement that there will be four

---

6. Fruit and vegetable growers' views on priorities in the upcoming farm bill debate may be found at www.uffva.org and at www.ffva.com, both accessed September 30, 2005.

tiers and that tariffs in the higher tiers will be cut more. As of early 2006 there was still no agreement on the size of the cuts in each tier, but more crucial to the outcome was the continued wrangling over how much flexibility countries would be given to depart from these general rules for an undetermined number of "sensitive products."

Adoption of an overall cap on tariffs seemed likely, though Japan and the other Group of 10 (G-10) countries remained adamantly opposed. Moreover, crucial details on how the cap would be implemented, such as the treatment of sensitive products, remained unclear. Beyond the crucial issues of the size of the cuts and the treatment of sensitive products, other outstanding issues included how to achieve expanded access under tariff-rate quotas (TRQs), what to do about tariff escalation and specific and other non–ad valorem tariffs, and whether to retain the special safeguard mechanism that allows developed countries to impose additional tariffs when imports of certain products surge.[7]

Tariff-Cutting Formula

The tariff-cutting formula used in the Uruguay Round required an unweighted average tariff cut of 36 percent and a minimum reduction of 15 percent for all tariff lines. This formula allowed countries to reach the average by taking large cuts in already low tariffs and cutting high tariffs by the minimum percentage. The chief alternative, preferred by US and Cairns Group negotiators, is the Swiss formula, which harmonizes tariffs downward, forcing larger cuts in the highest tariffs. The emerging compromise between these alternatives is four tiers with higher cuts in the higher tiers, which would help to reduce dispersion. The three main proposals, by US, EU, and Group of 20 (G-20) negotiators, are shown in table 5.4. The proposals seem to be converging around an overall average tariff cut of around 50 percent. But how much additional market access this would provide depends on how sensitive products are handled.[8]

Sensitive Products and Tariff-Rate Quotas

Ideally, the category of "sensitive products" would be dropped and the category of "special products" reserved for developing countries, with the

---

7. The special safeguard, which is far easier to use than the regular safeguard for dealing with import surges, is permitted only for products where the Uruguay Round required that quotas be converted to tariffs.

8. The fall 2005 EU proposal also sought agreement to allow use of a "pivot" for the lowest tier of tariffs (below 30 percent), which would allow a large number of tariffs to be cut by as little as 20 percent as long as the overall average of 35 percent was met. EU negotiators later appeared to back off this proposal in the face of unrelenting opposition from other negotiators.

Table 5.4 Key tariff-cutting proposals, March 2006 (percent)

	Thresholds	Tariff cut
United States	0–20	55–65
Tariff cap = 75	21–40	65–75
Sensitive products = 1	41–60	75–85
	>60	85–90
G-20	0–20	45
Tariff cap = 100	21–50	55
Sensitive products = 1	51–75	65
	>75	75
European Union	0–30	35, on average
Tariff cap = 100		(20 minimum,
Sensitive products = 8		45 maximum)
	31–60	45
	61–90	50
	>90	60

Notes: Developing-country cuts, other than by least developed countries, would be two-thirds of the final agreed-upon levels.

number of such products tightly limited on the basis of objective criteria such as the number of subsistence farmers or the population of consumers with insecure access to food. In the real world, some flexibility for sensitive products is probably necessary to reach agreement, and the negotiations will focus instead on constraining the degree of flexibility and using alternative means to ensure some degree of increased market access for sensitive commodities.

During negotiations in Geneva in May 2005, the European Union and the G-10 anchored one end of the debate, proposing that sensitive products not be limited to those currently under TRQs and that expansion of TRQs be linked to existing import levels rather than domestic consumption growth, as favored by exporting countries. The G-10 also proposed that the number of sensitive products be determined on a country-by-country basis and that each country be free to select the products it wanted to treat as sensitive.

Such provisions, if adopted, would gut meaningful liberalization of the most protected products, and were opposed by US, Cairns Group, and G-20 negotiators. On every point, meaningful market access depends on pursuing the opposite course:

■ Countries should be able to select a *limited* number of sensitive products, based on guidelines agreed to in the negotiations.

■ Only products already subject to TRQs should be eligible for designation as sensitive products, but countries with large numbers of TRQs, such as the European Union, South Korea, and the United States, should not be able to designate all of the affected products as sensitive.

- TRQs should be expanded and allowed to grow along with domestic consumption, and within-quota tariffs should be eliminated or sharply reduced (and bound) to ensure that the quotas are filled.

- A tariff cap on *all* products is needed to ensure that the exemptions for sensitive products do not completely negate any meaningful liberalization.

Table 2.5 gives an indication of which products the European Union, Japan, and United States are likely to declare sensitive. The initial proposals varied widely, with the European Union seeking to designate up to 8 percent of agricultural tariff lines as sensitive (more than 150 lines at the 8-digit level) and the G-10 wanting 15 percent. The United States and the G-20 coalition of developing countries have proposed that no more than 1 percent of tariff lines should be sensitive (1.5 percent for developing countries), which would be no more than 15 to 20 lines.

The data in table 2.5 on applied tariffs and TRQs suggest that sugar and dairy products are the most likely to be designated as sensitive, along with rice in Japan and beef in the European Union.[9] The bottom of the table shows the average production-weighted tariff applied against developing-country agricultural exports by Japan, the European Union, and the United States, as well as the simple average (mean) and median bound tariffs.[10] The median indicates that 50 percent of bound agricultural tariff lines are below 13 percent in the European Union and lower than that in Japan and the United States.

The combination shown in table 2.5 of moderate average tariffs and high numbers of TRQ lines for fruits, vegetables, and poultry suggests that the initial EU proposal to trade off the number of sensitive products for increased flexibility in determining the size of tariffs cuts in the lowest tier was aimed at protecting these products. EU negotiators have also proposed that the Uruguay Round's special safeguard mechanism for agriculture should be extended for these sectors, as well as for the more heavily protected beef, dairy, and sugar sectors. This stance also seems consistent with the analysis earlier in this chapter suggesting that the European Union will have to eliminate administered prices for fruits and vegetables to meet its domestic support commitments, meaning that tariffs and TRQs will be all it has to support domestic prices of these commodities.

---

9. CAP reform lowered the administered price for rice to the point that it is unlikely to be declared sensitive.

10. In developed countries, bound and applied tariffs are typically close. The difference between applied and average (mean) tariffs in table 2.5 is more likely due to the weights used (Roodman 2005).

But because the fruits and vegetables sector has not yet been reformed, this is also the only sector where EU negotiators have much flexibility to move on market access. Chapter 4 of this book and World Bank research (Aksoy 2005) also show that the fruits and vegetables sector is among the more dynamic sectors in global agricultural trade and is increasingly important for developing-country exporters. If the European Union and other rich countries insist on maintaining high levels of protection for the meat, dairy, and sugar sectors, fruits and vegetables is one area where they should give something up. Efforts by EU negotiators to declare fruits and vegetables sensitive should thus be opposed.

Tariff Escalation and Other Issues

With middle-income countries likely to be the primary near-term beneficiaries of any increased market access for fruits and vegetables, tariff escalation is an area where focused efforts could help low-income countries. The apparent agreement to have an overall cap on tariffs and to require larger cuts in tiers with higher tariffs will to some degree reduce tariff escalation and tariff peaks. Developing countries, however, have a particular interest in pushing for more progress in this area so that they have a chance to add value to primary products, diversify exports, and create jobs in rural areas. One approach would be to require that tariffs on processed products that are higher than the tariff on associated raw products be reduced by a multiple of whatever the formula reduction would otherwise be. For tropical products, of particular interest to many low-income countries, a more radical approach is justified. The WTO's Geneva framework agreement from July 2004 reiterated that full liberalization of tropical agricultural products is a "long-standing commitment" of WTO members that has not been fulfilled. In many cases, the tariff on raw products, such as coffee and cocoa beans, tea, and tropical fruits and vegetables is at or close to zero. In these cases, the tariff on processed products incorporating these commodities should also be at or close to zero, or at least in the single digits.

The final tariff issue is the treatment of specific, compound, and other types of non–ad valorem tariffs. As explained in chapter 2, these tariffs are less transparent and more trade distorting than ad valorem tariffs, and, where ad valorem equivalent estimates are available, they also tend to be higher. For purposes of the tariff-cutting negotiations, these tariffs have to be converted to their ad valorem equivalents. Fights over how to do this wasted several months of precious negotiating time over the winter of 2004–05. At issue was the base price that would be used to calculate the ad valorem equivalent of specific tariffs.

For a variety of reasons, import prices tend to be higher than world prices. This is especially true for products covered by TRQs. The European Union wanted to use the higher import price so that the calculated ad valorem equivalents would be lower and the required tariff cuts therefore lower. But EU negotiators and others taking this position did so expecting that they would be able to go back to the specific tariff after the cuts were made. A compromise using a hybrid price was reached, but the real issue is whether to require that all specific and compound tariffs be permanently converted to their ad valorem equivalents and bound at that level before being cut. Rather than spending months debating what price to use for the calculations, the time should have been spent negotiating a commitment to bind specific tariffs at whatever ad valorem equivalent was agreed to before getting to the technical issue of how to do the conversion. Developing countries use primarily ad valorem tariffs and are often the victim of higher specific tariffs in industrialized countries (Aksoy 2005, 44–45). Binding all tariffs at their ad valorem equivalents and then cutting them would thus be of particular interest to developing countries.

Finally, determining whether the special safeguard for developed countries is retained or eliminated should be deferred until the end of negotiations and then be decided on the basis of what has been settled in the rest of the agreement. The "special safeguard" for agriculture is much easier to use than regular safeguards permitted by the WTO and does not include the adjustment-oriented features requiring that safeguard actions be temporary and degressive. In the European Union, safeguards on some products have been in place continuously since the Uruguay Round Agreement on Agriculture was implemented in 1995. But if negotiators reach an ambitious market-opening agreement, especially if it is combined with ambitious results on domestic and export subsidies, then continuation of a special safeguard to allow countries to respond to import surges might be appropriate. Some additional disciplines to guard against abuse would still be needed, however. If, instead, the required cuts in tariffs are not deep or the list of sensitive products is long, then additional flexibility in regard to surges would not be appropriate. In that case, countries could still use the regular safeguard process to slow imports that threatened serious injury to their producers.

The final chapter summarizes the specific recommendations for commitments by rich countries in the Doha Round agricultural negotiations.

6

Delivering on Doha's Promise

The Doha Development Agenda was launched with at least a rhetorical commitment to promoting development and reducing poverty. But the argument that agriculture is central to making Doha a development round, because reducing agricultural barriers and subsidies would help billions of poor farmers, ignores a number of facts. First, it misses the fact that agriculture was also the key to breaking the impasse that delayed conclusion of the Uruguay Round for three years, an impasse that was not between North and South but between the United States and the European Union. Second, it ignores the fact that US negotiators in the current round, along with their counterparts from Australia, New Zealand, and Canada, are again demanding increased market access for their farmers in Europe, Japan, and in other markets. Third, it ignores the fact that developing countries are heterogeneous and agriculture is not necessarily a priority for all of them.

Whatever the rhetoric, then, agriculture is at the center of the Doha Development Agenda primarily because it is the sector with the highest remaining barriers in rich countries. These markets are mostly open to manufactured goods (with the important exception of textiles and apparel), and agricultural liberalization is the main thing rich countries can put on the table. Many developing countries also have a comparative advantage in agriculture, and the formation of the G-20, led by Brazil, India, and South Africa, has given the talks a more pronounced North-South flavor than in past rounds.[1] A successful conclusion to the Doha Round

---

1. The Cairns Group of agricultural exporters, which includes a mix of high- and middle-income exporters, was an important player in the Uruguay Round and remains active in the current talks but has been somewhat eclipsed by the developing-country exporters of the G-20.

is thus unlikely without significant concessions on agriculture from rich countries.

But that is not enough to deliver on Doha's promise to promote development in poor countries. Most recent trade models do show that agriculture accounts for most of the gains to be reaped from further trade liberalization. But most of those gains accrue to consumers and taxpayers in the rich countries with the highest barriers. For many countries outside Latin America, manufacturing liberalization, especially reductions in tariffs on textiles, apparel, footwear, and other labor-intensive light manufactures, are more important than agriculture. But, and this is an important caveat from the perspective of those concerned about poverty, agricultural trade is important for sub-Saharan Africa. While the numbers are small, World Bank scenarios of possible outcomes from the Doha Round suggest that sub-Saharan Africa could gain more from agricultural liberalization, as a share of national income, than any developing region outside Latin America (Anderson, Martin, and van der Mensbrugghe 2005).

But even among those developing countries for which agriculture is important, the benefits of the round will not be equally distributed. Some of the products that rich countries protect the most, for example dairy and meat, are unlikely to be major exports for many developing countries for some time, even if liberalized. In other cases, such as liberalization of quota systems for sugar and bananas, increased market access will help the most competitive developing-country exporters but harm others that rely on preferential access. Some of the more dynamic product sectors, such as fruits and vegetables, are not as heavily protected by traditional trade barriers, but many developing countries require assistance in meeting quality and safety standards to obtain access to rich countries' markets.

Agricultural liberalization will also have distributional effects within developing countries. Ending the "dumping" of subsidized food by industrialized countries on world markets would help farmers in poor countries. But the poorest are often net buyers of food, unable to produce enough on their own tiny plots to feed their families, and they could be hurt by higher prices in the short run. Alternatively, because many rural poor live in remote areas that are isolated from national and international markets, agricultural liberalization in rich countries might have little or no effect on them.

In sum, agriculture is where the greatest potential *global* gains lie in the Doha Round. And rural development—connecting the poor to markets—can be important to ensuring that growth benefits the poor while the development process proceeds. But agriculture is not the key for every developing country, and when it is, market access alone is often not enough. Developing-country governments and international donors also have to create an environment in which the poor can grasp new trade opportunities.

The previous chapter analyzed what developed countries could do in the Doha Round to help both themselves—since they pay most of the costs of agricultural protection—and developing countries. The present chapter looks, first, at what developing countries need to contribute to make the round successful and to ensure that they benefit from it. It analyzes the role of special and differential treatment and concludes that more balance is needed between giving poor countries "policy space" to adopt locally appropriate economic development strategies and disciplining the creation or spread of costly and inefficient agricultural support policies. Moreover, in order to sell politically difficult reforms to their respective legislatures, US, EU, and Japanese negotiators need increased market access in the more advanced developing countries. The second part of the chapter looks at the complementary policies that are needed alongside a Doha Round agreement. In particular, it examines the demands for increased aid-for-trade and suggests a framework for addressing them. The chapter concludes by briefly summarizing the recommendations for ensuring that these trade talks deliver as much as possible on the Doha *Development* Agenda.

Special and Differential Treatment

Special and differential treatment for developing countries under international trade rules has evolved significantly in some areas but very little in others. Countries still "self-designate" as either developing or developed, though the "least developed" country (LDC) designation developed by the United Nations has been adopted by the WTO for that group. Few countries, including South Korea after it achieved high-income status, have chosen to formally graduate from developing-country status, but neither have they taken advantage of the full range of flexibility that goes with that status.

The major changes are in how special and differential treatment operates, not for whom. Prior to the Uruguay Round, special and differential treatment effectively meant that most developing countries played little role in negotiations under the WTO's predecessor, the General Agreement on Tariffs and Trade (GATT), but also that little was expected of them. The "Quad"—the United States, the European Community, Canada, and Japan—negotiated among themselves and then presented the resulting agreement to the rest of the membership. Developing countries generally were not asked to make concessions, but they were able to reap gains from developed-country tariff cuts through the most favored nation principle, which requires that liberalization provided to one GATT member must be extended to all members.[2]

Some have argued that developing countries would have done better to engage and to accept liberalization of their own barriers in exchange for liberalization of areas of interest to them, including textiles and apparel

---

2. Article XXIV of the GATT provides an exception to the most favored nation principle for customs unions or regional or other preferential trade agreements that meet certain broad criteria.

and agriculture (Hoekman 2005). Given the political sensitivity of these sectors in the industrialized countries, however, as well as the small part that developing countries played in global trade in the 1960s and 1970s, it is not clear that much more could have been achieved in these sectors through this more offensive strategy.

By the 1980s, however, some countries had developed to the point and were growing rapidly enough that gaining access to their markets was of interest to developed-country exporters. Many developing countries were also gaining ground in export markets and wanted improved access to rich countries' markets for labor-intensive goods where they had comparative advantage. Another trend creating pressures for changes in special and differential treatment was increased attention to nontariff barriers and the need for rules to discipline them.

The Tokyo Round of trade talks in the 1970s addressed issues, such as domestic subsidies and customs valuation practices, that could distort trade and that required approaches other than traditional tariff-cutting negotiations. Developed countries tried to get developing countries to accept application of these rules, but most demurred, and the resulting agreements were implemented as plurilateral codes that applied only to those members who agreed to be bound by them.

Dissatisfaction with the evolution of the system on all sides led in the Uruguay Round to adoption of the "single undertaking" approach. In broad terms, in exchange for agreeing to negotiate liberalization of agriculture and the Multi-Fiber Arrangement (MFA) governing textiles and apparel, developed countries insisted that developing countries accept all parts of the resulting agreement, including new rules on services and intellectual property. In this case, universal application was the norm for most developing countries, and special and differential treatment took the form of longer phase-in periods for implementation and smaller tariff cuts than those made by the developed countries. LDCs were expected to eventually implement all the new rules that were adopted, but were given even longer phase-in periods and were not asked to open their own markets.

The Uruguay Round bargain generated a backlash as it became clear that very little agricultural liberalization was going to occur and that elimination of binding MFA quotas was going to be delayed until the end of the 10-year implementation period. The backlash was particularly strong, however, against the new rules on trade-related intellectual property and the realization that these rules could impede poor countries' access to cheap generic drugs, particularly with the AIDS epidemic spreading across sub-Saharan Africa. These and other new rules, for example, on customs valuation, required costly efforts to pass new laws and to set up enforcement mechanisms. Some researchers calculated that the potential costs of implementing these new agreements on rules and concluded that these were not necessarily areas that should be given priority when resources were inadequate to meet essential needs (Finger and Schuler 2002). Moreover, other studies noted that, whatever the costs of implementing new rules, they could be expected to be relatively higher for developing countries because the rules tended to be based on ones already being applied in the richer countries (Hoekman 2005). Thus, it appeared to many developing countries that they had been taken for a ride in the Uruguay Round, having been asked to shoulder expensive new obligations while receiving little new market access in return.

A number of proposals have been made for addressing the problems raised by the single undertaking approach and to reconcile the trend toward rules promoting "best practice" in a number of areas with the differing needs and capacity levels of developing countries. Bernard Hoekman, for example, has suggested that members might agree on a set of "core rules" related to market access (such as most favored nation, national treatment, the prohibition of quantitative restrictions, and the binding of tariffs) that would apply to all members, while the application of other rules would be based on a cost-benefit analysis for individual countries, along with an assessment of potential negative pecuniary spillovers to other members. This approach would mean that even the LDCs would accept the principles of forgoing quotas and agreeing to bind their tariffs, even if they were still allowed to make smaller tariff cuts or no cuts at all.

This approach is intuitively appealing from a development perspective, but it would be a sharp departure from GATT/WTO practice and raises a number of implementation questions. Moreover, since the current round is more narrowly focused on traditional market access issues, it may not be necessary to address these broad institutional issues in the Doha Round. The issues in agriculture are also rather different, and the approach to special and differential treatment developed in the Uruguay Round remains relevant in this area. Although the negotiations cover domestic support policies, as well as border measures, the aim is not to impose costly obligations but to discourage the adoption of new trade-distorting policies that could be quite costly over time. The large numbers of rural poor in most developing countries do suggest a need for caution in determining the pace and sequencing of liberalization. Governments should have the flexibility to adopt policies to provide food security for the poor and to promote rural development as part of pro-poor growth strategies. But the experience of the rich countries vividly illustrates the difficulties in unwinding support for farmers long after they are no longer poor. Thus, some degree of discipline on trade-distorting agricultural policies, even in the poorest countries, would be useful.

The Uruguay Round Agreement on Agriculture allowed developing countries, other than the least developed, to cut subsidies and tariffs by two-thirds as much as the rich countries. As a means of preventing new policies from undercutting the adopted disciplines, the agreement also prohibited countries that did not make reduction commitments from introducing new export or trade-distorting domestic subsidies. While the richer countries, including the more advanced middle-income countries, may not be so concerned about access to small, poor markets, they are likely to resist policies that would increase subsidized competition for their exporters in global markets in the future. Therefore, restrictions on new trade-distorting subsidies should be maintained, and countries that want to promote rural development should be encouraged to do so through minimally distorting green box mechanisms.

With respect to market access, flexibility for developing countries to protect food security and rural livelihoods will be a major issue. The Geneva framework proposes a combination of sensitive and special products that would be largely excluded from liberalization commitments. A special safeguard mechanism for agriculture, which was reserved for developed countries in the Uruguay Round, is likely to be extended to developing ones as well. In addition, LDCs will not be required to make any cuts, and cuts by other developing countries will likely be far smaller than they appear because most of these countries have bound tariffs, which they cannot legally raise, and which are well above currently applied levels. Thus, the risk is not too little flexibility but too much. If the agreement produces modest overall cuts in bound tariffs and adoption of a new special agricultural safeguard for developing countries that includes both volume and price triggers for temporarily raising tariffs, as appears likely, that is all the more reason for the list of special products to be limited.

The big question will be whether and how to differentiate among developing countries so that the more advanced emerging markets, such as Brazil, Thailand, and perhaps China and India, provide increased access to their markets as well. Table 6.1 shows indicators that might be used to guide such differentiation. The LDCs account for only a little more than 2 percent of global agricultural exports, yet roughly 7 in 10 of their citizens reside in rural areas and make a living from agriculture. Other low-income countries are somewhat less dependent on agriculture for employment, but the share of the economically active population in agriculture is still over 50 percent and these countries account for an even smaller share of global farm exports. Furthermore, with the exception of India, they are generally small markets. India poses something of a dilemma because it has high levels of rural poor but it is also a large potential market and a relatively large exporter, accounting for nearly as large a share of agricultural exports by itself as all other, non-LDC, low-income countries.

With the large exception of China, agriculture is on average a much less important source of employment in lower-middle-income countries, though it is still significant. When it joined the WTO, China made extensive commitments to liberalize its markets, including for agriculture, and it is not yet clear whether it will have to make substantial additional concessions in the current round. Pressure on Brazil as a successful exporter and leader of the G-20 to offer increased access to its market is particularly strong. Thailand is the only other lower-middle-income country with annual agricultural exports of more than a few billion dollars (an average of $9 bil-

Table 6.1 Possible indicators for differentiating special and differential treatment under an agricultural agreement

Country	2003 per capita income[a] (millions of dollars)	Share of total employment in agriculture (percent)	Share of total population in rural areas (percent)	Share of world agricultural exports (percent)
Least developed countries[b]	n.a.	n.a.	n.a.	2.3
Angola	740	75	64	n.a.
Djibouti	910	n.a.	15	n.a.
Maldives	2350	32	71	n.a.
Other	323	77	69	
Other low-income countries	505	54	60	1.6
India	540	64	72	1.3
Pakistan	520	52	66	0.2
Lower-middle-income countries	1,686	36	44	5.1
Brazil	2,420	23	17	3.9
China	1,100	72	61	3.2
Thailand	2,190	64	80	1.9

n.a. = not applicable

a. World Bank's Atlas method.
b. The United Nations designates countries as least developed based on a three-part formula that includes size, commodity dependence, and other indicators of vulnerability in addition to per capita income.

Sources: World Bank, *World Development Indicators;* UN Conference on Trade and Development, Trade Analysis and Information System (TRAINS) database.

lion per year from 2001 to 2003, compared with $2.5 billion for second-place Côte d'Ivoire); furthermore, its exports include products that are not primarily tropical and therefore compete with the output of the United States and of other temperate-product exporters. Thus, Thailand is another country that could come under pressure to accept relatively greater obligations on agriculture than other developing countries.

A formula based on objective criteria for determining how to treat countries according to level of development would be the cleanest approach to reforming special and differential treatment. But it would inevitably be arbitrary and the thresholds would be difficult to negotiate. An ad hoc approach that tried to balance concerns of both developed and developing countries might be more feasible and more consistent with past practice (Kleen and Page 2005). In the Uruguay Round, for example, deeper special and differential treatment under the subsidies code was provided to a list of non-LDC developing countries with incomes below $1,000 per capita (as measured by the World Bank). Under the Doha Round agriculture agreement, a similar approach might allow greater flexibility for countries with per capita incomes below $1,500 to select special products that would be exempt from formula tariff cuts. This would cover all low-income countries that are not LDCs plus 14 additional lower-middle-income countries with rural population shares of at least a third (half of them have rural population shares above 50 percent). Designation of a list of specific countries could also be used to address developed countries' concerns about large countries, if China and perhaps India are willing to accept the treatment accorded most middle-income developing countries. These countries would likely retain considerable flexibility in protecting special products for reasons of food security and rural development. At the other end of the spectrum, successful middle-income agricultural exporters, such as Brazil, Thailand, and Colombia, might agree to go beyond the commitments of other developing countries and further limit the number of special products they designated.

Aid-for-Trade and Supply Constraints

One legacy of the dissatisfaction with the results of the Uruguay Round is the demand by developing countries that rich countries and multilateral aid agencies do more to help them with the costs associated with trade liberalization, both their own and others'. The dissatisfaction arises from the higher than expected costs associated with implementing new rules, especially on intellectual property protection, but also in regard to product standards, customs, and other areas. The more insistent demands for financial and technical help also arise from the disappointing experience with past, unenforceable promises to provide such assistance.

The full range of costs worrying developing countries includes terms-of-trade losses from higher food prices and preference erosion, costs of implementing more new rules, lost tariff revenues, and costs of labor and firm adjustment arising from the liberalization of their country's markets. In addition, to help with adjustment costs, there is a need for external assistance to address the longer-term supply constraints that might otherwise prevent poor countries from grasping the opportunities offered by increased market access.

The key questions under debate are who should provide funding for which needs, how much is needed, what mechanisms should be used— existing or new—and who will be eligible. At the Development Committee meeting during the joint annual meetings of the International Monetary Fund (IMF) and the World Bank in September 2005, Bank and Fund staff presented a paper that recommended extending existing trade-focused facilities to address some of these costs. In particular, staff recommended substantially boosting the resources of the Integrated Framework, which had been created as a joint initiative of the WTO, the Bank, the IMF, the UN Development Programme, the UN Committee on Trade and Development, and the International Trade Center to mainstream trade in development strategies in the LDCs. The Integrated Framework does not provide direct funding for trade facilitation or other projects, but it helps LDCs identify trade priorities and coordinate them with other development priorities. Multilateral development banks or bilateral donors can then be approached to fund the identified projects. The staff paper argued against a new special fund focused on adjustment costs on the basis that these costs should not be addressed in isolation from broader development policies and domestic reforms, that various mechanisms already exist to address adjustment issues, that the costs of preference and tariff revenue erosion might not be as great as feared, and that the costs of setting up a separate fund might exceed the benefits (IMF and World Bank 2005).

This reasoning is compelling, but the argument for a new, dedicated fund arises out of political exigency—developing countries do not believe that sufficient resources will be provided on a timely basis to meet the needs they anticipate facing. That in turn makes them reluctant to take on new obligations, or gives them an incentive to block agreements among others that might result in terms-of-trade losses for them. Fearing a potential breakdown in negotiations at the WTO ministerial meeting in Hong Kong in December 2005, WTO Director-General Pascal Lamy used the occasion of the Bank-Fund meetings to call for a decision to be made to expand the Integrated Framework before or in Hong Kong, with a further agreement on expanded adjustment assistance by the end of 2006.

The Hong Kong ministerial declaration affirmed the commitment by WTO members to ensure that the enhanced Integrated Framework enters into force at the end of 2006, but left the details to a task force that was to report back at the end of April 2006 (another missed deadline). On broader aid-for-trade issues, including the problem of supply-side constraints, ministers in Hong Kong could agree only to "invite the Director-General to create a task force that shall provide recommendations on how to operationalize Aid for Trade" and to consult with member countries and the international financial institutions on where the resources might be found. In addition, Japan, the United States, and the EU member states announced increases in bilateral aid for trade infrastructure and other facilitation activities. If carried through, these promises could mean there would be roughly $8 billion a year from these sources (including the EU Commission, as well as the individual member states) for trade-related needs by 2010.

Both sides in the debate over the best way to approach aid-for-trade make valid points, and as with special and differential treatment, a pragmatic and ad hoc approach may be preferable. In analyzing the debate, it is helpful to divide the issues according to the sources of the need for assistance. Table 6.2 divides "adjustment" costs into four types, those arising from

- liberalization by others,

- one's own liberalization,

- institutional development, or

- broad economic development needs (which might better be termed investments rather than adjustment costs, as some have dubbed them).

Because LDCs will likely not be asked to make any commitments in the Doha Round, the most relevant potential costs for them arise from liberalization by others that is out of their control, for example, preference erosion, higher food import costs, and the need for assistance in addressing supply constraints. But as noted in chapter 4, LDCs are not receiving many of the benefits of existing preference programs, especially in agriculture, and food costs may not rise as much as feared. A recent World Bank paper also finds that the costs of preference erosion, which arise primarily from EU liberalization, are substantially reduced when all countries of the Organization for Economic Cooperation and Development (OECD) liberalize, thereby opening new opportunities in the US, Japanese, and other markets with less extensive preferences (Francois, Hoekman, and Manchin 2005). On food imports, most estimates of world price increases for staples are modest, and no one expects the long-term downward trend in commodity prices to reverse. Moreover, some food-insecure countries maintain relatively high tariffs that could be reduced unilaterally if import prices rise as a result of OECD reforms. With respect to other developing countries, the costs from tariff revenue loss, labor adjustment, and rule implementation depend on how much liberalization these countries ultimately accept and how special and differential treatment is applied to any new rules that are adopted.

In most of these areas there are existing mechanisms that could be expanded and adapted to ameliorate the costs. The Fund's Trade Integration Mechanism was designed in part to address potential trade balance problems arising from preference erosion, but special compensation arrangements are likely to be necessary, especially in the European Union, where arrangements with the African, Caribbean, and Pacific countries have more of a contract flavor, with exporters in some sectors, such as sugar, guaranteed a price above world market levels, as well as access. In the case of preference erosion, because of differences in the various programs, it seems preferable to deal with the issue of compensation bilaterally, but also promptly and credibly so that it does not impede the trade talks. Thus far, the EU offer on compensation to exporters that will lose rev-

Table 6.2 Categories of aid for trade (related to agricultural sector)

Costs arising from	Types of costs	Distribution of costs	Possible mechanisms for addressing costs
Liberalization by others	Preference erosion	Relatively small number of countries, often not the poorest	Mostly EU preferences for sugar and bananas, so a bilateral approach would be most appropriate
	Terms-of-trade losses due to higher food prices	An IFPRI study (Diaz-Bonilla et al. 2000) finds a high correlation between food insecurity and LDC status, but studies do not indicate large price increases for staples, except possibly rice	Reduced food importers' own tariffs; IMF Trade Integration Mechanism
Own liberalization	Tariff revenue losses	Size depends on degree of liberalization, which is zero for LDCs; import volume increases could offset rate reduction	IMF Trade Integration Mechanism for balance of payments; Integrated Framework for assistance in altering tax structure
	Labor adjustment	Again, these are minimal for LDCs if there are no liberalization commitments	Stronger case for dedicated facility because safety nets lacking, often neglected in programs
			But should be available for all dislocations, not just trade-related ones
Institutional development	Implementation of new WTO rules	Costs are inversely related to income level if rules generally are based on existing developed-country practices; LDCs may be exempt for some period	WTO Trade Capacity-Building Initiative; Special and differential treatment that requires implementation only as countries develop capacity and can benefit
Economic development	Amelioration of supply constraints	All developing countries, but LDCs most in need	Existing facilities, new funds, with important role for Integrated Framework to identify needs, coordinate responses

IFPRI = International Food Policy Research Institute
LDC = least developed country

enue from its announced sugar program reform is clearly insufficient.[3]

The area where the case for a dedicated facility seems strongest is labor adjustment, because safety nets and adjustment programs for workers are so neglected in most developing countries. But the US experience with the federal trade adjustment assistance program suggests caution because many of the programs do not appear to have been effective in key areas, particularly retraining. In addition, that experience illustrates how difficult it is to disentangle the reasons for a particular worker's dislocation and demonstrates, in a period of rapid globalization and technological change, that it is usually unwise to try. This conclusion lends support to the Bank-Fund staff recommendation to continue to try to better integrate adjustment assistance into broader farm development strategies.

Overall, the staff recommendations to increase resources and rely on existing mechanisms to address adjustment problems and capacity constraints seem basically sound. But the spate of *unilateral* commitments in Hong Kong to increase funds to build trade capacity raised the issue of a new mechanism to coordinate the flows. A proliferation of new projects in the absence of multilateral coordination creates the risk of redundancies and increased costs to recipients (Roodman 2006).

Moreover, using existing mechanisms and calling for increased resources elides the real problem: how to enhance the credibility of promises to commit *new* funds, and not just divert existing money. Donor countries have traditionally been unwilling to "bind" their technical and financial promises in trade negotiations, and that seems unlikely to change. Given these countries' low reputations with respect to fulfilling similar promises in the past and the likelihood that rich countries will again refuse to bind their financial commitments in a trade agreement, tangible progress in fulfilling these promises will have to be made before the Doha Round concludes. Creating a mechanism for coordinating the new promised funds from key donor countries could also increase the credibility of the aid-for-trade efforts.

Recommendations for a Doha Package Deal

Trade ministers in Hong Kong managed to agree on just enough at the end of 2005 to avoid a Cancún-style collapse of the talks. But the agricultural negotiations remained at an impasse, and that, in turn, prevented progress in the negotiations on nonagricultural market access and services. As of spring 2006, an agreement to eliminate export subsidies by 2013 was close, conditional on satisfactory progress in other areas of the negotiation. Market access remained the most difficult area, while the negotiations on

---

3. The amount offered by EU officials as compensation related to its sugar reform is a fraction of the roughly $400 million in losses estimated by Gillson, Hewitt, and Page (2005), and Francoise, Hoekman, and Machin (2005).

domestic subsidies were further along but in danger of setting ceilings so high as to render any reduction commitments meaningless, as happened in the Uruguay Round. Differences over how to define and discipline "less trade-distorting" subsidies eligible for the blue and green boxes also remained deep.

If these obstacles are overcome, current patterns of trade, as well as, economic modeling, suggest that Brazil and the other competitive Latin American exporters will reap most of the immediate gains. Agricultural trade is also important to sub-Saharan Africa, and a package that addresses tariff escalation and provides assistance in meeting food safety standards could deliver important benefits to that region. A few countries could lose, however, if they are not compensated for potential losses from higher food prices or preference erosion. And many poor farmers in low-income countries may not see much impact at all unless their governments take complementary steps to connect them to markets. A credible aid-for-trade package is thus also necessary to making Doha a development round.

As the talks proceed, the recommendations presented in the following sections may be used as a template for assessing the agreement as it takes shape. Detailed discussion of the recommendations under each of the three pillars in the agricultural negotiations can be found in chapter 5.

Export Competition

The value of export subsidies is small, but eliminating them is an essential part of a meaningful reform package. Specific goals toward that end should include

- phasing out export subsidies no later than 2013 and earlier if possible;

- ensuring that government-backed export credit programs are short-term and self-financing; and

- disciplining the use of food aid for surplus disposal and market development, while coordinating deliveries with the World Food Programme where possible.

Domestic Support

The keys to real cuts in agricultural subsidies are increased transparency and reduced flexibility, including clarification of the rules for allocating subsidies among the amber, green, and blue boxes and improvements in the reporting and monitoring requirements. Negotiators should work toward several specific objectives:

- Cuts in the aggregate measurement of support (AMS) in the amber box must be at least in the 60 to 70 percent range for the United States and the European Union, respectively, if there is to be a chance of imposing constraints on applied levels of support.

- The base period for setting product-specific caps in the AMS should be 1995–2000, not 1999–2001 as US negotiators proposed, because the latter period was a time of high subsidies, and using it as a benchmark would undermine the intended discipline.

- If market price support (MPS) is not removed from the AMS, product-specific caps should be supplemented with separate ceilings for MPS and subsidies. This would ensure that cosmetic reforms to MPS did not create room under the new AMS ceiling to maintain something close to current subsidy levels.

- The product-specific de minimis category should be eliminated.

- The non–product specific de minimis category should be cut immediately to 2.5 percent and eventually to no more than 1 percent of the value of production, as proposed by the European Union.

- The blue box should be immediately capped at 5 percent of the value of production and then cut to 2.5 percent; product-specific caps are needed to ensure that subsidies cannot be shifted among commodities. If US negotiators are unwilling to accept additional disciplines on counter-cyclical payments, which do not have the production-limiting features of other blue box programs, they should agree to an additional cut in the ceiling to 1.5 percent of the value of production. This level would exert at least some discipline on countercyclical payments when prices are low, which the 2.5 percent cap would not.

- The bases for calculating blue box payments and decoupled green box payments must be truly "fixed and unchanging," with no updating of base acreage or herd sizes allowed.

- The ruling from the WTO's United States–Brazil cotton dispute panel, which clarified eligibility conditions for allocating decoupled payments to the green box (neither requiring nor restricting production of particular commodities), should be codified in the agreement.

Market Access

To produce meaningful increases in market access, especially for developing countries, the agreement must address tariff dispersion and escalation, as well as the form tariffs take:

- Whatever the formula, the average developed-country bound tariff should be cut at least in half.

- A tariff cap is needed to reduce dispersion and should be applied to sensitive products.

- The agreement should limit the number of sensitive products and ensure increased market access for those items through meaningful expansion of tariff-rate quotas.

- All other tariff-rate quotas should be expanded even more, and in-quota tariffs should be reduced or eliminated.

- Tariff escalation should be eliminated or sharply reduced by cutting tariffs on processed products by a multiple of the cut for primary products.

- The remaining barriers to tropical commodities should be eliminated, including those on processed products.

- The agreement should bind specific tariffs at their ad valorem equivalents and then apply formula cuts.

- The special agricultural safeguard for developed countries should be disciplined or eliminated, depending on the degree of flexibility permitted in the rest of the agreement.

Monitoring

The Uruguay Round requirement to make timely notifications of all forms of support should be extended and made enforceable under the dispute settlement system to give countries an incentive to comply. One way to do this would be to require countries to immediately bring notifications up to date if their compliance with a provision of the agriculture agreement is challenged. Refusal to do so could be regarded as prima facie evidence of a violation.

Special and Differential Treatment for Developing Countries

The goals of special and differential treatment for developing countries should be flexibility and assistance in the meeting of development benchmarks, rather than superficial universality and adherence to arbitrary deadlines. The utility of trade disciplines in controlling rent seeking also needs to be recognized, and even the LDCs should bring their policies into compliance with core WTO rules. Negotiators should be mindful of several other specific objectives:

- Developing countries, including the least developed, should agree to bind all tariffs, with the size of any cuts to be determined separately.

- Product-specific subsidies and other new trade-distorting subsidies in developing countries that do not currently employ them should continue to be sharply restricted, as was done in the Uruguay Round.[4]

- Export subsidies should be tightly restricted, with as little differentiation as possible between the elimination schedules of developing and developed countries.

- Developing countries should be granted sufficient flexibility to manage food security and promote rural development, but through tariffs only and with no new quantitative restrictions. The degree of flexibility should be determined by objective indicators such as income level and rural share of the population.

- The agreement should limit the use of special products to as small a number as possible and forbid broad, across-the-board exemptions for products that are not typically grown or consumed by the poor.

- Public policies should focus on non–product-specific rural development programs aimed at "connecting the poor to markets"—infrastructure, research and development, extension services, education, health—which would be likely to go into the green box.

Assistance with Adjustment and Supply Constraints

Negotiators should broadly define aid for trade to include infrastructure and other supply-side constraints and it should not be restricted to training negotiators or customs inspectors. In general, the package should also draw on *additional* funds and not divert resources from other areas that may have higher priority in particular situations. Finally, since US and other donors are unlikely to bind their financial commitments in a trade agreement, tangible progress in specifying dollar amounts and mechanisms for allocating them needs to be made before the Doha Round is completed. Other specific actions that donors and international organizations need to take include:

- Bilateral compensation should be negotiated between preference-giving countries and recipients likely to suffer net losses from preference erosion. Efficient producers that can maintain or expand market shares and thus benefit from higher world prices in third markets need not be compensated beyond that.

---

4. The allowance for de minimis subsidies should be sufficient to cover special programs aimed at helping the poorest farmers, as recommended in a recent Overseas Development Institute brief (Howell 2005).

- Tax regimes and labor market policies should be addressed as part of broader country assistance and poverty reduction strategies because they significantly influence the overall business climate.

- Donors should ensure that the IMF's Trade Integration Mechanism has sufficient resources to address potential fiscal shortfalls arising from tariff cuts in developing countries or preference erosion that is not compensated.

- The Integrated Framework should be expanded and efforts to mainstream trade in overall development policies ratcheted up. The process should ensure that client countries, including through consultations with civil society, producer and other private sector groups, are the ones deciding where trade capacity-building fits in their overall priorities and how much aid trade promotion should get relative to other priorities.

- Donors should ensure that the multilateral development banks and other donor agencies have adequate resources to provide assistance for infrastructure improvements and other rural development programs.

- Donors should create a fund similar to the Global Fund to Fight AIDS, Tuberculosis, and Malaria, with the objective of pooling funds from recent unilateral pledges to increase aid-for-trade and reducing the costs and inefficiencies arising from donor and project proliferation.

Trade creates opportunities, and not just in terms of exports. A consistent finding from trade models is that developing countries do better the more they liberalize their own markets. Trade lowers the costs of food and other essentials that poor people disproportionately consume and allows poor countries to import capital goods and technologies that they cannot produce themselves.

But simply cutting tariffs will not get products to markets, and it will not reduce costly delays inflicted by corrupt customs inspectors. Open trade policies are important to foreign investors, but so are reliable electricity and a ready supply of skilled workers. A trade agreement that makes it easier for developing-country exporters to access global markets, including markets in other developing countries, would be an important step forward, but only the first of many.

Glossary

Ad valorem tariff. A tariff rate charged as a percentage of the value of a product.

Ad valorem equivalent (AVE). The ad valorem equivalent of a specific tariff.

Administered price. A WTO term covering the various national terms for price targets or floors that are used in calculating market price support, including intervention prices in the European Union and loan rates in the United States.

Amber box. WTO term indicating the most trade-distorting domestic support measures that do not qualify for exemption under the green box or blue box, as defined in the Uruguay Round Agreement on Agriculture. It includes both the aggregate measurement of support (AMS), which was capped and cut in the Uruguay Round, and de minimis subsidies that are permitted to a limited degree.

Aggregate measurement of support (AMS). WTO term indicating an agreed-upon measure of trade-distorting domestic support to agriculture that includes both market price support and subsidies. It is calculated for each commodity and then summed together with nonexempt, non–product-specific agricultural support (for example, input subsidies) if it is over 5 percent of the value of production to give a total AMS for agriculture.

Agreement on Agriculture. The first multilateral trade agreement dedicated to the agricultural sector, produced during the Uruguay Round, implementation of which began in 1995.

Blue box. WTO term indicating domestic subsidies that are linked to production-limiting programs and are therefore exempt from AMS calculations and reduction commitments and unlimited. Under the Uruguay Round agreement, these subsidies include (1) payments to farmers based on fixed historical areas or yields, (2) payments made on 85 percent or less of a base level of production, and (3) livestock payments made on a fixed number of head.

Cairns Group. Coalition of agricultural exporting nations lobbying for agricultural trade liberalization, formed in 1986 in Cairns, Australia, just before the beginning of the Uruguay Round. Members as of 2006 are Argentina, Australia, Bolivia, Brazil, Canada, Chile, Colombia, Costa Rica, Guatemala, Indonesia, Malaysia, New Zealand, Pakistan, Paraguay, Philippines, South Africa, Thailand, and Uruguay.

Countercyclical payment. Device created by the 2002 US farm bill to provide a safety net for farmers when prices decline. The payments are based on fixed historical acreage and do not require production of any specific crop, or of any crop at all, but are based on the difference between the higher of the loan rate or current market prices and a target price. From 1985 to 1996, there were similar payments, called deficiency payments, and between 1996 and 2002, Congress approved ad hoc emergency payments to compensate for low prices called marketing loss assistance.

De minimis. A provision of the WTO Agreement on Agriculture whereby otherwise nonexempt domestic support can be excluded from the calculation of total AMS for agriculture. If support on a product-specific basis is below 5 percent of the gross value of production for the product in question (10 percent for developing countries), that support is excluded from the AMS. If non-product-specific support (e.g., input subsidies) is less than 5 percent of the value of total agricultural production, it may also be excluded.

Decoupling (full decoupling). A policy is fully decoupled if it does not influence production decisions of farmers receiving payments and if it permits free-market determination of prices.

Deficiency payment. *See* countercyclical payment.

Generalized System of Preferences (GSP). An arrangement under which "selected products originating in developing countries are granted reduced or zero tariff rates over the [most favored nation] rates. The least developed countries . . . receive special and preferential treatment for a wider coverage of products and deeper tariff cuts" (www.unctad.org).

Green box. Under the Uruguay Round Agreement on Agriculture, certain domestic support measures that are minimally or non–trade distorting may be placed in the green box and will be exempt from reduction commitments and not be capped. Examples include decoupled direct payments, budgetary outlays on research, and subsidies for environmental purposes.

Group of 10 (G-10). Mostly higher-income agricultural importers with defensive interests in the Doha Round. As of August 2005 they were Bulgaria, Taiwan, South Korea, Iceland, Israel, Japan, Liechtenstein, Mauritius, Norway, and Switzerland.

Group of 20 (G-20). Group of developing-country agricultural exporters that came together just prior to the Cancún ministerial to oppose the joint EU-US proposal on agriculture. The membership has fluctuated, and as of August 2005 the members were Argentina, Bolivia, Brazil, Chile, China, Cuba, Egypt, India, Indonesia, Mexico, Nigeria, Pakistan, Paraguay, the Philippines, South Africa, Tanzania, Thailand, Venezuela, and Zimbabwe.

Intervention price. The internal market price that governments in the European Union seek to maintain through government policies for selected agricultural commodities.

Least developed countries (LDCs). An official category defined by the United Nations and accepted by the World Trade Organization. LDCs are a subcategory of low-income countries, and not all of the latter are LDCs.

Loan deficiency payment. The term used in the United States for payments made to farmers to compensate them when prices drop below the loan rate.

Loan rate. One of the government-set prices In the United States used to calculate payments to farmers under the marketing loan program, which sets the price floor for wheat, corn and other feed grains, cotton, rice, soybeans, and a few other crops. The term is also applied to the internal market prices the government tries to maintain through supply controls for dairy products and sugar.

Market price support (MPS). As defined by the OECD, "an indicator of the annual monetary value of gross transfers from consumers and taxpayers to agricultural producers arising from policy measures that create a gap between domestic market prices and border prices of a specific agricultural commodity, measured at the farm-gate level" (OECD 2004b). A slightly different definition is used by the WTO, with a fixed base-year price, rather than the current reference price used by the OECD, used to calculate the gap with the government-set administered price. The price gap is multiplied by the volume of eligible production to get the value of MPS that is included in each country's AMS. Products that are protected purely through trade barriers and with no administered price are not included in the WTO's measure of MPS.

Preference erosion. Reductions in the margin of preference that developing countries receive under programs created by developed countries aimed at encouraging export growth and economic development. The margin of preference is the difference between the most favored nation tariff, which is applied to most partners, and the preferential duty applied to eligible developing-country exports, or between an internal market price supported by quotas that is available to quota holders and the world price. Preference margins can be eroded by multilateral or unilateral liberalizations that lower most favored nation tariffs or expand quotas.

Producer support estimate (PSE). As defined by the OECD, "an indicator of the annual monetary value of gross transfers from consumers and taxpayers to agricultural producers, measured at the farm-gate level, arising from policy measures that support agriculture, regardless of their nature, objective, or impacts on farm production or income" (OECD 2004b).

Sanitary and phytosanitary (SPS) standards. Measures implemented by governments to protect human, animal, and plant life and health, and to help ensure that food is safe for consumption.

Specific tariff. A tariff rate charged as a fixed amount per quantity unit.

Tariff binding. A commitment not to increase a rate of duty beyond an agreed-upon level. Once a rate of duty is bound, it may not be raised unless the affected parties are compensated.

Tariff escalation. Imposing higher import duties on semiprocessed products than on raw materials, and still-higher duties on finished products. This practice protects domestic processing industries and discourages the development of processing activity in the countries where raw materials originate.

Tariff-rate quota (TRQ). A two-tiered tariff, with a lower in-quota tariff applied to a set volume of imports and a higher overquota tariff applied to all subsequent imports.

Total support estimate (TSE). An indicator of the annual monetary value of all gross transfers from taxpayers and consumers arising from policy measures that support agriculture, net of the associated budgetary receipts, regardless of their objectives and impacts on farm production and income, or consumption of farm products.

Variable levy. Import duty that varies in response to changes in world prices so as to maintain a given internal price; used heavily by the European Union until it was prohibited in the Uruguay Round.

References

Abdulai, Awudu, Christopher B. Barrett, and John Hoddinott. 2005. Does Food Aid *Really* Have Disincentive Effects? New Evidence from Sub-Saharan Africa. *World Development* 33, no. 10 (October): 1689–704.

Aksoy, M. Ataman. 2005. The Evolution of Agricultural Trade Flows. In *Global Agricultural Trade and Developing Countries,* ed. M. Ataman Aksoy and John C. Beghin. Washington: World Bank.

Aksoy, M. Ataman, and John C. Beghin. 2005. Introduction and Overview. In *Global Agricultural Trade and Developing Countries,* ed. M. Ataman Aksoy and John C. Beghin. Washington: World Bank.

American Farmland Trust. 2006. *Agenda 2007: A New Framework and Direction for U.S. Farm Policy.* Washington.

Anderson, Kym, Will Martin, and Dominique van der Mensbrugghe. 2006. Market and Welfare Implications of the Doha Reform Scenarios. In *Agricultural Trade Reform and the Doha Development Agenda,* ed. Kym Anderson and Will Martin. London and Washington: Palgrave Macmillan and World Bank.

Ashraf, Nava, Margaret McMillan, and Alix Peterson Zwane. 2005. My Policies or Yours: Have OECD Agricultural Policies Affected Incomes in Developing Countries? In *Globalization and Poverty,* ed. Ann Harrison. Chicago, IL: University of Chicago Press for National Bureau of Economic Research.

Badiane, Ousmane. 2004. Agricultural Trade Liberalization Under Doha: The Risks Facing African Countries. Paper presented at the H. E. Babock Workshop on Agricultural Trade Liberalization and the Least Developed Countries: How Should They Respond to Developments in the WTO? organized by Cornell University, Wageningen University, and the African Research Consortium, Wageningen, the Netherlands, December 2–3.

Baffes, John. 2005. Cotton: Market Setting, Trade Policies, and Issues. In *Global Agricultural Trade and Developing Countries,* ed. M. Ataman Aksoy and John C. Beghin. Washington: World Bank.

Baffes, John, and Harry de Gorter. 2005. Experience with Decoupling Agricultural Support. In *Global Agricultural Trade and Developing Countries,* ed. M. Ataman Aksoy and John C. Beghin. Washington: World Bank.

Balat, Jorge F., and Guido G. Porto. 2005. Globalization and Complementary Policies: Poverty Impacts in Rural Zambia. NBER Working Paper 11175. In *Globalization and*

Poverty, ed. Ann Harrison. Chicago, IL: University of Chicago Press for National Bureau of Economic Research.

Bayard, Thomas O., and Kimberly Ann Elliott. 1994. *Reciprocity and Retaliation in US Trade Policy*. Washington: Institute for International Economics.

Bhattacharya, Debapriya, and Kimberly Elliott. 2005. *Adjusting to the MFA Phase-Out: Policy Priorities*. CGD Brief. Washington: Center for Global Development.

Bouet, Antoine. 2006. *What Can the Poor Expect from Trade Liberalization? Opening the "Black Box" of Global Trade Modeling*. IFPRI Working Paper 93. Washington: International Food Policy Research Institute.

Bouet, Antoine, Simon Mevel, and David Orden. 2005. *More or Less Ambition? Modeling the Development Impact of U.S.-EU Agricultural Proposals in the Doha Round*. IFPRI Brief. Washington: International Food Policy Research Institute (December).

Bown, Chad P., and Bernard M. Hoekman. 2005. WTO Dispute Settlement and the Missing Developing Country Cases: Engaging the Private Sector. *Journal of International Economic Law* 8, no. 4 (December): 861–90.

Center for Responsive Politics. 2006. Agribusiness: Long-Term Contribution Trends. Available at www.opensecrets.org (accessed on April 14, 2006).

Cline, William R. 2004. *Trade Policy and Global Poverty*. Washington: Center for Global Development and Institute for International Economics.

Croome, John. 1998. *Reshaping the World Trading System: A History of the Uruguay Round*. The Hague: Kluwer Law International.

Diaz-Bonilla, Eugenio, Marcelle Thomas, and Sherman Robinson. 2000. *Food Security and Trade Negotiations in the World Trade Organization: A Cluster Analysis of Country Groups*. TMD Discussion Paper 59. Washington: International Food Policy Research Institute, Trade and Macroeconomics Division.

Elliott, Kimberly Ann. 2005a. *Looking for the Devil in the Doha Agricultural Negotiations*. CGD Brief. Washington: Center for Global Development.

Elliott, Kimberly Ann. 2005b. *Big Sugar and the Political Economy of US Agricultural Policy*. CGD Brief. Washington: Center for Global Development.

Environmental Working Group. n.d. Farm Subsidy Database. Available at www.ewg.org (accessed on April 14, 2006).

Finger, J. Michael, and Philip Schuler. 2002. Implementation of WTO Commitments: The Development Challenge. In *Development, Trade, and the WTO: A Handbook*, ed. Bernard Hoekman, Aaditya Mattoo, and Philip English. Washington: World Bank.

Food and Agriculture Organization. 2005. FAOSTAT: Agriculture and Food Trade. Available at http://faostat.fao.org (accessed on April 19, 2006).

Francois, Joseph, Bernard Hoekman, and Miriam Manchin. 2005. *Preference Erosion and Multilateral Trade Liberalization*. World Bank Policy Research Working Paper WPS3730. Washington: World Bank.

Gardner, Bruce L. 1990. The United States. In *Agricultural Protectionism in the Industrialized World*, ed. Fred H. Sanderson. Washington: Resources for the Future.

General Accounting Office. 1993. *Sugar Program: Changing Domestic and International Conditions Require Program Changes*. GAO Report GAO/RCED-93-84. Washington.

General Accounting Office. 2000. *Sugar Program: Supporting Sugar Prices Has Increased Users' Costs While Benefiting Producers*. GAO Report GAO/RCED-00-126. Washington.

Gibson, Paul, John Wainio, Daniel Whitley, and Mary Bohman. 2001. *Profiles of Tariffs in Global Agricultural Markets*. Agricultural Economic Report 796. Washington: US Department of Agriculture, Economic Research Service, Market and Trade Economics Division.

Gillson, Ian, Adrian Hewitt, and Sheila Page. 2005. Forthcoming Changes in the EU Banana/Sugar Markets: A Menu of Options for an Effective EU Transitional Package. Overseas Development Institute, London. Photocopy.

Harrison, Ann. 2005. *Globalization and Poverty*. Chicago: University of Chicago Press for National Bureau of Economic Research.

Hathaway, Dale E. 1987. *Agriculture and the GATT: Rewriting the Rules*. POLICY ANALYSES IN INTERNATIONAL ECONOMICS 20. Washington: Institute for International Economics.

Hertel, Thomas W., and Maros Ivanic. 2006. Assessing the World Market Impacts of Multilateral Trade Reforms. In *Putting Development Back into the Doha Agenda: Poverty Impacts of a WTO Agreement*, ed. Thomas W. Hertel and L. Alan Winters. Washington: World Bank.

Hertel, Thomas W., and Roman Keeney. 2006. What Is at Stake: The Relative Importance of Import Barriers, Export Subsidies, and Domestic Support. In *Agricultural Trade Reform and the Doha Development Agenda*, ed. Kym Anderson and Will Martin. London and Washington: Palgrave Macmillan and the World Bank.

Hertel, Thomas W., and L. Alan Winters. 2006. Poverty Impacts of a WTO Agreement: Synthesis and Overview. In *Putting Development Back Into the Doha Agenda: Poverty Impacts of a WTO Agreement*, ed. Thomas W. Hertel and L. Alan Winters. Washington: World Bank.

Hoekman, Bernard. 2005. Operationalizing the Concept of Policy Space in the WTO: Beyond Special and Differential Treatment. *Journal of International Economic Law* 8, no. 2: 405–24.

Honma, Masayoshi, and Yujiro Hayami. 1986. The Determinants of Agricultural Protection Level: An Econometric Analysis. In *The Political Economy of Agricultural Protection*, ed. Kym Anderson and Yujiro Hayami. Boston: Allen and Unwin.

Howell, John. 2005. *Farm Subsidies: A Problem for Africa Too*. Opinions, no. 47 (September). London: Overseas Development Institute.

Hufbauer, Gary Clyde, and Kimberly Ann Elliott. 1994. *Measuring the Costs of Protection in the United States*. Washington: Institute for International Economics.

Iceland, Charles. 1994. European Union: Oilseeds. In *Reciprocity and Retaliation in US Trade Policy*, ed. Thomas O. Bayard and Kimberly Ann Elliott. Washington: Institute for International Economics.

Ingco, Merlinda D., and John D. Nash. 2004. *Agriculture and the WTO: Creating a Trading System for Development*. Washington: World Bank.

IMF (International Monetary Fund) and World Bank. 2002. *Market Access for Developing Country Exports—Selected Issues*. Available at www.imf.org (accessed on April 19, 2006).

IMF (International Monetary Fund) and World Bank. 2005. *Doha Development Agenda and Aid for Trade*. Washington.

IPC (International Food and Agricultural Trade Policy Council). 2005. *Building on the July Framework Agreement: Options for Agriculture*. Washington.

Jackson, John. 1991. *The World Trading System: Law and Policy of International Economic Relations*. Cambridge, MA: MIT Press.

Josling, Tim. 1998. *Agricultural Trade Policy: Completing the Reform*. POLICY ANALYSES IN INTERNATIONAL ECONOMICS 53. Washington: Institute for International Economics.

Josling, Tim, and Dale Hathaway. 2004. *This Far and No Farther? Nudging Agricultural Reform Forward*. International Economics Policy Brief PB04-1. Washington: Institute for International Economics.

Josling, Tim, Donna Roberts, and David Orden. 2004. *Food Regulation and Trade: Toward a Safe and Open Global System*. Washington: Institute for International Economics.

Jotzo, Frank, Ivan Roberts, Neil Andrews, and Suthida Warr. 2003. 2003 EU CAP Reforms: A Step Forward on a Long Journey. *Australian Commodities* 10, no. 3 (September): 381–89.

Kelch, David, and Mary Anne Normile. 2004. European Union Adopts Significant Farm Reform. *Amber Waves* (September). Available at www.ers.usda.gov (accessed on April 20, 2006).

Kleen, Peter, and Sheila Page. 2005. *Special and Differential Treatment of Developing Countries in the World Trade Organization*. Global Development Studies 2. Stockholm and London: Overseas Development Institute for the Swedish Ministry for Foreign Affairs.

Kull, Steven. 2004. *Americans on Globalization, Trade, and Farm Subsidies*. Report and Associated Questionnaire. College Park, MD: Program on International Policy Attitudes, University of Maryland.

Levinsohn, James, and Margaret McMillan. 2005. Does Food Aid Harm the Poor? Household Evidence from Ethiopia. In *Globalization and Poverty*, ed. Ann Harrison. Chicago, IL: University of Chicago Press for National Bureau of Economic Research.

Lucas, Sarah, and C. Peter Timmer. 2005. *Connecting the Poor to Growth: Eight Key Questions.* CGD Brief. Washington: Center for Global Development.

Mensbrugghe, Dominique van der. 2006. Estimating the Benefits of Trade Reform: Why Numbers Change. In *Trade, Doha, and Development: A Window into the Issues,* ed. Richard Newfarmer. Washington: World Bank.

Mitchell, Donald. 2005. Sugar Policies: An Opportunity for Change. In *Global Agricultural Trade and Developing Countries,* ed. M. Ataman Aksoy and John C. Beghin. Washington: World Bank.

Moyer, H. Wayne, and Tim Josling. 1990. *Agricultural Policy Reform: Politics and Process in the EC and the USA.* Ames, IA: Iowa State University Press.

Newman, Mark, Tom Fulton, and Lewrene Glaser. 1987. *Comparison of Agriculture in the United States and the European Community.* Economic Research Service Staff Report AGES 870521. Washington: US Department of Agriculture.

Nicita, Alessandro. 2004. *Who Benefited from Trade Liberalization in Mexico? Measuring the Effects on Household Welfare.* World Bank Policy Research Working Paper 3265. Washington: World Bank.

OECD (Organization for Economic Cooperation and Development). 2002. *Methodology for the Measurement of Support and Use in Policy Evaluation.* Available at www.oecd.org (accessed on April 13, 2006).

OECD (Organization for Economic Cooperation and Development). 2003. *Agricultural Policies in OECD Countries: Monitoring and Evaluation, 2003.* Paris.

OECD (Organization for Economic Cooperation and Development). 2004a. *Analysis of the 2003 CAP Reform.* Paris.

OECD (Organization for Economic Cooperation and Development). 2004b. *Agricultural Support: How Is It Measured and What Does It Mean?* OECD Observer Policy Brief. Available at www.oecd.org (accessed on April 19, 2006).

OECD (Organization for Economic Cooperation and Development). 2005a. *Agricultural Policies in OECD Countries: Monitoring and Evaluation 2005, Highlights.* Paris.

OECD (Organization for Economic Cooperation and Development). 2005b. *The Development Effectiveness of Food Aid: Does Tying Matter?* Paris.

Orden, David. 2005. *Key Issues for the Next Farm Bill: Is a Farm Program Buyout Possible?* US Department of Agriculture Agricultural Outlook Forum 2005, Speech Booklet 5. Washington: US Department of Agriculture.

Orden, David, Robert Paarlberg, and Terry Roe. 1999. *Policy Reform in American Agriculture: Analysis and Prognosis.* Chicago, IL: University of Chicago Press.

Oxfam International. 2005. *Truth or Consequences: Why the EU and the USA Must Reform their Subsidies or Pay the Price.* Oxfam Briefing Paper 81. London.

Paarlberg, Robert. 1997. Agricultural Policy Reform and the Uruguay Round: Synergistic Linkage in a Two-Level Game? *International Organization* 51, no. 3 (summer): 413–44.

Paarlberg, Robert. 1999. The Political Economy of American Agricultural Policy: Three Approaches. *American Journal of Agricultural Economics* 81, no. 5 (December): 1157–64.

Polaski, Sandra. 2006. *Winners and Losers: The Impact of the Doha Round on Developing Countries.* Washington: Carnegie Endowment for International Peace.

Roodman, David. 2005. *Production-Weighted Estimates of Aggregate Protection in Rich Countries Toward Developing Countries.* Working Paper 66. Washington: Center for Global Development.

Roodman, David. 2006. *Aid Project Proliferation and Absorptive Capacity.* Working Paper 75. Washington: Center for Global Development.

Sharma, Devinder. n.d. *Western Cow Versus Eastern Farmer: The Absurdity of Inequality.* Available at the Hunger Notes Web site, www.worldhunger.org (accessed on April 12, 2006).

Sumner, Daniel A. 2005. *Boxed In: Conflicts Between US Farm Policies and WTO Obligations.* Trade Policy Analysis 32. Washington: Cato Institute.

Swinbank, Alan, and Carolyn Tanner. 1996. *Farm Policy and Trade Conflict: The Uruguay Round and CAP Reform.* Ann Arbor, MI: University of Michigan Press.

Thompson, Robert L. 2005. Essentials for the 2007 Farm Bill in a Global Context. *Trade Policy Analyses* 7, no. 6 (July). Washington: Cordell Hull Institute.

Timmer, C. Peter. 2002. Agriculture and Economic Development. In *Handbook of Agricultural Economics 2*, ed. Bruce L. Gardner and Gordon C. Rausser. New York: Elsevier.

Timmer, C. Peter. 2004. *Food Security and Economic Growth: An Asian Perspective.* Working Paper 51. Washington: Center for Global Development.

Timmer, C. Peter. 2005. *Agriculture and Pro-Poor Growth: An Asian Perspective.* Working Paper 63. Washington: Center for Global Development.

Timmer, C. Peter. Forthcoming. *Farmers and Global Trade: Market Dynamics.* Washington: Center for Global Development.

Tokarick, Stephen. 2003. *Measuring the Impact of Distortions in Agricultural Trade in Partial and General Equilibrium.* IMF Working Paper WP/03/110. Washington: International Monetary Fund.

USDA (US Department of Agriculture). 2000. U.S. Farm Program Benefits: Links to Planting Decisions and Agricultural Markets. *Agricultural Outlook* (October): 10–14.

USDA (US Department of Agriculture). 2003. *European Union Agricultural Situation: EU CAP Reform Deal Approved.* GAIN (Global Agriculture Information Network) Report E23121. Washington: USDA Foreign Agricultural Service.

USDA (US Department of Agriculture). 2004. *US-EU Food and Agriculture Comparisons.* Agriculture and Trade Report WRS-04-04. Washington.

Wailes, Eric J. 2005. Rice: Global Trade, Protectionist Policies, and the Impact of Trade Liberalization. In *Global Agricultural Trade and Developing Countries*, ed. M. Ataman Aksoy and John C. Beghin. Washington: World Bank.

Wainio, John, Shahia Shapouri, Michael Trueblood, and Paul Gibson. 2005. *Agricultural Trade Preferences and the Developing Countries.* Economic Research Report 6. Washington: US Department of Agriculture Economic Research Service.

World Bank. 2002. *Global Economic Prospects 2002: Making Trade Work for the Poor.* Washington: World Bank.

World Bank. 2005a. *Managing Food Price Risks and Instability in an Environment of Market Liberalization.* Report no. 32727. Washington: World Bank, Agriculture and Rural Development Department.

World Bank. 2005b. *Food Safety and Agricultural Health Standards: Challenges and Opportunities for Developing Country Exports.* Report no. 31207. Washington: World Bank, Poverty Reduction and Economic Management Trade Unit and Agriculture and Rural Development Department.

WTO (World Trade Organization). 2004. *WTO Agriculture Negotiations: The Issues, and Where We Are Now.* WTO Briefing Document. Geneva. Available at www.wto.org (accessed on April 19, 2006).

Index

ad valorem tariffs
  definition, 133
  description of, 16
  and equivalents, 112–13
  for selected developed countries, 26t
adjustment assistance
  costs, 123, 124t, 125
  recommendations for Doha Round, 126, 130–31
administered price, 19, 96n
  definition, 133
Afghanistan, 66t
African Growth and Opportunity Act (AGOA), 6
aggregate measurement of support (AMS), 18t,
     95–96. See also market price support
  definition, 133
  product-specific caps, 104
  recommendations for Doha Round, 127–28
  for US, European Union, 50t
Agreement on Textiles and Clothing, 4
Agreement on the Application of Sanitary and
    Phytosanitary Measures, 87
Agricultural Adjustment Act (1933), 42
agricultural liberalization, 1, 3, 83, 115–16
  domestic barriers to, 84–87
  impact on developing countries, 75–80, 80n
  impact on rural areas, 79
  potential country losses due to, 9–10
agricultural policy
  European, evolution of, 36–38
  impact of budget pressures on, 56, 58
  post–World War II, 3
  reform
    challenges for, 2
    developing countries' impact on, 59–60

EU single farm payments, 50
  external pressures for, 59–61
  internal (US, EU) pressures for, 53–56, 58–59
  strategies for, 37, 37b
  support costs, 17
  Uruguay Round approach to, 37
  US, 42–47, 45–47
    evolution of, 36–38, 48f
    farm lobby's impact on, 55–56
    payment mechanisms, 46–47
    politics of, 35–36
agricultural products. See also under names
    of products
  developing-country exports, 66t, 70f, 71f, 72t
    dependence on, 66t
    distribution of, 65, 65t, 66
  product categories, 68
  trade preference indicators, 81t
agricultural subsidies
  decoupled payments, 46
  impact of US farm lobby on, 55–56
  political economy theories for, 52–53
  unequal distribution of US payments, 54–55, 55t
agricultural support
  amber, green, and blue box descriptions, 95
  approaches to, 14
  country estimates, comparisons, 23t, 24, 24t
  de minimis exemptions, 18t
  domestic, categories for, 95
  mechanisms for, 13–17
  OECD estimates for, 20, 23t
  political economy theories for, 52–53
  products that are heavily supported, 28, 29t, 30t,
    31, 38

agricultural support—*continued*
  recommendations for Doha Round, 127–28
  three pillars of, 17
  WTO framework for reducing, 17, 18t, 19–20
agricultural trade
  barriers to, 5–6, 9
  compared with manufacturing, 5
  distortionary effects of, 5–6
  domestic barriers to, 83–87, 85t, 86t
  EC-10 imports, exports, 39f
  export diversification challenges for developing
    countries, 72–73
  export subsidies, 130
  import barriers, 81–82
  post–World War II policies, 3
  preference indicators, 81t
  special safeguards, 113
  US, 44f
Agricultural Trade Development and Assistance
    Act of (1954), 92–94
"aid for trade," 91–92, 122
  categories of, 124t
  recommended parameters for, 130
amber box subsidies, 18t, 95
  definition, 133
  EU, US agricultural support, 99t, 100t
  inclusion of aggregate measurement of support
    and market price support, 19
AMS. *See* aggregate measurement of support
Angola, 121t
Asia. *See also under country names*
  protection of rice, 35
  reliance on cereals, 77t
Australia, 60, 74b
  average and ad valorem tariffs, 26t
  dairy support, 28n
  producer support estimates, 22, 22t, 23t
AVE. *See* ad valorem tariff equivalents

bananas, 82
Bangladesh, 78
  effect of global trade liberalization on, 78t
beef
  agricultural support for, 28
  average tariffs, tariff peaks, and TRQs, 30t
Benin, 66t
beverages, exported by developing countries, 70f, 71f
Blair, Tony, 58
blue box subsidies, 18t, 95
  definition, 134
  EU subsidies, 50, 50n, 99t, 100t
  recommendations for Doha Round, 128
  US agricultural support, 99t, 100t
bovine spongiform encephalopthy (BSE), 87
Brazil, 59, 74b
  complaint against US over cotton, 40n, 51, 59,
    104b, 107
  against EU over sugar, 59, 82
  indicators for differentiating treatment under
    an agricultural agreement, 121t

Burkina Faso, 66t
Burundi, 66t
Bush, George W., 58, 60
business challenges, in developing countries,
    85–87, 86t

Cairns Group, 3, 115n
  definition, 134
  dissatisfaction with Uruguay Round, 4–5
  producer support estimates for, 22, 22t
Canada
  average tariffs, ad valorem tariffs, 26t
  producer support estimates for, 22, 22t, 23t
CAP. *See* Common Agricultural Policy
Caribbean, reliance on cereals, 77t
Castro, Fidel, 73b
CCP. *See* countercyclical payments
Chad, 66t
Chambliss, Saxby, 104b
"Chicken War," 3
China
  indicators for differentiating treatment, 121t
cocoa, chocolate
  exported by developing countries, 69, 70f, 71f
  tariffs, 27, 27t, 112
coffee
  exported by developing countries, 69, 70f, 71f
  tariffs, 27t, 112
Colombia, 74b
commodity loans, 42–43
Common Agricultural Policy (CAP), 3, 36
  evolution of, 40, 41f
  reforms, 39
  single farm payments and planting decisions,
    51–52
  tensions between UK and France, 58, 58n
Comoros, 66t
compensatory payments, 47, 48f
Conservation Reserve Program (CRP), 44, 55, 108
corn
  average tariffs, tariff peaks, and TRQs, 30t
  countercyclical payments for, 106t
  USDA payments for, 105f
Côte d'Ivoire, 66t
Cotonou arrangement, 81
cotton
  agricultural support for, 28, 29t
  Brazil-US dispute over, 51, 104b, 107
  countercyclical payments for, 106t
  nominal assistance coefficient for, 34t
  producer support estimates for, 32, 33t, 34t
  step-2 support for, 31t
  US support for, 15, 33t, 105f
countercyclical payments (CCP), 48f, 49–50, 98,
    98n, 106t
  definition, 134
  moving to blue box, 105
  for selected commodities, 106t
CRP. *See* Conservation Reserve Program
Cuba, 66t, 73b, 74b
customs valuation, 118

dairy, 30*t*
de minimis subsidies, 95–96, 129*n*
  definition, 134
  exemptions, 18*t*
decoupling, definition, 134
deficiency payments, 47, 48*f*, 49. *See also* countercyclical payments
developing countries. *See also* least developed
  countries
  agricultural advantages of, 63
  agricultural exports of, 67–69, 70*f*, 71*f*, 72, 72*t*
    dependence on, 66*t*
    distribution, 65*t*
    diversification challenges, 72–73
    domestic barriers to, 83–87, 85*t*, 86*t*
    sugar, 74*b*
    top, 66*t*
  agricultural income, employment, and produc-
    tivity, 64–65
  agricultural indicators for, 64*t*
  agricultural policy
    domestic reform, 10
    impact on reform, 59–60
  agricultural production categories, 68
  agricultural tariffs, 26*t*, 27
  agricultural trade positions of, 67, 67*t*
  business challenges in, 85–87, 86*t*
  changing status, designation of, 117–18
  as competitive exporters, 53
  compliance with SPS agreement, 87–88
  demand for financial support, 122–23
  dependence on agricultural exports, 66*t*
  impact on Uruguay Round, 59–60
  potential losses due to agricultural liberaliza-
    tion, 9–10
  special and differential treatment for, 117–22,
    121*t*, 129–30
direct payments, 46
  and planting decisions, 51, 52
Djibouti, 121*t*
Doha Round
  adjustment assistance issues, 126, 130–31
  agricultural liberalization scenarios, 7, 8*t*, 9
  "aid for trade," 91–92, 122
  cutting EU, US aggregate measurement of sup-
    port, 101, 104
  defensive vs. offensive interests in negotiations, 31
  domestic subsidies, impact on EU, US agricul-
    tural support, 99*t*, 100*t*, 127–28
  eliminating administered prices, 100
  eliminating export subsidies, 92–94, 127
  estimated gains from proposed scenarios, 8*t*
  and future 2007 US farm bill, 102*b*–104*b*
  goal to develop rural areas in poor countries, 116
  improving market access, 108–109
  market access, recommendations for, 128–29
  political influences on, 35–36
  reaching agreement on SPS measures, 87, 88, 90
  reducing tariff escalation, 112–13
  special and differential treatment for develop-
    ing countries, 120–22, 121*t*, 129–30

  rural livelihoods, 116, 120
  safeguards for food security, 120
  unresolved issues, 126–27
dynamic products, 68

electronics, telecommunications equipment
  distribution of developing-country exports,
    65*t*, 66
Ethiopia, 66*t*
European Union (EU)
  aggregate measurement of support, 97, 98
  agricultural import barriers, 82
  agricultural policy, 38–40, 41*t*, 42
  agricultural reform, 40, 58
  agricultural subsidies, 50*t*, 92
  agricultural trade, 39*f*
  decoupling issues, 107
  export subsidies, 92
  negotiation interests in Doha Round, 31
  population dependent on agriculture, 54*f*
  producer support estimates for, 22, 22*t*, 23*t*
  tariffs
    ad valorem, 26*t*
    by category, 5*t*
    escalation on cocoa and coffee, 27*t*
    peaks and TRQs, 30*t*
    proposals to cut, 109, 109*n*, 110*t*
  trade preference indicators, 81, 81*t*
Everything But Arms program, 6, 80
Export Enhancement Program, 44
external reference price, 96

Farm Security and Rural Investment Act
    (2002 farm bill), 105
  decoupling issues, 107
farming population, 54*f*
  relationship to total population, 63
Federal Agriculture Improvement and Reform
    (FAIR) Act (1996 farm bill), 45–47, 58
  impact on blue and green boxes, 49
Fiji, 82
food aid, 92–94
  impact on Africa, 93–94, 93*n*
  recommendations for reducing trade distortion,
    94
  reform of, 94
Food Security Act (1985 farm bill), 44, 44*n*
food stamps, 59
Freedom to Farm Act, 45, 46. *See also* Federal
    Agriculture Improvement and Reform Act
fruits and vegetables, 51*n*, 68, 69
  average tariffs, tariff peaks, and TRQs, 30*t*, 112
  decoupled payments for, 107–108
  exported by developing countries, 69, 70*f*, 71*f*

General Agreement on Tariffs and Trade (GATT),
    3, 117, 117*n*. *See also under* Doha Round;
    Tokyo Round; Uruguay Round
Generalized System of Preferences (GSP), 80, 134

global trade liberalization
  estimated gains of, 6–7, 7t
  impact on selected countries, commodities, 78t
  models for, 6, 7t
grains and cereals. See also rice; wheat
  agricultural support for, 28
  average tariffs, tariff peaks, and TRQs, 30t
  countercyclical payments for, 106t
  developing countries' reliance on, 76, 77t
  exported by developing countries, 69, 70f, 71f
green box subsidies, 18t, 95
  definition, 134
  eligibility of subsidies for, 52, 107–108
  for US, European Union, 50n
gross farm receipts, 21, 22t, 23t
Group of 10 (G-10)
  definition, 135
  negotiation interests in Doha Round, 31
  producer support estimates, 22, 22t
  sensitive-products tariff proposal, 110
Group of 20 (G-20), 37
  definition, 135
  dissatisfaction with Uruguay Round, 5
  tariff-cutting proposals, 109, 110t
Guatemala, 74b
Guyana, 82

honey. See also sugar
  exported by developing countries, 70f, 71f

Iceland, producer support estimates for, 23t
import quotas, description of, 16
India, 74b, 121t
Indonesia, effect of global trade liberalization on, 78t
Integrated Framework, 122–23, 130
intellectual property, 118
intervention price, definition, 135

Jamaica, 82
Japan
  aggregate measurement of support, 96, 97
  agricultural policy reform, 56
  green box support, 108
  market price support, 96, 97f, 98
  population dependent on agriculture, 54f
  producer support estimates for, 22, 22t, 23t
  protection of rice, 35
  tariffs
    applied, by category, 5t
    average, ad valorem, 26t
    peaks and TRQs, 30t
    escalation on cocoa and coffee, 27t
  trade preference indicators, 81, 81t
Johanns, Mike, 104b

Kenya, 66t, 89–90

labor adjustment, 126
Lamy, Pascal, 123
Latin America, reliance on cereals, 77t

least developed countries (LDC)
  definition, 135
  designation of, 117
  impact of preference erosion on, 80
loan deficiency payment, definition, 135
loan rates, 96n
  definition, 135
  US fluctuations in, 43
Lomé Convention, 81

MacSherry, Ray, 39, 41f
Madagascar, 82
maize, 77t
"Make Trade Fair," 13
Malawi, 66t
Maldives, 121t
Mali, 66t
Mandelson, Peter, 98
manufacturing
  applied tariffs, regional comparisons, 5t
  liberalization, 116
market access, 108–109, 128–29
market loans, 45, 48f
market loss assistance, 46, 48f
market price support (MPS), 18t
  calculation for, 18t
  description of, 14, 16, 135
  recommendations for Doha Round, 128
  role in aggregate measurement of support, 96
  US, European Union, 50t
Mauritius, 82
meats. See also beef
  average tariffs, tariff peaks, and TRQs, 30t
  exported by developing countries, 69, 70f, 71f
Mexico, 79
MFA. See Multi-Fiber Arrangement
monetization, 93
Mozambique, effect of global trade liberalization on, 78t
MPS. See market price support
Multi-Fiber Arrangement (MFA), 53, 83n, 118

Natsios, Andrew, 93, 94
net food importers, and impact of agricultural liberalization, 75–80, 80n
New Zealand, 22, 22t, 23t
nonrecourse loans, 45
Norway, 22, 22t, 23t, 26t
nuts, 30t

Organization for Economic Cooperation and Development (OECD)
  estimates of agricultural support, 20, 23t
  measurement of MPS, 21

Pakistan, 121t
Paraguay, 66t
peanuts, 102b, 106t
PFC. See production flexibility contracts
Philippines, 73b

Portman, Robert, 60
    proposed AMS cuts, 98
preference erosion, 80–83, 83n, 125
    for bananas, sugar, 82
    costs of, 125
    definition, 135–36
processed foods, 68, 70f, 71f
producer support estimates (PSE)
    country data, comparisons, 23t
    definition, 136
    description of, 21
    gross farm receipts, 21, 22t
    for US cotton, 32, 33t
production flexibility contracts (PFC), 48f, 49
product-specific caps, 104, 106

Quad, 117

rice
    agricultural support for, 28
    Asian protection of, 35
    average tariffs, tariff peaks, and TRQs, 30t
    countercyclical payments for, 106t
    developing countries' reliance on, 76, 77t
    effect of global trade liberalization on import
        prices, 78, 78t
    export prices, 76, 76n
    USDA payments for, 105f
rural development, 63, 130
Rwanda, 66t

sanitary and phytosanitary (SPS) standards, 87–90
    as an impediment to trade, 75, 87, 89–90
    definition, 136
    harmonization and equivalence recognition, 88
    mutual recognition agreements, 90
sensitive products, 111, 112
    tariff-cutting proposals for, 109, 110, 110t
services liberalization, 6n
single farm payments, 41f
    and CAP reform, planting decisions, 51–52
    description of, 40
    in lieu of blue box payments, 42
Sodbuster, 44n
South Africa, 74b
South Korea
    agricultural policy reform, 56
    average and ad valorem tariffs, 26t
    producer support estimates, 22, 22t, 23t
    protection of rice, 35
soybeans, 105f, 106t
special and differential treatment, recommenda-
        tions for Doha Round, 121t, 129–30
special products, 130
spices, exported by developing countries, 70f, 71f
squeeze-out, 43
St. Lucia, 66t
step-2 payments, 32
    for cotton, 31t

structural economic changes, impact on agricul-
        tural subsidies, 53–54
sub-Saharan Africa, reliance on cereals, 77t
subsidies. See also agricultural subsidies
    description of, 14
    European Union, 50t
    reducing associated budget costs, 15–16
    and relationship to prices, 25, 25t
    US, 50t
    vs. total support, 20–21
subsidies, decoupled, 42, 47
    2002 US farm bill issues, 107
    description of, 15
    implications for the Doha Round, 49–52
    payments, 46
    as a share of producer support, 49f
Sugar Protocol, 73b
sugar
    agricultural support for, 28
    average tariffs, tariff peaks, and TRQs, 30t
    EU prices for, 52n
    exported by developing countries, 70f, 71f
    history of trade in, 73b
    impact of liberalization on developing coun-
        tries, 72, 74b
    net importers, exporters of, 84t
    policy reform, potential winners and losers of, 84t
    US policy and politics, 57b
Sumner, Daniel, 104b
Swampbuster, 44n
Swaziland, 66t, 82
Switzerland, producer support estimates, 22, 22t, 23t

tariff rate quotas (TRQ), 16, 30t, 110–11, 136
tariffs, agricultural
    applied, bound, and average, 111, 111n
    averages, country comparisons, 26t
    definitions of, 136
    for developing countries, 26t, 27
    recommendations for Doha Round, 128–29
    regional comparisons, by category, 5t
    special, 16, 25, 27, 136
    binding, definition, 136
    cap, on sensitive products, 110t, 111
    escalation, 27, 27t, 112–13
    proposals to cut, 109, 109n, 110t
tea, 70f, 71f
temperate products, 68
    exported by developing countries, 69, 70f, 71f
textiles and apparel, 83n
    applied tariffs, regional comparisons, 5t
    distribution of developing-country exports, 65, 65t
Thailand, 74b
    agricultural exports of, 120–21
    indicators for differentiating treatment, 121t
tobacco, 70f, 71f, 102b
Tokyo Round, 118
Tonga, 66t
total support estimate (TSE), 23t, 136
Trade Integration Mechanism, 125, 130

tropical products, 68
   exported by developing countries, 69, 70f, 71f
TSE. *See* total support estimate

Uganda, 66t
United States
   2007 US farm bill and implications for the Doha
      Round, 102b–104b
   aggregate measurement of support, 96
   agricultural policy, 42–45
      dairy reform, 103b
      evolution of, 48f
      Freedom to Farm, 45–46
      impact on blue and green box payments, 49
      payment mechanisms, 46–47
      reform, 49, 56, 58, 103b
      sugar, 57b, 103b
   agricultural subsidies, 50t
   agricultural support, 14–15
      cotton, 33t
      green box, 108
   agricultural trade, 44f
      import barriers, 81
      postwar policies, 3
   farm budgets, 58–59
   farm crisis, 43–44
   farm lobby, influence on agricultural subsidies,
      55–56
   negotiation interests in Doha Round, 31
   population dependent on agriculture, 54f
   producer support estimates, 22, 22t, 23t
   Public Law 480, 92–94
   tariffs
      ad valorem, 26t
      average, peaks, and TRQs, 30t
      by category, 5t
      escalation on cocoa, coffee, 27t
      non–ad valorem, 112
      proposals to cut, 109, 110t
   trade preference indicators, 81, 81t
   trade-distorting agricultural support, 24–25, 24t
Uruguay, 104b
Uruguay Round, 118
   aggregate measurement of support, 95
   Agreement on Agriculture, 2, 19, 39–40, 119, 133
   agricultural policy reform, 37
   backlash to new rules, 118–19
   deficiencies relating to domestic support mea-
      sures, 19

developing countries' impact on, 59–60
   dissatisfaction with agreement, 4
   domestic support categories, 95
   effort to cut subsidies, 119–20
   impact on EU producer support, 39–40
   important contributions of agreement, 4
   tariff requirements, 19–20
   tariff-cutting proposal, 109
   WTO monitoring of tariff requirements, 20
US Agency for International Development's food
      aid proposal, 93
US Congress
   agricultural trade reform options, 103b
   influence on agricultural policy reform, 46–47
   and trade promotion authority, 61
US Department of Agriculture payments for
      selected commodities, 105f
Uzbekistan, 66t

variable levy, 38, 41f, 136
vegetable oils, 70f, 71f
Vietnam, 78t

wetlands, conversion to cropland, 44, 44n
WFP. *See* World Food Programme
wheat
   average tariffs, tariff peaks, and TRQs, 30t
   countercyclical payments for, 106t
   developing countries' reliance on, 77t
   effect of global trade liberalization on import
      prices, 78
   USDA payments for, 105f
World Bank
   estimated gains from global free trade, 6–7, 8t
   estimated gains from proposed Doha scenarios,
      8t
   estimated price effects of global free trade,
      78–79
   SPS study findings, 89–90
World Food Programme (WFP), 93
World Trade Organization (WTO)
   framework for reducing domestic agricultural
      support, 17, 18t, 19–20
   measurement of market price support, 21
   monitoring of Uruguay Round tariff require-
      ments, 20

Zambia, 80
Zimbabwe, 66t

Other Publications from the Institute for International Economics

WORKING PAPERS

94-1 APEC and Regional Trading Arrangements in the Pacific Jeffrey A. Frankel with Shang-Jin Wei and Ernesto Stein

94-2 Towards an Asia Pacific Investment Code Edward M. Graham

94-3 Merchandise Trade in the APEC Region: Is There Scope for Liberalization on an MFN Basis? Paul Wonnacott

94-4 The Automotive Industry in Southeast Asia: Can Protection Be Made Less Costly? Paul Wonnacott

94-5 Implications of Asian Economic Growth Marcus Noland

95-1 APEC: The Bogor Declaration and the Path Ahead C. Fred Bergsten

95-2 From Bogor to Miami . . . and Beyond: Regionalism in the Asia Pacific and the Western Hemisphere Jeffrey J. Schott

95-3 Has Asian Export Performance Been Unique? Marcus Noland

95-4 Association of Southeast Asian Nations (ASEAN) and ASEAN Free Trade Area (AFTA): Chronology and Statistics Gautam Jaggi

95-5 The North Korean Economy Marcus Noland

95-6 China and the International Economic System Marcus Noland

96-1 APEC after Osaka: Toward Free Trade by 2010/2020 C. Fred Bergsten

96-2 Public Policy, Private Preferences, and the Japanese Trade Pattern Marcus Noland

96-3 German Lessons for Korea: The Economics of Unification Marcus Noland

96-4 Research and Development Activities and Trade Specialization in Japan Marcus Noland

96-5 China's Economic Reforms: Chronology and Statistics Gautam Jaggi, Mary Rundle, Daniel Rosen, and Yuichi Takahashi

96-6 US-China Economic Relations Marcus Noland

96-7 The Market Structure Benefits of Trade and Investment Liberalization Raymond Atje and Gary Hufbauer

96-8 The Future of US-Korea Economic Relations Marcus Noland

96-9 Competition Policies in the Dynamic Industrializing Economies: The Case of China, Korea, and Chinese Taipei Edward M. Graham

96-10 Modeling Economic Reform in North Korea Marcus Noland, Sherman Robinson, and Monica Scatasta

96-11 Trade, Investment, and Economic Conflict Between the United States and Asia Marcus Noland

96-12 APEC in 1996 and Beyond: The Subic Summit C. Fred Bergsten

96-13 Some Unpleasant Arithmetic Concerning Unification Marcus Noland

96-14 Restructuring Korea's Financial Sector for Greater Competitiveness Marcus Noland

96-15 Competitive Liberalization and Global Free Trade: A Vision for the 21st Century C. Fred Bergsten

97-1 Chasing Phantoms: The Political Economy of USTR Marcus Noland

97-2 US-Japan Civil Aviation: Prospects for Progress Jacqueline McFadyen

97-3 Open Regionalism C. Fred Bergsten

97-4 Lessons from the Bundesbank on the Occasion of Its 40th (and Second to Last?) Birthday Adam S. Posen

97-5 The Economics of Korean Unification Marcus Noland, Sherman Robinson, and Li-Gang Liu

98-1 The Costs and Benefits of Korean Unification Marcus Noland, Sherman Robinson, and Li-Gang Liu

98-2 Asian Competitive Devaluations Li-Gang Liu, Marcus Noland, Sherman Robinson, and Zhi Wang

98-3 Fifty Years of the GATT/WTO: Lessons from the Past for Strategies for the Future C. Fred Bergsten

98-4 NAFTA Supplemental Agreements: Four Year Review Jacqueline McFadyen

98-5 Local Government Spending: Solving the Mystery of Japanese Fiscal Packages Hiroko Ishii and Erika Wada

98-6 The Global Economic Effects of the Japanese Crisis Marcus Noland, Sherman Robinson, and Zhi Wang

99-1 Rigorous Speculation: The Collapse and Revival of the North Korean Economy   Marcus Noland, Sherman Robinson, and Tao Wang

99-2 Famine in North Korea: Causes and Cures   Marcus Noland, Sherman Robinson, and Tao Wang

99-3 Competition Policy and FDI: A Solution in Search of a Problem?   Marcus Noland

99-4 The Continuing Asian Financial Crisis: Global Adjustment and Trade   Marcus Noland, Sherman Robinson, and Zhi Wang

99-5 Why EMU Is Irrelevant for the German Economy   Adam S. Posen

99-6 The Global Trading System and the Developing Countries in 2000   C. Fred Bergsten

99-7 Modeling Korean Unification   Marcus Noland, Sherman Robinson, and Tao Wang

99-8 Sovereign Liquidity Crisis: The Strategic Case for a Payments Standstill   Marcus Miller and Lei Zhang

99-9 The Case for Joint Management of Exchange Rate Flexibility   C. Fred Bergsten, Olivier Davanne, and Pierre Jacquet

99-10 Does Talk Matter After All? Inflation Targeting and Central Bank Behavior   Kenneth N. Kuttner and Adam S. Posen

99-11 Hazards and Precautions: Tales of International Finance   Gary Clyde Hufbauer and Erika Wada

99-12 The Globalization of Services: What Has Happened? What Are the Implications?   Gary C. Hufbauer and Tony Warren

00-1 Regulatory Standards in the WTO: Comparing Intellectual Property Rights with Competition Policy, Environmental Protection, and Core Labor Standards   Keith Maskus

00-2 International Economic Agreements and the Constitution   Richard M. Goodman and John M. Frost

00-3 Electronic Commerce in Developing Countries: Issues for Domestic Policy and WTO Negotiations   Catherine L. Mann

00-4 The New Asian Challenge   C. Fred Bergsten

00-5 How the Sick Man Avoided Pneumonia: The Philippines in the Asian Financial Crisis   Marcus Noland

00-6 Inflation, Monetary Transparency, and G-3 Exchange Rate Volatility   Kenneth N. Kuttner and Adam S. Posen

00-7 Transatlantic Issues in Electronic Commerce   Catherine L. Mann

00-8 Strengthening the International Financial Architecture: Where Do We Stand?   Morris Goldstein

00-9 On Currency Crises and Contagion   Marcel Fratzscher

01-1 Price Level Convergence and Inflation in Europe   John H. Rogers, Gary Clyde Hufbauer, and Erika Wada

01-2 Subsidies, Market Closure, Cross-Border Investment, and Effects on Competition: The Case of FDI in the Telecommunications Sector   Edward M. Graham

01-3 Foreign Direct Investment in China: Effects on Growth and Economic Performance   Edward M. Graham and Erika Wada

01-4 IMF Structural Conditionality: How Much Is Too Much?   Morris Goldstein

01-5 Unchanging Innovation and Changing Economic Performance in Japan   Adam S. Posen

01-6 Rating Banks in Emerging Markets: What Credit Rating Agencies Should Learn from Financial Indicators   Liliana Rojas-Suarez

01-7 Beyond Bipolar: A Three-Dimensional Assessment of Monetary Frameworks   Kenneth N. Kuttner and Adam S. Posen

01-8 Finance and Changing US-Japan Relations: Convergence Without Leverage — Until Now   Adam S. Posen

01-9 Macroeconomic Implications of the New Economy   Martin Neil Baily

01-10 Can International Capital Standards Strengthen Banks in Emerging Markets?   Liliana Rojas-Suarez

02-1 Moral Hazard and the US Stock Market: Analyzing the "Greenspan Put"?   Marcus Miller, Paul Weller, and Lei Zhang

02-2 Passive Savers and Fiscal Policy Effectiveness in Japan   Kenneth N. Kuttner and Adam S. Posen

02-3 Home Bias, Transaction Costs, and Prospects for the Euro: A More Detailed Analysis   Catherine L. Mann and Ellen E. Meade

02-4 Toward a Sustainable FTAA: Does Latin America Meet the Necessary Financial Preconditions?   Liliana Rojas-Suarez

02-5 Assessing Globalization's Critics: "Talkers Are No Good Doers???"   Kimberly Ann Elliott, Debayani Kar, and J. David Richardson

02-6   Economic Issues Raised by
        Treatment of Takings under NAFTA
        Chapter 11   Edward M. Graham
03-1   Debt Sustainability, Brazil, and
        the IMF   Morris Goldstein
03-2   Is Germany Turning Japanese?
        Adam S. Posen
03-3   Survival of the Best Fit: Exposure
        to Low-Wage Countries and the
        (Uneven) Growth of US
        Manufacturing Plants
        Andrew B. Bernard, J. Bradford
        Jensen, and Peter K. Schott
03-4   Falling Trade Costs,
        Heterogeneous Firms, and
        Industry Dynamics
        Andrew B. Bernard, J. Bradford
        Jensen, and Peter K. Schott
03-5   Famine and Reform in North Korea
        Marcus Noland
03-6   Empirical Investigations in
        Inflation Targeting   Yifan Hu
03-7   Labor Standards and the Free
        Trade Area of the Americas
        Kimberly Ann Elliott
03-8   Religion, Culture, and Economic
        Performance   Marcus Noland
03-9   It Takes More than a Bubble to
        Become Japan   Adam S. Posen
03-10   The Difficulty of Discerning
        What's Too Tight: Taylor Rules
        and Japanese Monetary Policy
        Adam S. Posen/Kenneth N. Kuttner
04-1   Adjusting China's Exchange Rate
        Policies   Morris Goldstein
04-2   Popular Attitudes, Globalization,
        and Risk   Marcus Noland
04-3   Selective Intervention and Growth:
        The Case of Korea   Marcus Noland
05-1   Outsourcing and Offshoring:
        Pushing the European Model Over
        the Hill, Rather Than Off the Cliff!
        Jacob Funk Kirkegaard
05-2   China's Role in the Revived
        Bretton Woods System:
        A Case of Mistaken Identity
        Morris Goldstein and Nicholas Lardy
05-3   Affinity and International Trade
        Marcus Noland
05-4   South Korea's Experience with International
        Capital Flows   Marcus Noland
05-5   Explaining Middle Eastern
        Authoritarianism   Marcus Noland
05-6   Postponing Global Adjustment:
        An Analysis of the Pending Adjustment
        of Global Imbalances   Edwin Truman
05-7   What Might the Next Emerging-
        Market Financial Crisis Look Like?
        Morris Goldstein, assisted by Anna Wong

05-8   Egypt after the Multi-Fiber
        Arrangement   Dan Magder
05-9   Tradable Services: Understanding
        the Scope and Impact of Services
        Offshoring   J. Bradford Jensen
        and Lori G. Kletzer
05-10   Importers, Exporters, and Multina-
        tionals: A Portrait of Firms in the
        U.S. that Trade Goods
        Andrew B. Bernard, J. Bradford
        Jensen, and Peter K. Schott
05-11   The US Trade Deficit: A Disaggre-
        gated Perspective   Catherine
        L. Mann and Katharina Plück
05-12   Prospects for Regional Free Trade
        in Asia   Gary Clyde Hufbauer
        and Yee Wong
05-13   Predicting Trade Expansion under
        FTAs and Multilateral Agreements
        Dean A. DeRosa and John P. Gilbert
05-14   The East Asian Industrial Policy
        Experience: Implications for the
        Middle East
        Marcus Noland and Howard Pack
05-15   Outsourcing and Skill Imports:
        Foreign High-Skilled Workers on
        H-1B and L-1 Visas in the United
        States   Jacob Funk Kirkegaard
06-1   Why Central Banks Should Not Burst
        Bubbles   Adam S. Posen
06-2   The Case for an International Reserve
        Diversification Standard
        Edwin M. Truman and Anna Wong
06-3   Offshoring in Europe — Evidence
        of a Two-Way Street from Denmark
        Peter D. Ørberg Jensen, Jacob Funk
        Kirkegaard, and Nicolai Søndergaard
        Laugesen
06-4   The External Policy of the Euro Area:
        Organizing for Foregn Exchange
        Intervention   C. Randall Henning

POLICY BRIEFS

98-1   The Asian Financial Crisis
        Morris Goldstein
98-2   The New Agenda with China
        C. Fred Bergsten
98-3   Exchange Rates for the Dollar,
        Yen, and Euro   Simon Wren-Lewis
98-4   Sanctions-Happy USA
        Gary Clyde Hufbauer
98-5   The Depressing News from Asia
        Marcus Noland, Sherman
        Robinson, and Zhi Wang
98-6   The Transatlantic Economic
        Partnership   Ellen L. Frost

98-7 **A New Strategy for the Global Crisis** C. Fred Bergsten

98-8 **Reviving the "Asian Monetary Fund"** C. Fred Bergsten

99-1 **Implementing Japanese Recovery** Adam S. Posen

99-2 **A Radical but Workable Restructuring Plan for South Korea** Edward M. Graham

99-3 **Crawling Bands or Monitoring Bands: How to Manage Exchange Rates in a World of Capital Mobility** John Williamson

99-4 **Market Mechanisms to Reduce the Need for IMF Bailouts** Catherine L. Mann

99-5 **Steel Quotas: A Rigged Lottery** Gary C. Hufbauer and Erika Wada

99-6 **China and the World Trade Organization: An Economic Balance Sheet** Daniel H. Rosen

99-7 **Trade and Income Distribution: The Debate and New Evidence** William R. Cline

99-8 **Preserve the Exchange Stabilization Fund** C. Randall Henning

99-9 **Nothing to Fear but Fear (of Inflation) Itself** Adam S. Posen

99-10 **World Trade after Seattle: Implications for the United States** Gary Clyde Hufbauer

00-1 **The Next Trade Policy Battle** C. Fred Bergsten

00-2 **Decision-making in the WTO** Jeffrey J. Schott and Jayashree Watal

00-3 **American Access to China's Market: The Congressional Vote on PNTR** Gary C. Hufbauer and Daniel Rosen

00-4 **Third Oil Shock: Real or Imaginary? Consequences and Policy Alternatives** Philip K. Verleger Jr.

00-5 **The Role of the IMF: A Guide to the Reports** John Williamson

00-6 **The ILO and Enforcement of Core Labor Standards** Kimberly Ann Elliott

00-7 **"No" to Foreign Telecoms Equals "No" to the New Economy!** Gary C. Hufbauer/Edward M. Graham

01-1 **Brunei: A Turning Point for APEC?** C. Fred Bergsten

01-2 **A Prescription to Relieve Worker Anxiety** Lori Kletzer/Robert E. Litan

01-3 **The US Export-Import Bank: Time for an Overhaul** Gary C. Hufbauer

01-4 **Japan 2001 — Decisive Action or Financial Panic** Adam S. Posen

01-5 **Fin(d)ing Our Way on Trade and Labor Standards?** Kimberly Ann Elliott

01-6 **Prospects for Transatlantic Competition Policy** Mario Monti

01-7 **The International Implications of Paying Down the Debt** Edwin M. Truman

01-8 **Dealing with Labor and Environment Issues in Trade Promotion Legislation** Kimberly Ann Elliott

01-9 **Steel: Big Problems, Better Solutions** Gary Clyde Hufbauer/Ben Goodrich

01-10 **Economic Policy Following the Terrorist Attacks** Martin Neil Baily

01-11 **Using Sanctions to Fight Terrorism** Gary Clyde Hufbauer, Jeffrey J. Schott, and Barbara Oegg

02-1 **Time for a Grand Bargain in Steel?** Gary C. Hufbauer and Ben Goodrich

02-2 **Prospects for the World Economy: From Global Recession to Global Recovery** Michael Mussa

02-3 **Sovereign Debt Restructuring: New Articles, New Contracts — or No Change?** Marcus Miller

02-4 **Support the Ex-Im Bank: It Has Work to Do!** Gary Clyde Hufbauer and Ben Goodrich

02-5 **The Looming Japanese Crisis** Adam S. Posen

02-6 **Capital-Market Access: New Frontier in the Sanctions Debate** Gary C. Hufbauer and Barbara Oegg

02-7 **Is Brazil Next?** John Williamson

02-8 **Further Financial Services Liberalization in the Doha Round?** Wendy Dobson

02-9 **Global Economic Prospects** Michael Mussa

02-10 **The Foreign Sales Corporation: Reaching the Last Act?** Gary Clyde Hufbauer

03-1 **Steel Policy: The Good, the Bad, and the Ugly** Gary Clyde Hufbauer and Ben Goodrich

03-2 **Global Economic Prospects: Through the Fog of Uncertainty** Michael Mussa

03-3 **Economic Leverage and the North Korean Nuclear Crisis** Kimberly Ann Elliott

03-4 **The Impact of Economic Sanctions on US Trade: Andrew Rose's Gravity Model** Gary Clyde Hufbauer and Barbara Oegg

03-5 **Reforming OPIC for the 21st Century** Theodore H. Moran/C. Fred Bergsten

03-6   The Strategic Importance of
        US-Korea Economic Relations
        Marcus Noland
03-7   Rules Against Earnings Stripping:
        Wrong Answer to Corporate
        Inversions
        Gary Clyde Hufbauer and Ariel Assa
03-8   More Pain, More Gain: Politics
        and Economics of Eliminating Tariffs
        Gary C. Hufbauer and Ben Goodrich
03-9   EU Accession and the Euro: Close
        Together or Far Apart?
        Peter B. Kenen and Ellen E. Meade
03-10   Next Move in Steel: Revocation or
        Retaliation?   Gary Clyde Hufbauer
        and Ben Goodrich
03-11   Globalization of IT Services and
        White Collar Jobs: The Next Wave
        of Productivity Growth
        Catherine L. Mann
04-1   This Far and No Farther? Nudging
        Agricultural Reform Forward
        Tim Josling and Dale Hathaway
04-2   Labor Standards, Development,
        and CAFTA   Kimberly Ann Elliott
04-3   Senator Kerry on Corporate Tax
        Reform: Right Diagnosis, Wrong
        Prescription   Gary Clyde Hufbauer
        and Paul Grieco
04-4   Islam, Globalization, and Economic
        Performance in the Middle East
        Marcus Noland and Howard Pack
04-5   China Bashing 2004
        Gary Clyde Hufbauer and Yee Wong
04-6   What Went Right in Japan
        Adam S. Posen
04-7   What Kind of Landing for the
        Chinese Economy?   Morris Goldstein
        and Nicholas R. Lardy
05-1   A Currency Basket for East Asia,
        Not Just China   John Williamson
05-2   After Argentina   Anna Gelpern
05-3   Living with Global Imbalances:
        A Contrarian View   Richard N. Cooper
05-4   The Case for a New Plaza Agreement
        William R. Cline
06-1   The United States Needs German
        Economic Leadership
        Adam S. Posen
06-2   The Doha Round after Hong Kong
        Gary C. Hufbauer and Jeffrey J. Schott
06-3   Russia's Challenges as Chair of the G-8
        Anders Åslund
06-4   Negotiating the Korea–United States
        Free Trade Agreement   Jeffrey J. Schott,
        Scott C. Bradford, and Thomas Moll
06-5   Can Doha Still Deliver on the Develop-
        ment Agenda?   Kimberly Ann Elliott

* = out of print

POLICY ANALYSES IN
INTERNATIONAL ECONOMICS Series

1   The Lending Policies of the International
     Monetary Fund*   John Williamson
     August 1982   ISBN 0-88132-000-5
2   "Reciprocity": A New Approach to World
     Trade Policy?*   William R. Cline
     September 1982   ISBN 0-88132-001-3
3   Trade Policy in the 1980s*
     C. Fred Bergsten and William R. Cline
     November 1982   ISBN 0-88132-002-1
4   International Debt and the Stability of the
     World Economy*   William R. Cline
     September 1983   ISBN 0-88132-010-2
5   The Exchange Rate System,* Second Edition
     John Williamson
     Sept. 1983, rev. June 1985   ISBN 0-88132-034-X
6   Economic Sanctions in Support of Foreign
     Policy Goals*
     Gary Clyde Hufbauer and Jeffrey J. Schott
     October 1983   ISBN 0-88132-014-5
7   A New SDR Allocation?*   John Williamson
     March 1984   ISBN 0-88132-028-5
8   An International Standard for Monetary
     Stabilization*   Ronald L. McKinnon
     March 1984   ISBN 0-88132-018-8
9   The Yen/Dollar Agreement: Liberalizing
     Japanese Capital Markets*   Jeffrey A. Frankel
     December 1984   ISBN 0-88132-035-8
10   Bank Lending to Developing Countries: The
     Policy Alternatives*   C. Fred Bergsten,
     William R. Cline, and John Williamson
     April 1985   ISBN 0-88132-032-3
11   Trading for Growth: The Next Round of
     Trade Negotiations*
     Gary Clyde Hufbauer and Jeffrey J. Schott
     September 1985   ISBN 0-88132-033-1
12   Financial Intermediation Beyond the Debt
     Crisis*   Donald R. Lessard, John Williamson
     September 1985   ISBN 0-88132-021-8
13   The United States-Japan Economic Problem*
     C. Fred Bergsten and William R. Cline
     October 1985, 2d ed. January 1987
                     ISBN 0-88132-060-9
14   Deficits and the Dollar: The World Economy
     at Risk*   Stephen Marris
     December 1985, 2d ed. November 1987
                     ISBN 0-88132-067-6
15   Trade Policy for Troubled Industries*
     Gary Clyde Hufbauer and Howard R. Rosen
     March 1986   ISBN 0-88132-020-X

16 The United States and Canada: The Quest for Free Trade*   Paul Wonnacott, with an appendix by John Williamson
March 1987   ISBN 0-88132-056-0

17 Adjusting to Success: Balance of Payments Policy in the East Asian NICs*
Bela Balassa and John Williamson
June 1987, rev. April 1990   ISBN 0-88132-101-X

18 Mobilizing Bank Lending to Debtor Countries*   William R. Cline
June 1987   ISBN 0-88132-062-5

19 Auction Quotas and United States Trade Policy*   C. Fred Bergsten, Kimberly Ann Elliott, Jeffrey J. Schott, and Wendy E. Takacs
September 1987   ISBN 0-88132-050-1

20 Agriculture and the GATT: Rewriting the Rules*   Dale E. Hathaway
September 1987   ISBN 0-88132-052-8

21 Anti-Protection: Changing Forces in United States Trade Politics*
I. M. Destler and John S. Odell
September 1987   ISBN 0-88132-043-9

22 Targets and Indicators: A Blueprint for the International Coordination of Economic Policy
John Williamson and Marcus H. Miller
September 1987   ISBN 0-88132-051-X

23 Capital Flight: The Problem and Policy Responses*   Donald R. Lessard and John Williamson
December 1987   ISBN 0-88132-059-5

24 United States-Canada Free Trade: An Evaluation of the Agreement*
Jeffrey J. Schott
April 1988   ISBN 0-88132-072-2

25 Voluntary Approaches to Debt Relief*
John Williamson
Sept.1988, rev. May 1989   ISBN 0-88132-098-6

26 American Trade Adjustment: The Global Impact*   William R. Cline
March 1989   ISBN 0-88132-095-1

27 More Free Trade Areas?*
Jeffrey J. Schott
May 1989   ISBN 0-88132-085-4

28 The Progress of Policy Reform in Latin America*   John Williamson
January 1990   ISBN 0-88132-100-1

29 The Global Trade Negotiations: What Can Be Achieved?*   Jeffrey J. Schott
September 1990   ISBN 0-88132-137-0

30 Economic Policy Coordination: Requiem or Prologue?*   Wendy Dobson
April 1991   ISBN 0-88132-102-8

31 The Economic Opening of Eastern Europe*
John Williamson
May 1991   ISBN 0-88132-186-9

32 Eastern Europe and the Soviet Union in the World Economy*
Susan M. Collins and Dani Rodrik
May 1991   ISBN 0-88132-157-5

33 African Economic Reform: The External Dimension*   Carol Lancaster
June 1991   ISBN 0-88132-096-X

34 Has the Adjustment Process Worked?*
Paul R. Krugman
October 1991   ISBN 0-88132-116-8

35 From Soviet disUnion to Eastern Economic Community?*
Oleh Havrylyshyn and John Williamson
October 1991   ISBN 0-88132-192-3

36 Global Warming: The Economic Stakes*
William R. Cline
May 1992   ISBN 0-88132-172-9

37 Trade and Payments After Soviet Disintegration*   John Williamson
June 1992   ISBN 0-88132-173-7

38 Trade and Migration: NAFTA and Agriculture*   Philip L. Martin
October 1993   ISBN 0-88132-201-6

39 The Exchange Rate System and the IMF: A Modest Agenda   Morris Goldstein
June 1995   ISBN 0-88132-219-9

40 What Role for Currency Boards?
John Williamson
September 1995   ISBN 0-88132-222-9

41 Predicting External Imbalances for the United States and Japan*   William R. Cline
September 1995   ISBN 0-88132-220-2

42 Standards and APEC: An Action Agenda*
John S. Wilson
October 1995   ISBN 0-88132-223-7

43 Fundamental Tax Reform and Border Tax Adjustments*   Gary Clyde Hufbauer
January 1996   ISBN 0-88132-225-3

44 Global Telecom Talks: A Trillion Dollar Deal*
Ben A. Petrazzini
June 1996   ISBN 0-88132-230-X

45 WTO 2000: Setting the Course for World Trade   Jeffrey J. Schott
September 1996   ISBN 0-88132-234-2

46 The National Economic Council: A Work in Progress*   I. M. Destler
November 1996   ISBN 0-88132-239-3

47 The Case for an International Banking Standard   Morris Goldstein
April 1997   ISBN 0-88132-244-X

48 **Transatlantic Trade: A Strategic Agenda***
Ellen L. Frost
May 1997 ISBN 0-88132-228-8

49 **Cooperating with Europe's Monetary Union**
C. Randall Henning
May 1997 ISBN 0-88132-245-8

50 **Renewing Fast Track Legislation*** I. M. Destler
September 1997 ISBN 0-88132-252-0

51 **Competition Policies for the Global Economy**
Edward M. Graham and J. David Richardson
November 1997 ISBN 0-88132-249-0

52 **Improving Trade Policy Reviews in the World Trade Organization** Donald Keesing
April 1998 ISBN 0-88132-251-2

53 **Agricultural Trade Policy: Completing the Reform** Timothy Josling
April 1998 ISBN 0-88132-256-3

54 **Real Exchange Rates for the Year 2000**
Simon Wren Lewis and Rebecca Driver
April 1998 ISBN 0-88132-253-9

55 **The Asian Financial Crisis: Causes, Cures, and Systemic Implications** Morris Goldstein
June 1998 ISBN 0-88132-261-X

56 **Global Economic Effects of the Asian Currency Devaluations**
Marcus Noland, LiGang Liu, Sherman Robinson, and Zhi Wang
July 1998 ISBN 0-88132-260-1

57 **The Exchange Stabilization Fund: Slush Money or War Chest?** C. Randall Henning
May 1999 ISBN 0-88132-271-7

58 **The New Politics of American Trade: Trade, Labor, and the Environment**
I. M. Destler and Peter J. Balint
October 1999 ISBN 0-88132-269-5

59 **Congressional Trade Votes: From NAFTA Approval to Fast Track Defeat**
Robert E. Baldwin and Christopher S. Magee
February 2000 ISBN 0-88132-267-9

60 **Exchange Rate Regimes for Emerging Markets: Reviving the Intermediate Option**
John Williamson
September 2000 ISBN 0-88132-293-8

61 **NAFTA and the Environment: Seven Years Later** Gary Clyde Hufbauer, Daniel Esty, Diana Orejas, Luis Rubio, and Jeffrey J. Schott
October 2000 ISBN 0-88132-299-7

62 **Free Trade between Korea and the United States?** Inbom Choi and Jeffrey J. Schott
April 2001 ISBN 0-88132-311-X

63 **New Regional Trading Arrangements in the Asia Pacific?**
Robert Scollay and John P. Gilbert
May 2001 ISBN 0-88132-302-0

64 **Parental Supervision: The New Paradigm for Foreign Direct Investment and Development** Theodore H. Moran
August 2001 ISBN 0-88132-313-6

65 **The Benefits of Price Convergence: Speculative Calculations**
Gary Clyde Hufbauer, Erika Wada, and Tony Warren
December 2001 ISBN 0-88132-333-0

66 **Managed Floating Plus**
Morris Goldstein
March 2002 ISBN 0-88132-336-5

67 **Argentina and the Fund: From Triumph to Tragedy** Michael Mussa
July 2002 ISBN 0-88132-339-X

68 **East Asian Financial Cooperation**
C. Randall Henning
September 2002 ISBN 0-88132-338-1

69 **Reforming OPIC for the 21st Century**
Theodore H. Moran
May 2003 ISBN 0-88132-342-X

70 **Awakening Monster: The Alien Tort Statute of 1789**
Gary C. Hufbauer and Nicholas Mitrokostas
July 2003 ISBN 0-88132-366-7

71 **Korea after Kim Jong-il**
Marcus Noland
January 2004 ISBN 0-88132-373-X

72 **Roots of Competitiveness: China's Evolving Agriculture Interests** Daniel H. Rosen, Scott Rozelle, and Jikun Huang
July 2004 ISBN 0-88132-376-4

73 **Prospects for a US-Taiwan FTA**
Nicholas R. Lardy and Daniel H. Rosen
December 2004 ISBN 0-88132-367-5

74 **Anchoring Reform with a US-Egypt Free Trade Agreement**
Ahmed Galal and Robert Z. Lawrence
April 2005 ISBN 0-88132-368-3

75 **Curbing the Boom-Bust Cycle: Stabilizing Capital Flows to Emerging Markets**
John Williamson
July 2005 ISBN 0-88132-330-6

76 **The Shape of a Swiss-US Free Trade Agreement**
Gary Clyde Hufbauer and Richard E. Baldwin
February 2006 ISBN 978-0-88132-385-6

77 **A Strategy for IMF Reform**
Edwin M. Truman
February 2006 ISBN 978-0-88132-398-6

BOOKS

IMF Conditionality* John Williamson, editor
1983 ISBN 0-88132-006-4
Trade Policy in the 1980s* William R. Cline, ed.
1983 ISBN 0-88132-031-5

Subsidies in International Trade*
Gary Clyde Hufbauer and Joanna Shelton Erb
1984   ISBN 0-88132-004-8
International Debt: Systemic Risk and Policy
Response*   William R. Cline
1984   ISBN 0-88132-015-3
Trade Protection in the United States: 31 Case
Studies* Gary Clyde Hufbauer, Diane E. Berliner,
and Kimberly Ann Elliott
1986   ISBN 0-88132-040-4
Toward Renewed Economic Growth in Latin
America* Bela Balassa, Gerardo M. Bueno, Pedro-
Pablo Kuczynski, and Mario Henrique Simonsen
1986   ISBN 0-88132-045-5
Capital Flight and Third World Debt*
Donald R. Lessard and John Williamson, editors
1987   ISBN 0-88132-053-6
The Canada-United States Free Trade Agreement:
The Global Impact*
Jeffrey J. Schott and Murray G. Smith, editors
1988   ISBN 0-88132-073-0
World Agricultural Trade: Building a Consensus*
William M. Miner and Dale E. Hathaway, editors
1988   ISBN 0-88132-071-3
Japan in the World Economy*
Bela Balassa and Marcus Noland
1988   ISBN 0-88132-041-2
America in the World Economy: A Strategy for
the 1990s*   C. Fred Bergsten
1988   ISBN 0-88132-089-7
Managing the Dollar: From the Plaza to the
Louvre*   Yoichi Funabashi
1988, 2d. ed. 1989   ISBN 0-88132-097-8
United States External Adjustment and the World
Economy*   William R. Cline
May 1989   ISBN 0-88132-048-X
Free Trade Areas and U.S. Trade Policy*
Jeffrey J. Schott, editor
May 1989   ISBN 0-88132-094-3
Dollar Politics: Exchange Rate Policymaking in
the United States*
I. M. Destler and C. Randall Henning
September 1989   ISBN 0-88132-079-X
Latin American Adjustment: How Much Has
Happened?*   John Williamson, editor
April 1990   ISBN 0-88132-125-7
The Future of World Trade in Textiles and
Apparel*   William R. Cline
1987, 2d ed. June 1999   ISBN 0-88132-110-9
Completing the Uruguay Round: A Results-
Oriented Approach to the GATT Trade
Negotiations*   Jeffrey J. Schott, editor
September 1990   ISBN 0-88132-130-3

Economic Sanctions Reconsidered (2 volumes)
Economic Sanctions Reconsidered:
Supplemental Case Histories
Gary Clyde Hufbauer, Jeffrey J. Schott, and
Kimberly Ann Elliott
1985, 2d ed. Dec. 1990   ISBN cloth 0-88132-115-X
                           ISBN paper 0-88132-105-2
Economic Sanctions Reconsidered: History and
Current Policy   Gary Clyde Hufbauer,
Jeffrey J. Schott, and Kimberly Ann Elliott
December 1990   ISBN cloth 0-88132-140-0
                       ISBN paper 0-88132-136-2
Economic Sanctions Reconsidered: History
and Current Policy   Gary Clyde Hufbauer,
Jeffrey J. Schott, and Kimberly Ann Elliott
December 1990   ISBN cloth 0-88132-140-0
                       ISBN paper 0-88132-136-2
Pacific Basin Developing Countries: Prospects
for the Future*   Marcus Noland
January 1991   ISBN cloth 0-88132-141-9
                      ISBN paper 0-88132-081-1
Currency Convertibility in Eastern Europe*
John Williamson, editor
October 1991   ISBN 0-88132-128-1
International Adjustment and Financing: The
Lessons of 1985-1991* C. Fred Bergsten, editor
January 1992   ISBN 0-88132-112-5
North American Free Trade: Issues and
Recommendations*
Gary Clyde Hufbauer and Jeffrey J. Schott
April 1992   ISBN 0-88132-120-6
Narrowing the U.S. Current Account Deficit*
Alan J. Lenz/June 1992   ISBN 0-88132-103-6
The Economics of Global Warming
William R. Cline/June 1992   ISBN 0-88132-132-X
US Taxation of International Income: Blueprint
for Reform*   Gary Clyde Hufbauer,
assisted by Joanna M. van Rooij
October 1992   ISBN 0-88132-134-6
Who's Bashing Whom? Trade Conflict in High-
Technology Industries Laura D'Andrea Tyson
November 1992   ISBN 0-88132-106-0
Korea in the World Economy* Il SaKong
January 1993   ISBN 0-88132-183-4
Pacific Dynamism and the International
Economic System*
C. Fred Bergsten and Marcus Noland, editors
May 1993   ISBN 0-88132-196-6
Economic Consequences of Soviet Disintegration*
John Williamson, editor
May 1993   ISBN 0-88132-190-7
Reconcilable Differences? United States-Japan
Economic Conflict*
C. Fred Bergsten and Marcus Noland
June 1993   ISBN 0-88132-129-X

Does Foreign Exchange Intervention Work?
Kathryn M. Dominguez and Jeffrey A. Frankel
September 1993　　　ISBN 0-88132-104-4
Sizing Up U.S. Export Disincentives*
J. David Richardson
September 1993　　　ISBN 0-88132-107-9
NAFTA: An Assessment
Gary Clyde Hufbauer and Jeffrey J. Schott/*rev. ed.*
October 1993　　　ISBN 0-88132-199-0
Adjusting to Volatile Energy Prices
Philip K. Verleger, Jr.
November 1993　　　ISBN 0-88132-069-2
The Political Economy of Policy Reform
John Williamson, editor
January 1994　　　ISBN 0-88132-195-8
Measuring the Costs of Protection
in the United States
Gary Clyde Hufbauer and Kimberly Ann Elliott
January 1994　　　ISBN 0-88132-108-7
The Dynamics of Korean Economic Development*
Cho Soon/*March 1994*　　ISBN 0-88132-162-1
Reviving the European Union*
C. Randall Henning, Eduard Hòchreiter, and
Gary Clyde Hufbauer, editors
April 1994　　　ISBN 0-88132-208-3
China in the World Economy　Nicholas R. Lardy
April 1994　　　ISBN 0-88132-200-8
Greening the GATT: Trade, Environment, and
the Future　　　Daniel C. Esty
July 1994　　　ISBN 0-88132-205-9
Western Hemisphere Economic Integration*
Gary Clyde Hufbauer and Jeffrey J. Schott
July 1994　　　ISBN 0-88132-159-1
Currencies and Politics in the United States,
Germany, and Japan　　C. Randall Henning
September 1994　　　ISBN 0-88132-127-3
Estimating Equilibrium Exchange Rates
John Williamson, editor
September 1994　　　ISBN 0-88132-076-5
Managing the World Economy: Fifty Years after
Bretton Woods　　　Peter B. Kenen, editor
September 1994　　　ISBN 0-88132-212-1
Reciprocity and Retaliation in U.S. Trade Policy
Thomas O. Bayard and Kimberly Ann Elliott
September 1994　　　ISBN 0-88132-084-6
The Uruguay Round: An Assessment*
Jeffrey J. Schott, assisted by Johanna W. Buurman
November 1994　　　ISBN 0-88132-206-7
Measuring the Costs of Protection in Japan*
Yoko Sazanami, Shujiro Urata, and Hiroki Kawai
January 1995　　　ISBN 0-88132-211-3
Foreign Direct Investment in the United States,
3d ed., Edward M. Graham and Paul R. Krugman
January 1995　　　ISBN 0-88132-204-0

Asia Pacific Fusion: Japan's Role in APEC*
Yoichi Funabashi
October 1995　　　ISBN 0-88132-224-5
Korea-United States Cooperation in the New
World Order*
C. Fred Bergsten and Il SaKong, editors
February 1996　　　ISBN 0-88132-226-1
Why Exports Really Matter!*　ISBN 0-88132-221-0
Why Exports Matter More!*　ISBN 0-88132-229-6
J. David Richardson and Karin Rindal
July 1995; February 1996
Global Corporations and National Governments
Edward M. Graham
May 1996　　　ISBN 0-88132-111-7
Global Economic Leadership and the Group of
Seven　　C. Fred Bergsten and C. Randall Henning
May 1996　　　ISBN 0-88132-218-0
The Trading System after the Uruguay Round*
John Whalley and Colleen Hamilton
July 1996　　　ISBN 0-88132-131-1
Private Capital Flows to Emerging Markets after
the Mexican Crisis*　　　Guillermo A. Calvo,
Morris Goldstein, and Eduard Hochreiter
September 1996　　　ISBN 0-88132-232-6
The Crawling Band as an Exchange Rate Regime:
Lessons from Chile, Colombia, and Israel
John Williamson
September 1996　　　ISBN 0-88132-231-8
Flying High: Liberalizing Civil Aviation in the
Asia Pacific*
Gary Clyde Hufbauer and Christopher Findlay
November 1996　　　ISBN 0-88132-227-X
Measuring the Costs of Visible Protection
in Korea*　　　Namdoo Kim
November 1996　　　ISBN 0-88132-236-9
The World Trading System: Challenges Ahead
Jeffrey J. Schott
December 1996　　　ISBN 0-88132-235-0
Has Globalization Gone Too Far?　Dani Rodrik
March 1997　　　ISBN paper 0-88132-241-5
Korea-United States Economic Relationship*
C. Fred Bergsten and Il SaKong, editors
March 1997　　　ISBN 0-88132-240-7
Summitry in the Americas: A Progress Report
Richard E. Feinberg
April 1997　　　ISBN 0-88132-242-3
Corruption and the Global Economy
Kimberly Ann Elliott
June 1997　　　ISBN 0-88132-233-4
Regional Trading Blocs in the World Economic
System　　　Jeffrey A. Frankel
October 1997　　　ISBN 0-88132-202-4

Sustaining the Asia Pacific Miracle:
Environmental Protection and Economic
Integration   Andre Dua and Daniel C. Esty
October 1997   ISBN 0-88132-250-4
Trade and Income Distribution   William R. Cline
November 1997   ISBN 0-88132-216-4
Global Competition Policy
Edward M. Graham and J. David Richardson
December 1997   ISBN 0-88132-166-4
Unfinished Business: Telecommunications
after the Uruguay Round
Gary Clyde Hufbauer and Erika Wada
December 1997   ISBN 0-88132-257-1
Financial Services Liberalization in the WTO
Wendy Dobson and Pierre Jacquet
June 1998   ISBN 0-88132-254-7
Restoring Japan's Economic Growth
Adam S. Posen
September 1998   ISBN 0-88132-262-8
Measuring the Costs of Protection in China
Zhang Shuguang, Zhang Yansheng,
and Wan Zhongxin
November 1998   ISBN 0-88132-247-4
Foreign Direct Investment and Development:
The New Policy Agenda for Developing
Countries and Economies in Transition
Theodore H. Moran
December 1998   ISBN 0-88132-258-X
Behind the Open Door: Foreign Enterprises
in the Chinese Marketplace
Daniel H. Rosen
January 1999   ISBN 0-88132-263-6
Toward A New International Financial
Architecture: A Practical Post-Asia Agenda
Barry Eichengreen
February 1999   ISBN 0-88132-270-9
Is the U.S. Trade Deficit Sustainable?
Catherine L. Mann
September 1999   ISBN 0-88132-265-2
Safeguarding Prosperity in a Global Financial
System: The Future International Financial
Architecture, Independent Task Force Report
Sponsored by the Council on Foreign Relations
Morris Goldstein, Project Director
October 1999   ISBN 0-88132-287-3
Avoiding the Apocalypse: The Future of the
Two Koreas   Marcus Noland
June 2000   ISBN 0-88132-278-4
Assessing Financial Vulnerability: An Early
Warning System for Emerging Markets
Morris Goldstein, Graciela Kaminsky, and
Carmen Reinhart
June 2000   ISBN 0-88132-237-7

Global Electronic Commerce: A Policy Primer
Catherine L. Mann, Sue E. Eckert, and Sarah
Cleeland Knight
Intellectual Property Rights in the Global
Economy   Keith E. Maskus
August 2000   ISBN 0-88132-282-2
The Political Economy of the Asian Financial
Crisis   Stephan Haggard
August 2000   ISBN 0-88132-283-0
Transforming Foreign Aid: United States
Assistance in the 21st Century
Carol Lancaster
August 2000   ISBN 0-88132-291-1
Fighting the Wrong Enemy: Antiglobal Activists
and Multinational Enterprises
Edward M. Graham
September 2000   ISBN 0-88132-272-5
Globalization and the Perceptions of American
Workers
Kenneth F. Scheve and Matthew J. Slaughter
March 2001   ISBN 0-88132-295-4
World Capital Markets: Challenge to the G-10
Wendy Dobson and Gary Clyde Hufbauer,
assisted by Hyun Koo Cho
May 2001   ISBN 0-88132-301-2
Prospects for Free Trade in the Americas
Jeffrey J. Schott
August 2001   ISBN 0-88132-275-X
Toward a North American Community:
Lessons from the Old World for the New
Robert A. Pastor
August 2001   ISBN 0-88132-328-4
Measuring the Costs of Protection in Europe:
European Commercial Policy in the 2000s
Patrick A. Messerlin
September 2001   ISBN 0-88132-273-3
Job Loss from Imports: Measuring the Costs
Lori G. Kletzer
September 2001   ISBN 0-88132-296-2
No More Bashing: Building a New
Japan–United States Economic Relationship
C. Fred Bergsten, Takatoshi Ito,
and Marcus Noland
October 2001   ISBN 0-88132-286-5
Why Global Commitment Really Matters!
Howard Lewis III and J. David Richardson
October 2001   ISBN 0-88132-298-9
Leadership Selection in the Major Multilaterals
Miles Kahler
November 2001   ISBN 0-88132-335-7
The International Financial Architecture:
What's New? What's Missing?
Peter Kenen
November 2001   ISBN 0-88132-297-0

Delivering on Debt Relief: From IMF Gold
to a New Aid Architecture
John Williamson and Nancy Birdsall,
with Brian Deese
April 2002   ISBN 0-88132-331-4
**Imagine There's No Country: Poverty,
Inequality, and Growth in the Era
of Globalization**   Surjit S. Bhalla
September 2002   ISBN 0-88132-348-9
Reforming Korea's Industrial Conglomerates
Edward M. Graham
January 2003   ISBN 0-88132-337-3
**Industrial Policy in an Era of Globalization:
Lessons from Asia**
Marcus Noland and Howard Pack
March 2003   ISBN 0-88132-350-0
Reintegrating India with the World Economy
T. N. Srinivasan and Suresh D. Tendulkar
March 2003   ISBN 0-88132-280-6
**After the Washington Consensus:
Restarting Growth and Reform
in Latin America**   Pedro-Pablo Kuczynski
and John Williamson, editors
March 2003   ISBN 0-88132-347-0
**The Decline of US Labor Unions and
the Role of Trade**   Robert E. Baldwin
June 2003   ISBN 0-88132-341-1
**Can Labor Standards Improve
under Globalization?**
Kimberly Ann Elliott and Richard B. Freeman
June 2003   ISBN 0-88132-332-2
**Crimes and Punishments? Retaliation
under the WTO**   Robert Z. Lawrence
October 2003   ISBN 0-88132-359-4
Inflation Targeting in the World Economy
Edwin M. Truman
October 2003   ISBN 0-88132-345-4
**Foreign Direct Investment and Tax
Competition**   John H. Mutti
November 2003   ISBN 0-88132-352-7
**Has Globalization Gone Far Enough?
The Costs of Fragmented Markets**
Scott Bradford and Robert Z. Lawrence
February 2004   ISBN 0-88132-349-7
**Food Regulation and Trade:
Toward a Safe and Open Global System**
Tim Josling, Donna Roberts, and David Orden
March 2004   ISBN 0-88132-346-2
**Controlling Currency Mismatches
in Emerging Markets**
Morris Goldstein and Philip Turner
April 2004   ISBN 0-88132-360-8
**Free Trade Agreements: US Strategies
and Priorities**   Jeffrey J. Schott, editor
April 2004   ISBN 0-88132-361-6

Trade Policy and Global Poverty
William R. Cline
June 2004   ISBN 0-88132-365-9
**Bailouts or Bail-ins? Responding
to Financial Crises in Emerging Economies**
Nouriel Roubini and Brad Setser
August 2004   ISBN 0-88132-371-3
Transforming the European Economy
Martin Neil Baily and Jacob Kirkegaard
September 2004   ISBN 0-88132-343-8
**Chasing Dirty Money: The Fight Against
Money Laundering**
Peter Reuter and Edwin M. Truman
November 2004   ISBN 0-88132-370-5
**The United States and the World Economy:
Foreign Economic Policy for the Next Decade**
C. Fred Bergsten
January 2005   ISBN 0-88132-380-2
**Does Foreign Direct Investment Promote
Development** ?   Theodore Moran, Edward
M. Graham, and Magnus Blomström, editors
April 2005   ISBN 0-88132-381-0
American Trade Politics, 4th ed.
I. M. Destler
June 2005   ISBN 0-88132-382-9
**Why Does Immigration Divide America?
Public Finance and Political Opposition
to Open Borders**   Gordon Hanson
August 2005   ISBN 0-88132-400-0
Reforming the US Corporate Tax
Gary Clyde Hufbauer and Paul L. E. Grieco
September 2005   ISBN 0-88132-384-5
The United States as a Debtor Nation
William R. Cline
September 2005   ISBN 0-88132-399-3
**NAFTA Revisited: Achievements
and Challenges**
Gary Clyde Hufbauer and Jeffrey J. Schott,
assisted by Paul L. E. Grieco and Yee Wong
October 2005   ISBN 0-88132-334-9
**US National Security and Foreign Direct
Investment**
Edward M. Graham and David M. Marchick
May 2006   ISBN 0-88132-391-8
                    ISBN 978-0-88132-391-7
**Accelerating the Globalization of America:
The Role for Information Technology**
Catherine L. Mann, assisted by Jacob Kirkegaard
June 2006   ISBN 0-88132-390-X
                    ISBN 978-0-88132-390-0
Delivering on Doha: Farm Trade and the Poor
Kimberly Ann Elliott
July 2006   ISBN 0-88132-392-6
                    ISBN 978-088132-392-4

SPECIAL REPORTS

1 **Promoting World Recovery: A Statement on Global Economic Strategy***
   by 26 Economists from Fourteen Countries
   December 1982   ISBN 0-88132-013-7
2 **Prospects for Adjustment in Argentina, Brazil, and Mexico: Responding to the Debt Crisis***   John Williamson, editor
   June 1983   ISBN 0-88132-016-1
3 **Inflation and Indexation: Argentina, Brazil, and Israel***   John Williamson, editor
   March 1985   ISBN 0-88132-037-4
4 **Global Economic Imbalances***
   C. Fred Bergsten, editor
   March 1986   ISBN 0-88132-042-0
5 **African Debt and Financing***
   Carol Lancaster and John Williamson, eds.
   May 1986   ISBN 0-88132-044-7
6 **Resolving the Global Economic Crisis: After Wall Street***   by Thirty-three Economists from Thirteen Countries
   December 1987   ISBN 0-88132-070-6
7 **World Economic Problems***
   Kimberly Ann Elliott/John Williamson, eds.
   April 1988   ISBN 0-88132-055-2
   Reforming World Agricultural Trade*
   by Twenty-nine Professionals from Seventeen Countries/1988   ISBN 0-88132-088-9
8 **Economic Relations Between the United States and Korea: Conflict or Cooperation?***
   Thomas O. Bayard and Soogil Young, eds.
   January 1989   ISBN 0-88132-068-4
9 **Whither APEC? The Progress to Date and Agenda for the Future***
   C. Fred Bergsten, editor
   October 1997   ISBN 0-88132-248-2
10 **Economic Integration of the Korean Peninsula**   Marcus Noland, editor
   January 1998   ISBN 0-88132-255-5
11 **Restarting Fast Track*** Jeffrey J. Schott, ed.
   April 1998   ISBN 0-88132-259-8
12 **Launching New Global Trade Talks: An Action Agenda** Jeffrey J. Schott, ed.
   September 1998   ISBN 0-88132-266-0
13 **Japan's Financial Crisis and Its Parallels to US Experience**
   Ryoichi Mikitani and Adam S. Posen, eds.
   September 2000   ISBN 0-88132-289-X
14 **The Ex-Im Bank in the 21st Century: A New Approach**   Gary Clyde Hufbauer and Rita M. Rodriguez, editors
   January 2001   ISBN 0-88132-300-4
15 **The Korean Diaspora in the World Economy**
   C. Fred Bergsten and Inbom Choi, eds.
   January 2003   ISBN 0-88132-358-6
16 **Dollar Overvaluation and the World Economy**
   C. Fred Bergsten and John Williamson, eds.
   February 2003   ISBN 0-88132-351-9
17 **Dollar Adjustment: How Far? Against What?**
   C. Fred Bergsten and John Williamson, eds.
   November 2004   ISBN 0-88132-378-0
18 **The Euro at Five: Ready for a Global Role?**
   Adam S. Posen, editor
   April 2005   ISBN 0-88132-380-2
19 **Reforming the IMF for the 21st Century**
   Edwin M. Truman, editor
   April 2006   ISBN 0-88132-387-X
                     ISBN 978-0-88132-387-0

WORKS IN PROGRESS

Case Studies in US Trade Negotiation, Vols. 1 and 2
Charan Devereaux, Robert Z. Lawrence, and Michael Watkins
US-China Trade Disputes: Rising Tide, Rising Stakes
Gary Clyde Hufbauer
Trade Relations Between Colombia and the United States
Jeffrey J. Schott
Sustaining Reform with a US-Pakistan Free Trade Agreement Gary Clyde Hufbauer and Shahid Javed Burki
Reform in a Rich Country: Germany
Adam S. Posen
Global Forces, American Faces: US Economic Globalization at the Grass Roots   J. David Richardson
The Future of Chinese Exchange Rates
Morris Goldstein and Nicholas R. Lardy
The Arab Economies in a Changing World
Marcus Noland and Howard Pack
Economic Regionalism in East Asia
C. Fred Bergsten
The Strategic Implications of China-Taiwan Economic Relations
Nicholas R. Lardy
Financial Crises and the Future of Emerging Markets
William R. Cline
US Taxation of International Income, 2d ed.
Gary Clyde Hufbauer and Ariel Assa

Prospects for a Middle East Free Trade
Agreement
Robert Z. Lawrence
Prospects for a Sri Lanka Free Trade
Agreement
Dean DeRosa
Workers at Risk: Job Loss from Apparel,
Textiles, Footwear, and Furniture
Lori G. Kletzer
Economic Sanctions Reconsidered, 3d. ed.
Kimberly Ann Elliott, Gary C. Hufbauer,
and Jeffrey J. Schott
The Impact of Global Services Outsourcing
on American Firms and Workers
J. Bradford Jensen, Lori G. Kletzer,
and Catherine L. Mann

Rethinking US Social Security:
Drawing on World Best Practices
Martin N. Baily and Jacob Kirkegaard
Policy Reform in Mature Industrial
Economies
John Williamson, ed.
The Impact of Financial Globalization
William R. Cline
Banking System Fragility
in Emerging Economies
Morris Goldstein and Philip Turner
Second among Equals: The Middle-Class
Kingdoms of India and China
Surjit Bhalla

Australia, New Zealand,
and Papua New Guinea
D. A. Information Services
648 Whitehorse Road
Mitcham, Victoria 3132, Australia
Tel: 61-3-9210-7777
Fax: 61-3-9210-7788
Email: service@dadirect.com.au
www.dadirect.com.au

India, Bangladesh, Nepal, and Sri Lanka
Viva Books Private Limited
Mr. Vinod Vasishtha
4737/23 Ansari Road
Daryaganj, New Delhi 110002
India
Tel: 91-11-4224-2200
Fax: 91-11-4224-2240
Email: viva@vivagroupindia.net
www.vivagroupindia.com

Mexico, Central America, South America,
and Puerto Rico
US PubRep, Inc.
311 Dean Drive
Rockville, MD 20851
Tel: 301-838-9276
Fax: 301-838-9278
Email: c.falk@ieee.org
www.uspubrep.com

Southeast Asia (*Brunei, Burma, Cambodia,*
Indonesia, Malaysia, the Philippines,
Singapore, Taiwan, Thailand, and Vietnam)
APAC Publishers Services PTE Ltd.
70 Bendemeer Road #05-03
Hiap Huat House
Singapore 333940
Tel: 65-6844-7333
Fax: 65-6747-8916
Email: service@apacmedia.com.sg

Canada
Renouf Bookstore
5369 Canotek Road, Unit 1
Ottawa, Ontario K1J 9J3, Canada
Tel: 613-745-2665
Fax: 613-745-7660
www.renoufbooks.com

Japan
United Publishers Services Ltd.
1-32-5, Higashi-shinagawa
Shinagawa-ku, Tokyo 140-0002
Japan
Tel: 81-3-5479-7251
Fax: 81-3-5479-7307
Email: purchasing@ups.co.jp
For trade accounts only. Individuals will find
IIE books in leading Tokyo bookstores.

Middle East
MERIC
2 Bahgat Ali Street, El Masry Towers
Tower D, Apt. 24
Zamalek, Cairo
Egypt
Tel. 20-2-7633824
Fax: 20-2-7369355
Email: mahmoud_fouda@mericonline.com
www.mericonline.com

United Kingdom, Europe
(*including Russia and Turkey*), **Africa,**
and Israel
The Eurospan Group
c/o Turpin Distribution
Pegasus Drive
Stratton Business Park
Biggleswade, Bedfordshire
SG18 8TQ
United Kingdom
Tel: 44 (0) 1767-604972
Fax: 44 (0) 1767-601640
Email: eurospan@turpin-distribution.com
www.eurospangroup.com/bookstore

Visit our Web site at:
www.iie.com
E-mail orders to:
IIE mail@PressWarehouse.com